Racism and social change
in the Republic of Ireland

MANCHESTER
1824

Manchester University Press

Racism and social change in the Republic of Ireland

Second edition

BRYAN FANNING

Manchester University Press

Manchester and New York

distributed exclusively in the USA by Palgrave Macmillan

The right of Bryan Fanning to be identified as the author of this work has been asserted
by him in accordance with the Copyright, Designs and Patents Act 1988.

Published by Manchester University Press
Oxford Road, Manchester M13 9NR, UK
and Room 400, 175 Fifth Avenue, New York, NY 10010, USA
www.manchesteruniversitypress.co.uk

Distributed in the United States exclusively by
Palgrave Macmillan, 175 Fifth Avenue, New York,
NY 10010, USA

Distributed in Canada exclusively by
UBC Press, University of British Columbia, 2029 West Mall,
Vancouver, BC, Canada V6T 1Z2

British Library Cataloguing-in-Publication Data
A catalogue record for this book is available from the British Library

Library of Congress Cataloging-in-Publication Data applied for

ISBN 978 0 7190 8663 2 *paperback*

First published 2012

The publisher has no responsibility for the persistence or accuracy of URLs for any
external or third-party internet websites referred to in this book, and does not guarantee
that any content on such websites is, or will remain, accurate or appropriate.

Typeset in Palatino with Frutiger display by
Koinonia, Manchester
Printed in Great Britain by
Bell & Bain Ltd, Glasgow

Contents

List of tables

Acknowledgements

When the news came on the radio that Barack Obama had been elected President of the United States I was in a taxi in Dublin. I was leafing through an academic book on racism by David Theo Goldberg. My taxi glided past a car that had been stopped by the Irish police. The occupants were two young black men. The Gardaí were young white men. I recalled the anger of an African friend, an Irish citizen, who had been stopped with his son nearby some months earlier for no other reason, he believed, than because he was black. Having his son see how the police treated him was what upset him the most. I pondered Obama's victory alongside Goldberg's insistence in *The Threat of Race* that Western racisms had metastasised into new insidious twenty-first-century forms in trying to make sense of the racial profiling that may or may not have led to those black men being pulled over. I can date my decision to prepare a second edition of *Racism and Social Change in the Republic of Ireland* from about then.

The original edition of this book birthed two follow-up volumes and these, alongside this much-expanded and updated second edition of *Racism and Social Change*, constitute a larger composite work on immigration and social change, about Irish responses to such change, on the experiences of immigrants and on the challenges now facing an irreversibly diverse Irish society. I owe debts of gratitude to the many people who participated in the various research projects along the way or who provided advice and support. Gabriel Kiely encouraged my first published writings about racism (on the experiences of Travellers and asylum seekers in County Clare) and gave me the opportunity to teach the course at University College Dublin (UCD) from which the first edition of this book grew. Sean Spellessy provided valuable advice while I undertook research on Travellers in Ennis during the late 1990s. Susannah Riordan, Michael Kennedy and Tom Garvin were crucial sounding boards at UCD when it came to writing chapters on Irish nation-building and Irish treatment of Jews before, during and after the Holocaust. I learned much from Orla Ni Eli, then of the Irish Refugee Council branch office in

Ennis and now of the Clare Integration Centre. James Stapleton inducted me into the world of pro-migrant NGOs. The Irish Refugee Council, the Combat Poverty Agency, the Africa Centre, the Irish Research Council for the Social Sciences and the Immigrant Council of Ireland funded and enabled various research projects on Irish responses to immigration and studies of the experiences of immigrants that I became involved in over the last twelve years.

The bibliography to this book identifies many co-authors of various studies and articles that I draw upon here; I owe debts to them all. The last three chapters draw upon field work undertaken with Neil O'Boyle, Kevin Howard, Saorlaith Ní Bhroin and Brian Killoran. I stand on many shoulders but particularly wish to acknowledge those of Fidèle Mutwara-sibo who has coaxed me out of my ivory tower a few times over the years. This book is dedicated to my three daughters: Caitriona, Eilis and Ellie.

Abbreviations and Irish terms

AkiDwa	Akina Dada wa Africa [African Women's Organisation]
CADIC	Campaign Against the Deportation of Irish Children
CERD	UN Convention on the Elimination of Racial Discrimination
CSO	Central Statistics Office
Dáil	Parliament [lower house]
DJELR	Department of Justice, Equality and Law Reform
ECRE	European Council for Refugees and Exiles
ESRI	Economic and Social Research Institute
FAS	Irish industrial training agency
Gardaí Síochána	Irish police
GCIM	Global Commission on International Migration
HSCL	Home School Community Liaison
HSE	Health Services Agency
ICI	Immigrant Council of Ireland
ICTU	Irish Congress of Trades Unions
IHRC	Irish Human Rights Commission
INO	Irish Nurses Organisation
IOM	International Organization for Migration
MRCI	Migrants Rights Centre Ireland
NASC	Cork immigrant support group
NCCRI	National Consultative Committee on Racism and Interculturalism
NPAR	National Action Plan Against Racism
Oireachtas	Parliament [both houses]
PPS	Personal Public Service [number]
RTE	Raidió Teilifís Éireann [Irish televisión]
Taoiseach	prime minister

1

Introduction

This is the revised second edition of a book first published a decade ago. During the first decade of the twenty-first century, Irish society was changed through immigration to an extent that could not have been imagined beforehand. In 2002 there were clear indications, addressed in the first edition of *Racism and Social Change in the Republic of Ireland*, that new immigrant communities of black and ethnic minorities were becoming established in Dublin and some other parts of the country. Back then, media, political and academic discourses focused mostly on the arrival of asylum seekers in discernible and rapidly increasing numbers. Debates on racism in Ireland at the time tended to depict it as a new phenomenon and even as one imported by asylum seekers. The first edition of *Racism and Social Change in the Republic of Ireland* emphasised a wider historical context. It argued that Ireland was never immune from the racist ideologies that governed relationships between the West and the rest notwithstanding a history of colonial anti-Irish racism.

Like many other such concepts – such as the concept of poverty – racism suggests no single precise meaning (though useful definitions can be offered) but instead signals a debate about something that constitutes a fact or facts about the world (racism exists; some people experience racism) and a series of debates about its nature and extent. One might oppose poverty (an anti-poverty strategy) but how one does so very much depends on how the problem of poverty is understood and explained and how poverty becomes defined as a problem to be addressed. Just as the term poverty signals a series of debates about inequalities, barriers and remedies so too does the term racism signal such a range of debates. The term racism is variously used to describe actions, behaviour, social norms and processes and their consequences on the lives of those affected by them. At its root is the fact that at least some members of society are likely to make racialised distinctions between different members of society. These distinctions are expressed cognitively as stereotypes, behaviourally as prejudice and institutionally as discrimination.

To some extent the politicisation of asylum issues in Ireland mirrored responses throughout 'Fortress Europe' and in other Western countries. Newspaper headlines during 1997 depicted Ireland as being swamped by asylum seekers. Yet the number which arrived in that year was fewer than 4,000 or about 9 per cent of overall immigration.[1] The number of asylum seekers that arrived in Ireland rose year by year yet totalled fewer than 10,000 by the end of the decade. Throughout 2000 and 2001 quarterly figures of between 2,500 and 3,000 or about 10,000 per annum were recorded. Ireland continued to receive proportionately fewer asylum seekers than many other European countries. They formed just one part of a larger wave of immigration consisting of returned emigrants, people from other European Union (EU) countries and immigrant workers from non-EU countries. For example, some 18,000 work permits were granted to non-EU nationals in 2000. A further 32,823 such permits were granted between January and November 2001.[2] Some 78 per cent of those who arrived in 2001 came from Eastern Europe, the Baltic States and the Russian Federation. The highest numbers of work permits were granted to people from Latvia, Lithuania and Poland. Many of these arrived in response to labour recruitment campaigns run by the Irish government. Just a small proportion arrived from the countries of origin of asylum seekers.[3] A useful analogy might be drawn with Britain during the 1950s when labour shortages resulted in policies of seeking immigrants from Commonwealth countries. The emergence of race within British politics and the experiences of immigrants of racism from that time have been echoed to an extent within contemporary Irish society.

Nevertheless Ireland came to be transformed by a new wave of globalised migration, one that often had little to do with old post-colonial ties, yet one experienced by Ireland as its own first wave. By 2006 some 420,000 migrants had moved to Ireland; various commentators including government ministers argued that the 2006 census underestimated the size of Ireland's immigrant population.[4] Within a few years these observed that Ireland had acquired a black and new ethnic community population proportionally larger than that built up within many Western countries over several decades. In this context Ireland entered twenty-first-century policy and academic debates without having directly experienced, as did a number of Western countries, generations of immigration and decades of thinking and debating the consequences of racism. Such experience cannot be bought off the shelf. The approach of the first edition of *Racism and Social Change* was to focus, wherever possible, upon indigenous lessons, upon hidden histories of Irish racisms, anti-Semitisms and the squeezing out of ethnic minorities in processes of nation-building that could count as Irish experience.

To a considerable extent the first edition was oriented towards debates within Irish historiography and Irish studies rather towards the mainstream of international academic debates about racism. Rather than claim that such theories applied a priori to the Irish case, the focus was on contesting what Tom Dunne refers to as self-affirming community narratives capable of denying that the Irish with their histories of colonial oppression could not also be at times the oppressors of others. For example, accounts of ethnic violence towards Protestants during the war of independence by Peter Hart, have been fiercely rejected by nationalists but also by post-colonial and anti-racist theorists such as Luke Gibbons.[5] These as discussed in Chapter 3 recall similar controversies about the 1798 Rebellion in Wexford addressed by Dunne. In the Wexford case the issue was a tendency to de-emphasise sectarian killings, notably the killing of 126 men, women and children, many of whom were burned to death alive in a barn at Scullabogue, in populist celebrations of the uprising. Dunne discussed how any interpretation of the past, based on analysis of the evidence but at odds with traditional accounts, 'can meet with powerful resistance from people emotionally attached to self-affirming community narratives'.[6] This second edition does not break with this approach. For example, no changes are made to Chapter 3 which examines Jewish, Protestant and Traveller exclusions within the nation-building processes that came to define after independence what it was to be Irish.

Chapter 3 explores how the processes of nation-building which shaped contemporary Irish society and the Irish state were accompanied by a politics of national identity within which claims of social membership of various minority groups were discounted. It is not suggested that there is a simplistic link between nationalism and racism. However, it is argued that nationalism is bound up with processes of inclusion and exclusion within a terrain where cultural authenticity and social membership are contested. Nation-building in Ireland, a process of political, religious, social and economic modernisation, resulted in the ideological and material exclusion of minorities as dominant understandings of 'Irishness' narrowed and combined with other forms of social and economic closure. As such, it produced what John O'Connell referred to as one of the myths of Irishness; that Ireland has always been a homogeneous society and that Irish identity is something which remains fixed and unchanged.[7]

Writers such as Benedict Anderson have argued that nations are socially constructed 'imagined communities'.[8] Nationalisms make specific ideological claims about the nature and composition of societies. Nation states tend to institutionalise dominant constructions of social membership.

Chapter 3 examines the exclusionary and assimilationist consequences of Irish nation-building for Protestant, Jewish and Traveller minority communities. The chapter argues that past and present myths of homogeneity preclude inquiry into racism within contemporary Irish society. It aims to locate contemporary responses to asylum seekers, immigrant minority communities and the Travelling People, an indigenous ethnic minority, within a history of ideological and material exclusions.

In recent decades some breaks with past dominant constructions of Irishness could be noted. Yet, it continues to be implicitly defined in monocultural terms. A post-colonial conception of national identity formed in opposition to Britishness was reinvigorated by the Northern Ireland conflict even as secularisation and urbanisation unravelled the earlier project of nation-building on which this drew. The Robinson presidency (1990–97) was marked by a symbolism which acknowledged the Irishness of emigrants and their descendants. Mary Robinson employed the phrase 'the fifth province' to refer to Irish communities outside the four provinces of the Island. A more generally used concept was that of an Irish Diaspora. Such concepts have been employed alongside a commodification of Irishness which sells high and low Irish 'culture' to the consumers of the developed world. The consumption of Irishness can occur via James Joyce websites, a U2 concert in Australia, a production of Riverdance in New York or in a theme pub in Beijing. The notion of a global Irish community has found expression in the lobbying of American politics to further a political settlement in Northern Ireland, cheaper air travel for emigrants and, as a result of economic prosperity, the return of some former emigrants. Globalisation has reconstituted Irishness in other ways. Increased social diversity can be seen as part of an ongoing process of nation-building whereby past constructions of Irish society become unsettled. Ireland is a multicultural society. Yet, even after two decades of ongoing immigration Irish society continues to be represented as homogeneous and monocultural. Immigrants remain invisible within mainstream politics and hence remain ignored within mainstream debates about social policy. Responses to them by the Irish state vacillate between benign neglect (their presence is mostly ignored) and malign neglect (racism and barriers to integration that likewise tend to be ignored).

Chapter 4 considers anti-Semitism in Irish society from independence in 1922 until the 1950s. Only minor changes have been made to the version of the chapter that was first published in 2002. Most aim to reflect new scholarly contributions to the study of Jews in Ireland and Irish anti-Semitisms. There is a specific focus upon Ireland's response to Jewish refugees before, during and after the Holocaust. Here, as in earlier chapters, the relationship between racialised portrayals of minority groups and exclusionary ideologies of social belonging within the nation state is examined. It is argued that there has been a tendency among Irish historians to underestimate the extent and consequences of anti-Semitism within Irish society. Some have taken the view that anti-Semitism in the era after independence was of little consequence. This is disputed in the chapter on a number of grounds. A recurring theme in responses to minorities, throughout the twentieth century, has been the depiction of a homogeneous Irish society under threat. This can be seen in ideological justifications for the 'pogrom' against the Jewish community in Limerick in 1904, for explicitly anti-Semitic refugee policies, in political responses to Travellers and in responses to asylum seekers.

Yet the use of the term pogrom to describe 'the most serious outbreak of anti-Semitism in recent Irish history' has been disputed by Cormac Ó'Gráda.[9] He argues that what occurred is better explained by the Irish term 'boycott'. In the 2002 edition I argued that what occurred was in effect a pogrom because Limerick's Jewish community were driven from the city, never to return. One of these, Gerald Goldberg, later Lord Mayor of Cork, recalled how his father's house was 'attacked, its windows broken, its front door battered and the family driven into refuge in an upper room'.[10] Yet, the *Oxford English Dictionary* defines a pogrom as an organised massacre of Jews, the word etymologically rooted in a Russian word for devastation. Accordingly, I have removed the term in Chapter 5. I draw attention to this change because many of the intellectual debates in writings about racism, especially those by academics, turn on semantic distinctions and specialist terminologies. I will come back to this point below in discussing the gaps between language used by some academics and the wider community which pays little heed to academic work that purports to expose and challenge racism.

Chapter 5 examines how contemporary responses to refugees and asylum seekers in Ireland have been shaped by a legacy of exclusionary state practices. It deals with the period from 1956 when Ireland ratified the UN Convention on the Status of Refugees (1951) to the end of the first decade of the twenty-first century. In essence, the original chapter is updated. An ongoing emphasis upon control and containment owed much to the dominant monoculturalism that governed state practices. Exclusionary policies and practices in both cases were justified by a dominant ideology of homogeneity. The Irish state stratifies groups of non-citizens on the basis of decisions about their entitlements. A distinction between citizen rights and what Christian Joppke refers to as 'alien rights' underlies a state process which allows non-citizen groups to be treated differently from each other by the state.[11] Non-EU immigrant workers, immigrants with Irish-born children, people with refugee status and asylum seekers are each deemed by the state to have different rights and entitlements. In all cases these are less than the entitlements of citizens. A hierarchy of differing 'alien rights' has been shaped by a mixture of indigenous legislation, notably the Aliens Act (1935) and the Refugee Act (1996), and international agreements. Asylum seekers in Ireland have been further split into a number of groups with different entitlements. Most of the policies which defined how asylum seekers were to be treated in Ireland had been put in place by the time the first edition was published. In updating the chapter a decade later the focus, to some extent, is upon the consequences of such policies.

Chapters 6 and 7 examine anti-Traveller racism in Irish society since the 1960s. Chapter 6 consists of a detailed 'blow by blow' case study of the politics of Traveller exclusion in County Clare. It examines the period from 1963, when Travellers first became the focus of social policies with the publication of the *Report of the Commission on Itinerancy*, to the end of 1999. The research had particular personal resonance as I grew up in Ennis, the largest town in the county, alongside many of the county's present Traveller population. I gave little thought to the inequalities and discriminations experienced by Traveller neighbours until, as an adult working as a local authority official in London, I encountered Travellers as fellow emigrants. Social and economic modernisation during the twentieth century displaced Travellers from rural society to the margins of urban and suburban Ireland. Travellers in Ireland have faced deepening hostility from settled communities opposed to their presence since the 1960s when policies of assimilation were first sanctioned by the state. Accounts of such hostility have been a staple of the Irish media on an ongoing basis over the last four decades yet this remains the only detailed study of Traveller spatial exclusion to be published. It would be difficult to exaggerate the extent of racism and discrimination against Travellers in Irish society and the extent to which it remains justified within racialised discourses that depict Travellers as deviant and inferior.

Chapter 7 explores state responses to Travellers as a legacy of extremely flawed social policies with implications for new immigrant black and ethnic minority communities. Again, it has been updated to reflect events during the last decade. These have included an ongoing denial of Traveller ethnicity and consequentially denials by the state that Travellers experience racism. In the original 2002 introduction I argued that an unwillingness to address ways in which racism perpetrates inequality in the case of Travellers augured poorly for how the Irish state might address racism experienced by other groups in Irish society. In the last decade an unwillingness to acknowledge experiences of racism of immigrants can also be identified.

Chapter 8 introduces a new emphasis on experiences of racism. It draws mostly on interviews conducted in early 2011 among immigrants who have lived in Ireland for several years. These describe how racism blights lives, hurts and wounds. It considers how these effects are compounded by the denial of racism within mainstream society and its institutions. Some of these accounts describe how difficult it is, given prevailing Irish norms, to have experiences of racism acknowledged or redressed.

Something needs to be said about the very different ways in with racism is understood or ignored in different social settings. The Irish case is somewhat unusual in so far as Ireland has been an early adopter of international anti-racism protocols such as the EU Race Directive (2000). It also introduced an Equal Status Act in 2000 which prohibited discrimination in the provision of goods and services on the basis of 'race' as well as upon various other grounds. But these have remained very much paper policies in the absence of thick normative understandings of what racism is and how it affects the lives of people. Understandings of racism within Irish society, among Irish policy makers and within the Irish state remain thin.

The situation is arguably not helped by the very different uses of language by many academics and the wider population. The former often write for international specialist audiences. Scholastic writings designed to play well in academic periodicals often do not speak to policy makers or even to victims of racism. Within wider society racism is often narrowly defined and often ignored and the ability of some academic analyses of racism in Ireland to meaningfully challenge racism in terms understandable to those outside academia must be questioned. While this book engages with such academic accounts (particularly in Chapter 8) the aim is to contribute to wider societal debates and to be accessible enough to do so.

The final chapter is substantially different from that which appeared in the first edition. The 2002 version evaluated efforts to contest racism and discrimination faced by minorities in Ireland as expressions of multiculturalism. It argued that the discriminations encountered by black and ethnic minorities could only be overcome through measures that acknowledge and address the structural inequalities resulting from racism within society. Such measures began, by definition, with a full measure of liberal democratic individual rights to equal treatment but also include measures designed to contest the racism and inequalities experienced by minorities.

That argument still holds. Yet, even as the first edition appeared, the term multiculturalism fell out of favour within international debates to be replaced by the term integration. In the wake of 9/11 in New York and the subsequent 'war on terror' mainstream liberalism in the West became increasingly intolerant of debate about cultural diversity. In a muscular liberal climate where notions of a clash of civilisations were taken seriously, nuanced debates about the benefits of recognising black and ethnic minority cultural distinctiveness fell out of favour. However, one of the problems of anti-multiculturalism is that it has made racism easier to ignore and easier to deny. In this context, the final chapter examines the challenges of acknowledging and addressing racism within Irish policy debates.

Notes

1 P. Faughnan, *Refugees and Asylum Seekers in Ireland* (Dublin: Social Science Research Centre University College Dublin, 1999), p. 6.
2 M. Woods and N. Humphries, *Seeking Asylum in Ireland: Comparative Figures for Asylum Seekers in Ireland and Europe in 2000 and 2001* (Dublin: Social Science Research Centre University College Dublin, 2001), p. 8.
3 *Ibid.*, p. 18.
4 Conor Lenihan cited in Office of the Minister for Integration, *Migration Nation: Statement on Integration Strategy and Diversity Management* (Dublin: Stationery Office, 2007), p. 7.
5 P. Hart, *The IRA and Its Enemies: Violence and Community in Cork 1916–23* (Oxford: Oxford University Press, 1980); L. Gibbons, 'Memory without walls: From Kevin Barry to Osama Bin Laden', *Village*, 20 October 2005. About this, see B. Fanning, *New Guests of the Irish Nation* (Dublin: Irish Academic Press, 2009), p. 136.
6 T. Dunne, *Rebellions: Memoir, Memory and 1798* (Dublin: Lilliput Press, 2010) p. 279.
7 J. O'Connell, 'Myths of Innocence', in B. Baumgartl and A. Favell (eds), *A New Xenophobia in Europe* (London: Kluwer Law International, 1995).
8 B. Anderson, *Imagined Communities: Reflections on the Origin and Spread of Nationalism* (London: Verso, 1983).
9 C. Ó'Gráda, *Jewish Ireland in the Age of Joyce: A Socioeconomic History* (New Jersey: Princeton University Press, 2006), p. 193.
10 *Ibid.*, p. 192.
11 C. Joppke, 'The Legal–Domestic Sources of Immigrant Rights: The United States, Germany and the European Union', *Comparative Political Studies*, 34(4) (2001), p. 345.

2

Racism in Ireland

This chapter examines the origins and changing context of racism in Irish society. This, in the first instance, relates to shifting understandings of race and racial distinctiveness, which have impacted upon Irish society. It is argued that Ireland was never insulated from the racisms that justified the subjugation of black people by the West. Understandings of racial difference in Ireland, as elsewhere, were the product of colonial ideologies of Western superiority. To some extent popular debates on prejudice and intolerance towards new refugee and immigrant minority communities have implied that these are the natural response of a homogeneous society which knows no better. There has been considerable emphasis on the concept of xenophobia, literally 'fear of the stranger', to explain such prejudice and intolerance rather than the concept of racism. Such distinctions ignore how such fear of the other is often rooted in understandings of cultural difference superimposed upon beliefs about the biological difference of races. It remains the case that 'race' provides an ongoing basis for both the stereotyping and self-labelling of groups.[1] Assumptions of biological superiority and inferiority are often regarded with contempt in public discourse, but many contemporary prejudices and intolerances against black and ethnic minority communities in Ireland, as elsewhere, rely upon a code of common assumptions about racial distinctiveness.

Until recently the existence of such racisms in Irish society could easily be contested because of dominant presumptions of social homogeneity. This notion was itself an ideological construct. It was born, in part, out of nineteenth-century nationalist claims that there was such a thing as an Irish race. Nineteenth-century Irish nationalism, along with the nation-building ideologies of other European countries, emphasised the superiority of the Irish and the inferiority of the non-Irish. Irish identity was not just constructed in opposition to Britishness. It was expressed in a sense of national pride in Irish missionary efforts. Assumptions of Irish spiritual superiority combined with colonial ideologies of Western superiority within enduring relationships between Ireland, as part of the

West, and Western colonies in Africa and Asia. Dominant constructions of Irishness also placed indigenous minorities outside the nation. A history of Irish racisms has been revealed as monocultural presumptions about the nature of Irishness which have become eroded.

Race and racism

The term racism describes negative attitudes and practices towards persons because of their membership of groups perceived to differ in physical or cultural characteristics from the perceiver. The starting points for such claims are beliefs that different races exist and that membership of a 'race' makes a person innately superior or inferior. The justifications offered for such beliefs have shifted over time. Claims made about racial superiority or inferiority have cited religious proofs. These were subsequently repackaged as scientific and, more recently as, social scientific 'truth'. Racism, as such, describes a number of interlocking discourses which emerged in turn, were superimposed upon each other, and which can be seen to persist within ideological and everyday understandings of social difference.

The concept of race was first used to refer to the genealogy of groups of people with common ancestry, customs and a common native history. Writers have discussed the characteristics of the Irish, the Germans or the English as distinct races with due emphasis on the nobility of their own race and the inferiority of other races. The notion of an Irish race was employed in late nineteenth-century Catholic Irish nationalism to negate claims of the inferiority of the Irish within colonial ideology. This emerging cultural nationalism ideologically contested such constructions through the evocation of a mythology which constructed the Irish Celt or Gael as an ideal type, who was pure of race, loved his religion and country and, was above all, Catholic. These racial undertones were, for example, described in the *Gaelic Annual* (1907–8):

> The Irish Celt is distinguished among the races for height and strength, manly vigour and womanly grace: despite wars and domestic disabilities, the stamina of the race has survived in almost pristine perfection. The ideal Gael is a matchless athlete, sober, pure in mind, speech and deed, self possessed, self-reliant, self-respecting, loving his religion and his country with a deep and restless love, earnest in thought and effective in action.[2]

Claims that nations constituted races, based upon presumed common ancestry, were, in effect, claims about blood ties or shared biological heritage. Most notably, the Nazi assertion of an Aryan or German master race centred upon beliefs that the Jews were an inferior race who had biologically and culturally corrupted the German nation. European nationalisms all distinguished, to some extent, the 'true' Germans, French, English or Irish from lesser peoples and races through sectarianism, anti-Semitism or colonial ideologies of racial superiority. The linking of race and nation continues to have a degree of resonance in popular Irish discourse. During 1999 and 2000, for instance, the Irish Electricity Supply Board ran a billboard campaign across the country which used slogans such as 'This Island Race' and 'Heating the Nation' interchangeably.

The concept of race acquired a second meaning within a series of successive yet overlapping accounts of phenotypical difference in the relationship between 'the West and the rest'. 'Explanations' of racial differences emerged alongside shifting Western understandings of the world from the Middle Ages onwards. Before the Enlightenment the main ideological justifications for racism emerged from religious doctrine. A long-standing primitive colour prejudice had equated blackness with ugliness, evil, danger and sexual transgression. Black was the colour of the devil in a European folklore that drew upon encounters with the Moors.[3] Subsequently, folklore racisms became theologically refined to justify slavery and colonialism. For example, from the seventeenth century onwards the account in the book of Genesis of how the children of Ham were cursed by Ham's father Noah to be slaves was cited as proof that the oppression of black people was part of God's plan. In societies where literal interpretations of the Bible were accepted as the truth such an argument was difficult to contest.[4] Claims that black people were inferior to white people could be asserted as truth on the back of religious beliefs.

Religious proofs of the legitimacy of racism were in part superseded by so-called 'scientific' proofs of the biological inferiority of black people. According to Lively this was very much a case of pouring old wine into new bottles.[5] Distinctions made in the nineteenth century between superior and inferior races were part of a broader discourse of progress within the West. Enlightenment notions of Western superiority and a (mis)reading of evolutionary theories combined with earlier racisms to suggest that there was a hierarchy among races stretching from the ape-like 'lower races' to the more evolved, and thus superior (white) races.

Race as a contested concept

A number of social scientists have questioned whether the terms 'race' and 'racial' should be used at all. Gilroy, for instance, argues that the use of such terms reifies 'race'.[6] Some French intellectuals have tried to eliminate the word 'race' from the French constitution, claiming that racism is real, races are not.[7] However, there are problems with such approaches. Foremost among these, according to Body-Gendtrot, would be the difficulty of opposing biological racism if the term race was suppressed.[8] During the twentieth century 'race' has been ever present within bureaucratic, technical, academic and political discourse. This legacy needs to be faced if racism is to be addressed. Race may not be a valid social science concept, yet it often provides the basis of forms of social identity.[9] As Gilroy acknowledges, an antipathy to race 'may be viewed as a betrayal of those groups whose oppositional, legal and even democratic claims have come to rest on identities and solidarities forged at great cost from the categories given to them by their oppressors'.[10]

It is important not to conflate all forms of prejudice under the label of racism. It is possible, even useful, to distinguish between racisms, xenophobias, sectarianisms and other forms of prejudice while at the same time acknowledging the impact and consequences of race thinking on beliefs about distinctive groups within dominant ideologies, beliefs and stereotypes. One problem with a narrow definition of racism is that the concept of race has more than one meaning. Solomos argues that race and ethnicity are not 'natural' categories, even though both concepts are often represented as if they were. Their boundaries are not fixed, nor are their memberships uncontested. Racial and ethnic groups, like nations, are imagined communities.[11]

The term racialisation describes a process of race thinking by which specific groups of people are 'constructed' as a 'type' with reference to a limited number of physical and cultural characteristics. Their actual or assumed behaviour, abilities and values are then explained by reference to those selected features. The concept of racialisation describes processes of labelling and stereotyping by which particular groups are identified by direct or indirect reference to their real or imagined phenotypical characteristics in such a way as to suggest that they can only be understood as a supposedly biological unity.[12] Nation-building ideologies have employed race thinking to justify processes of external and internal colonisation. Various writers have identified anti-Irish prejudice in Britain as a form of racism rooted in colonial ideologies of racial superiority.[13] One example of this was an account of the Irish written by Charles Kingsley in 1860:

I am haunted by the human chimpanzees I saw along that hundred miles of horrible country … to see white chimpanzees is dreadful; if they were black, one would not feel it so much, but their skins, except where tanned by exposure, are as white as ours.[14]

The idea that the white Irish, or other white populations such as the Irish Travelling people, can experience racism warrants specific examination. Race thinking can embody forms of self-labelling as well as the stereotyping and racialisation of the other. At the same time outgroups may be racialised in opposite to implicit ideas of normalcy. Dyer argues that there is a tendency to regard whites as a non-race within some forms of race discourse.[15] White is constructed as normal. Whites, unlike non-white racialised populations, are 'just' human, yet, to paraphrase Orwell, some whites are whiter than others. Some white groups have been racialised as inferior within colonialism and nation-building.

Since the 1960s use of the term racism has expanded to refer to a whole complex of factors which produce racial discrimination, and ever more loosely, to designate those which produce racial disadvantage.[16] For example, the concept of institutional racism describes how minorities suffer from discrimination when racism within society becomes reflected in organisations and institutions. The discriminations experienced by minorities may be unintentional but they are often profound. They emanate from the inability or unwillingness of organisations and institutions to take into account the diversity of society in providing services. They may be linked with a denial of the possibility of racism within unwarranted assumptions of social homogeneity. They may even be a product of narrow definitions of racism.

The Parekh Report entitled *The Future of Multi-Ethnic Britain* (2000) defined racism broadly to include the experiences of Jews, Muslims and Irish as well as black people. It argued that anti-Irish racism has many of the same features as most racisms. The report criticised race equality organisations, academics and other specialists for promoting a narrow definition of racism which tacitly denied the existence of anti-Irish racism within a 'myth of homogeneity'; a false belief that the Irish were indistinguishably part of the British white majority.[17] It argued that denial of anti-Irish racism was part of the institutional structure of anti-Irish racism. Mac an Ghaill states that such responses to the Irish in Britain illustrate the limits of the black–white dualistic model of racial discrimination.[18] Conceptions of racial difference, based exclusively on skin colour, served to position the Irish as racially the same as the white English while at the same time anti-Irish racism held that they were racially inferior to the white British.[19] Travellers experience a similar ambivalence within the

Irish nation to that experienced by the Irish in Britain. Denials of Traveller distinctiveness in Ireland have served to justify state policies of assimilation as a form of internal colonisation. Arguably the structure of anti-Traveller racism in Ireland is somewhat similar to that of anti-Irish racism in Britain.

Irish racisms and colonial legacies

Ireland has a shared history of race and racism with other Western countries as well as its own specific engagements with black societies through colonialism. The legacy of colonialism in Irish society as elsewhere is complex. Just as British colonial expansion in Asia and Africa resulted in the development of Asian communities in Kenya or South Africa so also were soldiers, colonial police, administrators and missionaries from Ireland part of the history of Western colonialism. Throughout the nineteenth century the British army, colonial police forces and, at times, the Indian civil service, were disproportionately of Irish origin.[20] In 1831 42.2 per cent were Irish born at a time when 32.3 per cent of the population of Britain and Ireland, were Irish born. Even as the population declined during the nineteenth century Irish people continued to be disproportionately represented in the British army. Irish soldiers, police and administrators served imperial interests all around the world.[21] Irish regiments proved as capable of brutality towards native populations as any other colonial troops.[22] Those who made their living directly from colonialism, their families and their communities of origin were part of an intersection between Ireland and other colonised countries marked by racist ideologies of 'white' Western superiority as well as other racisms which held the Irish to be inferior. According to Holmes, Ireland acquired an 'unwelcome heritage' of colonialism that sits ill at ease with its reputation as a country that struggled against colonialism.[23]

McVeigh notes that Philip Sheridan, an Irish emigrant to the United States who rose to be commander in chief of the American army, coined and lived by the phrase that 'the only good injun is a dead one'.[24] The genocide of Native Americans found ongoing ideological justification in the Hollywood westerns that entertained generations of Irish people in the decades that followed. Generations of little boys in Ireland, as elsewhere, played at cowboys and Indians. Through the nineteenth and twentieth centuries Irish people, along with those of other Western countries, imbibed a popular culture which presented tales of colonial adventure and conquest alongside white supremacist beliefs about race. Novels of the era of colonial expansion, or the twentieth-century films based upon these, were part of a broad popular culture which represented Africans as primitive and as the 'white man's burden'. Collectively, these promoted and reproduced racist beliefs within Western society:

> In particular the notion of atavism – the belief that the 'primitive' people of Africa constituted an earlier stage of human development – often recurs: all references to primeval swamps, to primitive rituals, the colonial subjects' perceived deficiency of language, intellect and culture attest to this belief.[25]

Irish missionaries were part of an expansion of Christianity within the empires of Europe. They aided the spread of empire with remorseless effectiveness.[26] They convinced indigenous populations to abandon their own cultural systems and to embrace those of the conquering peoples. The development of the Irish missions can be dated from the early decades of the nineteenth century, after Catholic emancipation in 1829, when the Irish church underwent a process of renewal and reform.[27] Catholic orders from the continent that played a role in this revitalisation were often referred to as missionaries. In 1842 the first Irish seminary, All Hallows, aimed at training priests for the 'foreign missions' was opened. A prospectus for the college outlined the purpose of such missions as; 'to extend the Empire of Jesus Christ and to rescue from slavery of the devil some millions of our fellow creatures who are at present either buried in the darkness of idolatry, or labouring under the greatest spiritual distress for a want of priests'.[28]

The organisation of such missions became an integral part of Irish life and identity. For example, the Association of the Propagation of the Faith, which was established in Dublin in 1838 to promote the foreign missions, soon had branches in every diocese. The Association was as much concerned with heightening missionary consciousness among Catholics as with the task of fundraising. By 1841 its journal, aimed at clergy and educated Catholics, sold 12,000 copies each month. By 1930 similar publications had achieved an established circulation of 130,000.[29]

It is perhaps no accident that the zenith of Irish missionary efforts coincided with the emergence of the Irish nation state and the subsequent half-century of Catholic hegemony in Irish life. In the early twentieth century the missionary magazines reflected nationalist sentiments in proclaiming the emergence of a 'golden age of Irish civilisation'. National pride and religiosity were constructed in relation to each other.[30] The extension of Ireland's spiritual glory in the missions was linked to the emergence of a Catholic Irish nation at home:

The imaginative link between Irish freedom and Irish Catholicism had already been forged by nationalists such as Pearse and Plunkett. But the advocates of the missionary movement gave it a new dimension by extending it to include those 'fighting the battle for Christ in Africa and Asia'. Freedom, it was argued was the object for which the nationalists were fighting. Freedom of a spiritual order – a higher freedom – was the object of the 'warriors' on the missions. Thus a common objective, a common idealism, differing only in degree, was at the root of both struggles.[31]

The missionary magazines depicted the missions as part of the life of the nation before and after independence. After the civil war, the war for Christ in Africa and Asia was portrayed as struggle that could reunite Irishmen whatever their political persuasion. National identity was constructed in terms of spiritual superiority. The heroic sacrifices of the missions were necessary to 'assure millions unborn a faith permanent and pure as the faith of the Gael'.[32] This missionary nationalism drew upon colonial ideologies of racial superiority. A generation still living remembers the 'black babies' as a central image of the Irish missions. As recalled by Tim Pat Coogan in *Wherever Green Is Worn*:

We were brought up believing that Africans as a class were much in need of the civilising influences of the Irish religions as parched earth was of water. It was an image propagated by missionary magazines with their pictures of a big beaming Irish priest, generally robed in white, surrounded by a group of adoring, chubby little black children.[33]

Clare Boylan's novel *Black Baby* tells the story of an old Irish woman who meets a black woman who she believes to be the baby she 'purchased' with her first communion money. As recounted in the novel:

The Irish always had an intense sentimental preoccupation with distant pagans. There was no tradition of nursery stories. Instead, it was the dusky heathen who stirred the infant imagination. There was romance in these stories and terror too, for the missionary fell prey to foul disease, to the leopard's tooth and the cannibal's pot. Children loved to hear such tales and were schooled early to sacrifice for God's unchosen. 'Penny for the black baby', was one of the first phrases learnt. There was as much pleasure in putting a penny in the mission box, with its nodding black head on top, as spending it on an orange.[34]

Such paternalistic understandings of black people have contributed to contemporary responses to refugees and asylum seekers in Irish society even if the missionary movement itself has reduced in scale, and has been superseded, to a degree, by secular aid and development organisations in recent decades. A 1998 magazine article described refugee children in an Irish primary school as black babies. The author commented that 'all over the country the nuns who have spent years collecting for the little black babies have finally saved up enough to get some'.[35] Such comments suggest an ongoing legacy of racism and paternalism, rooted in the collective Irish imagination, which impacts upon black people in Irish society.

Race, ethnicity and nation

The sociologist Max Weber defined racial identities, ethnicity and nationality in ways that highlighted common presumptions shared between them. Racial identities were predicated on presumptions of common inherited and inheritable traits understood to derive from common descent. Ethnicity referred to human groups that entertain a belief in their common descent because of similarities of physical type or of customs or of both, or because of memories of colonisation or migration. Weber emphasised that ethnic identities depended on such belief; it did not matter whether or not an objective blood relationship existed. He defined nationality as a sense of common distinctiveness which is felt to derive from common descent. Whether racial, ethnic or national differences were real or not was irrelevant to Weber, what mattered were the consequences of such beliefs upon how societies were organised and segregated. He noted that beliefs in ethnic identities often came to set limits upon how a community was politically defined.[36]

Weber for his part believed that ethnicity and nationalism would decline in importance as societies modernised, industrialised and individualised.[37] The experiences of the twentieth and twenty-first centuries have been otherwise. The twentieth century produced explicitly racial states such as Nazi Germany. These could be viewed as extreme legacies of beliefs in race-as-nation. Many Western countries still have 'national front'-style political parties who overtly profess nineteenth-century beliefs in racial nations whereas such essentialist beliefs have arguably been consigned to history within the political mainstream of these Western countries. Beliefs about racial, ethnic and nationalist distinctiveness – all shared core presumptions that identity was a matter of blood relations and shared primordial biological origins – arguably persist as a kind of race thinking software or ghost within the machinery of the modern nation state.

Such essentialist roots are evident for example in the names of some Irish political parties. Sinn Féin translates as we, ourselves or 'us' (as distinct from 'them'), Fianna Fáil translated into English means the Soldiers of

Destiny and Fine Gael as the tribe of Ireland. Such names are echoes from a time when declarations that there existed an Irish race would hardly have raised a sceptical eyebrow. Nationalism within the political mainstream and in popular discourse became increasingly tempered in the second half of the twentieth century, partly due, in the Irish case, to the Northern Ireland conflict. Aspects of a key founding event, the 1916 Rising led by Patrick Pearce, an essentialist nationalist who promoted the necessity of blood sacrifice to achieve Ireland's national destiny, were played down by successive governments and it is only since the end of violence in the North, that a degree of triumphal celebration – military parades of the kind found in many nation states – has crept back into annual commemoration of 1916 by the Irish state.

In early twentieth century (before Weber was translated into English) the term race was often used to denote what would now be described as ethnicity. This section examines debates from that period within the Irish journal *Studies* so as to illustrate the intersections between race thinking, what we would now call ethnicity and nationalism within Irish debates. These debates paralleled political efforts to promote independence, by considering the distinctiveness of the Irish nation, examine the dangers of extreme nationalism and highlight racism in Nazi Germany and the United States.

A key intellectual influence on the former was Ernest Renan's classic 1882 essay 'Qu'est-ce qu'une nation?'. Renan criticised scientific racism as ignorant of human history and a dangerous influence on politics. 'Race' as historians understood the term – here he meant how given beliefs about the origins of peoples could be invented or forgotten over time – was 'something that makes and unmakes itself', not a fixed truth about human beings:

> Human history is essentially different from zoology. Race is not everything, as it is in the case of rodents and felines; and we have no right to go about the world, feeling the heads of people, then taking them by the throat, and saying, 'You are our blood; you belong to us!' Beyond anthropological characteristics there are reason, justice, truth and beauty; and these are the same in all.

That which purported to be racial science, he argued, was inevitably falsified science.[38]

Two 1913 essays by Stephen Brown, 'What Is a Nation?' and 'The Question of Irish Nationality', applied Renan's analysis to the Irish case and instigated an ongoing debate in the Jesuit journal *Studies* about race, ethnicity and nation.[39] Brown outlined and discused the extent to which the Irish case fitted criteria for nationhood identified by 'anthropologists and sociologists' in the 'truly vast body of literature dealing with the connection between national character and *race*'.[40] 'Race' as used by Brown followed Renan's ethnographic focus on presumed national characteristics rather than those presumed to relate to genetic phenotype. Brown, like Renan, identified custom, the unwritten and traditional codes which rule the habits of people and 'by long iteration, furrows deep traits in its character' as a 'nation-building force'.[41] Linguistic distinctiveness too could have a nation-building role.

However, Brown emphasised that the boundaries of language and national belonging were by no means the same even if a common language – here he was thinking of the United States – had the power 'to weld into some sort of oneness' the 'jumble of races as is to be found within its borders'.[42] Religion, he argued was 'the strongest and most important of the elements which go to constitute nationality'.[43] Before the Reformation, he argued, the idea of a common Christianity was stronger than that of loyalty to separate nationalities; 'The enemies of Christianity were, so to speak, the national enemies of all'.[44] Since the Reformation, religious differences had prevented devotion to a common country but the experience of modern nations had shown 'the absurdity of the notion that there can be no national unity without religious unity'. Brown emphasised the role of historical consciousness – of Fatherland as 'the patrimony of memories that unite us to our fathers and in terms of an understanding of common origin' – as the crucial block of nation-building.[45] Nations were held together by common memories:

A nation looks back on its past as a lesson for its national life in the present, and as a justification of its continued national life in the future. Common memories are the nourishment of patriotism, the foundation of national consciousness and by the common hopes and aspirations that sprung from these.[46]

Taking these elements together, 'race', language, custom, religion and common understandings of history, Brown drew a few conclusions about what constituted a nation. A nation consisted of a relatively large group living together in common territory in organised social relations held together by a peculiar kind of spiritual oneness. There was, he insisted, nothing mystic about this sense of oneness. National consciousness consisted, 'of common memories of historic things wrought in common and suffered in common in the past, and secondly the actual consent to carry on that common life, as a distinct people, master of its destinies, shaper of its future'.[47]

Another article by Brown in 1920 addressed the problem of using the terms 'race' and 'nationality' interchangeably.[48] Here, in the absence of the concept of ethnicity he sought to explain how the term 'race', as used by anthropologists, acknowledged no racial distinctions between Europeans.[49] Race understood as nation admitted 'absurd and often unjust explanations' of the inherent qualities of different types; 'the Latin decadent, the Slav politically incapable, the Irish lazy and mendacious' and so on. Brown's literature review examined the use of abstractions such as the Teutonic, Anglo-Saxon or Celtic races. It cited refutations of the German idea of nationality which was understood to be 'based on the ethnographic or race theory'. Brown's account, to use a later terminology, was sceptical of accounts that presumed intrinsic characteristics of any race as nationality. Yet, Brown presumed a psychology of national character.[50] Different peoples (Brown used the term 'race' for want of an alternative) cultivated distinctiveness. Ethnic distinctiveness, in effect, was presented as grounds for national self-determination. Another article in *Studies* argued that the white Irish deserved parity with other white nations and colonial powers:

> Ireland is now the only white nationality in the world (let us leave coloured possessions out of the discussion) where the principle of self-determination is not, at least in theory, conceded.[51]

During the First World War a number of writers preoccupied with national character discussed the role of the German state in promoting national culture, or *Kultur.* As put in one 1915 article:

> *Kultur* is not primarily an attribute of the individual, as culture is, but of the group, and especially of the nation. It is what makes a nation a state, it is its organic life. It consists, in a word, in ordered cooperation. Its scope is not merely intellectual, but is moral, spiritual and material as well. It is the action of the state in stimulating and guiding the energies of its subjects and in co-ordinating them with one another for a common purpose, and the reciprocal devotion of the citizens to the state. It is the product of education; perhaps the most wonderful of its products, for it implies the universal, willing, and above all, intelligent acceptance of a common ideal.[52]

Several articles criticised the fusion of state and nation implied by this definition of *Kultur.* Alfred O'Reilly, later President of University College Cork, citing Hegel and Fichte, argued that in Germany, 'culture bears a government stamp, it is a state product, manufactured in school and camp'.[53]

A 1925 article, 'Nationality as a Claim to Sovereignty' by John Marcus O'Sullivan echoed much of Brown's argument.[54] The nation, O'Sullivan maintained, had a quasi-personality:

> There is a feeling of oneness, a will to be and to act as one; a distinct culture has been evolved, which at least tends to desire and even create its own governmental machinery. Its members have grown together, so as to have developed a corporate consciousness, a spiritual oneness, a feeling that they can live happily when they live together, unhappily when forcibly separated or subordinated to others.[55]

O'Sullivan accepted that a vigorous national feeling combined with a strong spirit of independence was perhaps one of the most solid foundations that a state can have. However, it could be taken too far. Extreme forms of nationalism were not to be condoned. In the end, nationalism, as an ideology, rested upon abstraction and as such differed, or should differ, from the real loves people could have for individuals or family.

In 1933 Daniel Binchy, the Irish Minister to Germany from 1929 to 1932 published an astute article on Adolf Hitler immediately after Hitler's rise to power.[56] Binchy had first heard Hitler speak in Munich in 1921. His article detailed the role of anti-Semitism in building the National Socialist movement from 1920 onwards and explicitly described such anti-Semitism as racism.[57] Binchy took care to refute various anti-Semitic claims noting, for instance, that thousands of Jews (denounced by Hitler as traitors) had fought bravely for Germany during the Great War, and to challenge the self-contradictory claims that Jews were at once 'the leaders of international capital and of the Bolsheviks who seek to destroy it'.[58] Binchy detailed plans, outlined in *Mein Kampf*, for the withdrawal of citizenship from Jews and the confiscation of their property. He outlined Nazi eugenics proposals. Hitler, Binchy explained, would extend sterilisation policies to those who were either corporally or mentally unfit to have vigorous offspring.[59] Binchy's scrupulous refutation of anti-Semitism contrasted vividly with the extreme anti-Semitism of Charles Bewley, the Irish diplomat who succeeded him in Berlin and from the kinds of anti-Semitism (considered in Chapter 4) that became institutionalised within the Irish state.

A number of critiques of Nazi racial theories appeared in *Studies* in the wake of Binchy's article. One 1935 article argued that such race theories found a ready ally in extreme nationalism and totalitarianism.[60] A 1938 article argued that Nazi racial theories were 'pseudo-scientific nonsense'. Their real importance, this implied, were as psychological tools of nation-building:

It is a natural tendency for nations to seek an escape from the inadequacies of the present in a mythical past. This is a common experience in
all countries. But it requires a portentous absence of humour to accept
the theory in the form given to it in Nazi literature – in this form it
is altogether pathological. A certain minimum of self-esteem is, no
doubt, necessary for the nation as for the individual. And unsuccessful
peoples, in moments of stress, may have difficulty in reaching it. This
is the purpose of mass-propaganda. It aims at restoring self-respect to
a defeated people. In moderation racial feeling may be at the worst an
amiable weakness, at best a proper pride. The Greek, with much justice,
thought himself superior to the barbarian. And in a negative way we
have all heard, nearer home, of 'lesser breeds without the law' and of
the 'wild hysterics of the Celt'.[61]

Beliefs about race and ethnicity became integral to development of nation
states such as the Republic of Ireland. Chapter 3 outlines how Irish nation-
building, by which is meant processes of social modernisation affecting
how societies became organised and regulated and national identities
promulgated, worked to exclude internal minorities and others defined
as outside the nation.

The reinvention of racism

Scientific racisms have become widely discredited, especially in the aftermath of the Holocaust, and have been largely expunged from political
discourse in Western countries. However, the discrediting of racism, so
defined, does not mean that racisms have not persisted in Western society.
The social sciences provided new 'justifications' for racist beliefs through
assumptions that the cultures and ways of life of black and minority
ethnic groups were inferior or less valid than the dominant ways of life of
Western white society. These beliefs drew upon the colonial assumptions
of white superiority that was part and parcel of the Western Enlightenment. Anthropology, eugenics, social biology and social ecology retained
the use of racial categories and have suggested, to some extent, a physical
or biological basis for social and cultural difference.[62]

The term 'new racism' emerged in an attempt to explain a racist
discourse about black and minority ethnic groups in Britain which was
not grounded in claims that such groups were biologically inferior. It
was a sophisticated discourse with many levels. At the apex, politicians
opposed to the presence of such minorities could deny racism ('of course
we don't believe that black people are inferior'). They could, at the same
time, pursue racist goals of exclusion within an anecdotal discourse that

represented the imagined grievances of the (white) community against black people.[63] This might be understood as a response to a prohibition of 'race' talk in public space.[64] Contemporary manifestations of racism are often coded in a language that aims to circumvent accusations of racism. In the case of 'new racism' race is coded as culture. However, biological or phenotypic distinctions are at the heart of the distinctions made between cultures. It is assumed, within a pseudo-biologically defined culturalism, that the qualities of social groups are fixed, and are in fact natural.[65]

Race and underclass

Contemporary racisms continue to be justified by widely held assumptions of the cultural inferiority of 'racially' or phenotypically distinct populations. The term phenotype describes visible or measurable physical characteristics such as hair or eye colour, bone structure or skin colour. The new racism implies that cultural inferiority can be identified on the basis of physical characteristics. Such assumptions of inferiority are often manifested within coded academic and political discourses preoccupied with the threat to social order posed by the existence of deviant 'underclasses' who happen to be black.

The term underclass is generally used to describe groups, such as the chronically unemployed, vagrants, the criminal 'underground' or occupational groups defined as immoral that are, in essence, deemed to exist beyond the pale of respectable society.[66] The concept harks back to nineteenth-century Victorian engagements with urban poverty that employed language and metaphors derived from colonialism in discussion of areas inhabited by the urban poor. The concept drew upon racialised conceptions of society. The poor were depicted in the journalism and social research of the day as 'the people of the abyss'. Their children were described as 'street Arabs'. The journalists and researchers, such as Charles Mayhew, who wrote about them were referred to as 'social explorers' and their visits to the slums were likened to journeys to darkest Africa. The language used to depict the lives of the poor was a language of 'domestic colonisation'. Domestic missionaries went among the poor; 'who lived in parishes "as dark as Africa", in "darkest" Liverpool or London, or in *Darkest England*, as put in the title of a book by General Booth who founded the Salvation Army'.[67] Within these discourses the poor were a race apart and poverty was constructed as a moral problem. The poor were perceived as living outside of society. They were deemed to constitute a threat to the social order.

The Victorian intersection between race as national type, where the underclass fell below the socially constructed moral attributes of nation, and race as a biological 'fact' has re-emerged in contemporary uses of the term underclass as a code for depicting black and ethnic minorities in contemporary societies as culturally inferior and deviant. There are a number of reasons for this. First, the influence of neo-liberalism has to some extent reinstated nineteenth-century understandings of poverty as an individual problem of moral failing. Neo-liberal critiques of state provided welfare have been blamed for a breakdown of 'traditional' social structures, family values and work ethics.

Second, a new emphasis on the deviant and transgressive nature of the poor emerged in the United States as a coded racialised discourse which discussed black families and communities within cultural stereotypes rooted in colonial racisms. These implied that only black single mothers have children by different fathers, that dysfunctional black families were part of dysfunctional black cultures and that crime was a product of the deviance of black men. This discourse has been promulgated within academia as well as through media stereotypes of black people as pimps, pushers and prostitutes. The work of right-wing academics such as Charles Murray has reasserted the biological foundations of racism.[68] The argument by Hernstein and Murray's *The Bell Curve* (1994) is that IQ is genetic and exists and can be measured independently of environment by conventional IQ testing, that intelligence is biologically inherited and that some groups, notably African-Americans, have lower average intelligence and that this in turn explains why they occupy the lowest strata of society. The research for the book was largely funded by a right-wing organisation founded by eugenicists in the 1930s.[69] Steinberg argues that the underclass thesis points to a resurgence in the popularity of biological determinism during the 1990s. He notes that biological determinism was an attractive ideology in societies where social hierarchies were fixed or caste-like. In the past, social mobility and change had undermined this ideology, along with other ideologies that consigned black and ethnic minorities, women and the poor to positions of social inferiority. *The Bell Curve* arrived at a time when American society had become more static and when the gaps between the haves and the have-nots were expanding. In this context, biological determinism seemingly accounted for the permanently subordinate position of black people.[70] Such an account ignores the negative impact of racism upon social mobility. If the 'people of the abyss' in Western societies have become black, then the black urban ghettos in the United States are themselves a product of virulent racism in housing markets and discrimination in employment.[71]

The term underclass has gained some currency within British and Irish welfare debates. A degree of acceptance of the underclass thesis, stripped to a degree of underlying racialised assumptions and therefore employed interchangeably with terms such as social exclusion, has been absorbed by the British left and has underpinned New Labour welfare-to-work measures. The use of the term in such a manner remains problematic because the racialised assumptions about deprived communities all too easily become reasserted when such communities include black and ethnic minorities. In the Irish case, descriptions of Travelling People as an economically disadvantaged underclass by advocates of Traveller rights have emerged alongside racialised depictions of Travellers as a culturally, and even biologically, inferior underclass.[72] In such a context there is a tendency to explain Traveller economic and social exclusion in racialised terms. For instance, an article in the *Sunday Independent* in July 2000 suggested that high rates of Traveller infant mortality, found to be more than double those of Irish society as a whole, 'might' be explained by interbreeding and that shorter life expectancies 'might' be explained by alcohol problems.[73] The article in question was a response to a briefing for journalists organised by Traveller organisations. This briefing had outlined the findings of research into the causes of Traveller health disadvantage that identified poverty and institutional barriers in accessing health care as the most likely explanations of higher Traveller mortality rates.[74] However, within popular discourse, the marginalisation of Travellers within Irish society continues to be explained in terms of their presumed deviance.

Institutional racisms

During the 1990s the issue of institutional racism became highlighted in the United Kingdom. The consequences of institutional racism include unequal access to services and unequal outcomes on the basis of race or ethnicity. This is illustrated by the following definition of institutional racism by the McPherson Inquiry:

> The collective failure of an organisation to provide an appropriate and professional service to people because of their colour, culture or ethnic origin. It can be seen in processes, attitudes and behaviour which amount to discrimination through unwitting prejudice, ignorance thoughtlessness and racist stereotyping which disadvantage ethnic minority people.[75]

The focus of the Macpherson Inquiry was the response of the London Metropolitan Police to the killing of Steven Lawrence, a black teenager.

The Inquiry found that the police had pursued the investigation less vigorously than they would have done if Steven had been white. The findings of the Inquiry emphasised institutional tendencies to treat black victims of crime as if they were criminals more so than would be the case if such victims were white. The wider context was one where black people were far more likely to be criminalised than white people, and of widespread racism towards black and ethnic minority police officers by their white colleagues. In short, racism informed how some police tended to deal with black people. Black people were more likely to be stopped and searched, charged with an offence and then imprisoned than white people. Part of this was due to overt racism but institutional practices were also seen to have produced differential outcomes for black and white people.

Within debates on institutional racism the focus has been on racist outcomes rather than racist intentions. Institutional barriers can be deliberate (overt discrimination) or unwitting. These might be identified on the basis of race or ethnicity in areas such as employment, education, health and policing. There is growing evidence of such institutional barriers in the Irish case. Here are some examples:

- Some 446 Africans were committed to prison in 2002 amounting to almost 4.6 per cent of the overall prison population; compared to the other members of Irish society these were hugely overrepresented.[76] That year the percentage of Africans in prison was more than eight times higher than the overall percentage of the Irish population in prison.
- A 2005 ESRI study found that black Africans were more likely than other non-EU migrants to experience harassment by neighbours or on the street but least likely to report such an incident to the police.[77] This suggests that the Gardaí (Irish police) may be less responsive to black victims of crime than to white victims. The ESRI study suggests that high levels of under-reporting of racist incidents and discrimination in Ireland. Again, this may point to institutional barriers to having such crimes acknowledged and taken seriously.
- The *Our Geels: All-Ireland Traveller Health Study* (2010) concluded that Travellers in twenty-first-century Ireland were experiencing 'the mortality experience of previous generations 50–70 years ago' and that the mortality gap between Travellers and the general population has widened in the past twenty years.[78] Like previous studies of Traveller health *Our Geels* reported high levels of discrimination from and low levels of trust in health service providers.[79]

Services configured towards a culture's expectations and needs of majority groups which wittingly or unwittingly neglect those of minority ethnic groups are likely to produce unequal outcomes for minority ethnic groups. A lack of intentionality can mask indifference. In the absence of explanations that focus on how institutions respond to different groups, outcomes may come to be explained in terms of the presumed deviance of the groups affected by institutional barriers. Areas to be considered include employment, education, health, education, housing and policing. Institutional forms of discrimination contribute to unequal outcomes on the basis of ethnicity; for example, where minority ethnic groups experience disproportionately poor standards of health. It must also be emphasised that people are inevitably faced with institutional barriers where they have fewer rights and entitlements than other members of society. This can be particularly seen in the case of immigrants from non-EU countries or asylum seekers.

Notes

1 J. Solomos and L. Back, *Racism and Society* (London: Macmillan, 1996), p. xiv.
2 J. Sugden and A. Bairner, *Sport, Sectarianism and Society in a Divided Ireland* (Leicester: Leicester University Press, 1993), p. 29.
3 A. Lively (1998) *Masks: Blackness, Race and the Imagination* (London: Chatto & Windus, 1998), pp. 13–52.
4 Fredrick Douglas contested the 'curse of Ham' as a justification for slavery in America by arguing that many slaves, perhaps including himself, had some white ancestry. See F. Douglas, *Narrative of the Life of Fredrick Douglas, an American Slave* (London: Penguin, 1986), p. 50.
5 Lively, *Masks*, pp. 13–52.
6 P. Gilroy (1998) 'Race Ends Here', *Ethnic and Racial Studies*, 21(5) (1998), p. 840.
7 S. Body-Gendrot, 'Now You See It, Now You Don't', *Ethnic and Racial Studies*, 21(5) (1998), p. 849.
8 *Ibid.*
9 Solomos and Back, *Racism and Society*, p. xiv.
10 Gilroy, 'Race Ends Here', p. 842.
11 J. Solomos, 'Race, Multiculturalism and Difference', in N. Stevenson (ed.), *Culture and Citizenship* (London: Sage, 2001) p. 119.
12 R. Miles, 'Racialisation', *Dictionary of Race and Ethnic Studies* (London: Routledge, 1996), p. 307.
13 L. P. Curtis, *Apes and Angels: The Irishman in Victorian Caricature* (New York: New York University Press, 1971) and C. Husband (1987) *Race in Britain: Continuity and Change* (London: Hutchinson, 1987).
14 Cited in Husband, *Race in Britain*, p. 12.
15 R. Dyer 'The Matter of Whiteness', in L. Back and J. Solomos (eds), *Theories of Race and Racism* (London: Routledge, 2000), p. 543.
16 M. Banton and R. Miles, 'Racism', in E. Cashmore (ed.), *Dictionary of Race and Ethnic Relations* (London: Routledge, 1995), p. 308.
17 B. Parekh, *The Future of Multi-Ethnic Britain* (London: Runnymede Trust, 2000), p. 61.

18 M. Mac an Ghaill, *Contemporary Racisms and Ethnicities* (Buckingham: Open University Press, 1999), p. 81.

19 *Ibid.*, p. 51.

20 D. H. Akenson, *The Irish Diaspora: A Primer* (London: Harman, 1993), p. 143.

21 *Ibid.*, p. 145.

22 Irish soldiers, referred to as 'Rishti', as distinct from 'Angrese' (English), were 'noted for their contempt for and brutal treatment of the Indian population'. See M. Holmes 'The Irish and India: Imperialism, Nationalism and Internationalism', in Bielenberg, *The Irish Diaspora*, p. 237.

23 Holmes, 'The Irish and India', p. 242.

24 R. McVeigh, *The Racialisation of Irishness: Racism and Anti-Racism in Ireland* (Belfast: Centre for Research and Documentation, 1997), pp. 42–3.

25 L. Young, 'Imperial Culture', in Back and Solomos, *Theories of Race and Racism*, p. 269.

26 Akenson, *The Irish Diaspora*, p. 147.

27 E. Hogan, *The Irish Missionary Movement: A Historical Survey, 1830–1980* (Dublin: Gill & Macmillan, 1992), p. 2.

28 *Ibid.*, p. 21.

29 *Ibid.*, pp. 63, 67, 146.

30 *Ibid.*, p. 151.

31 *Ibid.*, pp. 147–8.

32 Cited from *The African Missionary* (1914) in Hogan, *Irish Missionary Movement*, p. 152.

33 T. P. Coogan, *Wherever Green Is Worn: The Story of the Irish Diaspora* (London: Hutchinson, 2000), p. 508.

34 C. Boylan, *Black Baby* (New York: Doubleday, 1989).

35 *Magpie* (October 1998).

36 M. Weber, *Wirtshaft und Gesellschaft*, pp. 234–40, first published posthumously in 1922, trans. E. Matthews, in W. G. Runciman (ed.), *Max Weber: Selections in Translation* (Cambridge: Cambridge University Press, 1978).

37 I. Law, *Racism and Ethnicity: Global Debates, Dilemmas, Directions* (Harlow: Pearson, 2010) p. 65.

38 E. Renan, *The Poetry of the Celtic Races and Other Studies* (Kennikat Press, 1970), pp. 74–5.

39 'What Is a Nation?', *Studies*, 1 (1913), pp. 496–510; 'The Question of Irish Nationality', *Studies*, 1 (1913), pp. 634–55.

40 Original italics, Brown, 'What Is a Nation?', p. 499.

41 *Ibid.*, p. 503.

42 *Ibid.*

43 Sir John Seeley, *The Expansion of England*, p. 261, cited *ibid.*, p. 504.

44 *Ibid.*, p. 505.

45 L. Legrand, *L'Idée de Patri*, p. 58 cited *ibid.*

46 *Ibid.*, p. 505.

47 *Ibid.*, p. 509.

48 Brown, 'Recent Studies in Nationality', *Studies*, 9 (1920), pp. 20–464.

49 *Ibid.*, pp. 458–9.

50 *Ibid.*, p. 463.

51 See p. 226, John J. Horgan, 'Precepts and Practices: 1914–1919', *Studies*, 7 (1918), pp. 220–6, p. 226.

52 *Ibid.*, p. 214.
53 'Ideals at Stake', *Studies*, 4 (1915), pp. 16–33, p. 26.
54 Minister of Education 1926–32, see T. Garvin, *Preventing the Future: Why Ireland Remained So Poor for So Long* (Dublin: Gill & Macmillan, 2005), p. 134.
55 John. M. O'Sullivan, 'Nationality as a Claim to Sovereignty', *Studies*, 14 (1925), pp. 633–47, p. 634.
56 Prof. Daniel A. Binchy, 'Adolf Hitler', *Studies*, 22 (1933), pp. 29–47.
57 *Ibid.*, pp. 37–8.
58 *Ibid.*, p. 39.
59 *Ibid.*, p. 41.
60 J. Coyne, 'Alfred Rosenberg as German Prophet', *Studies*, 24 (1935), pp. 177–88, p. 180.
61 Rev. Prof. Denis O'Keefe, 'The Nazi Movement in Germany', *Studies*, 27 (1938), pp. 1–12, p. 6.
62 Notably in the work of the Chicago school of social ecology. From this socio-logical perspective 'races' were real things which interacted within processes that came to be known as race relations.
63 E.g., A. Brown, '"The Other Day I Met a Constituent Of Mine": A Theory of Anecdotal Racism', *Ethnic and Racial Studies*, 22(1) (1999), pp. 23–55.
64 *Ibid.*, p. 23.
65 Solomos and Back, *Racism and Society*, pp. 18–19.
66 P. van den Berghe, 'The Underclass', *Dictionary of Race and Ethnic Studies* (London: Routledge, 1996), p. 367.
67 G. Mooney, 'Remoralizing the Poor? Gender, Class and Philanthropy in Victorian Britain', in G. Lewis (ed.), *Forming Nation, Framing Welfare* (London: Routledge, 1999), p. 57.
68 R. Hernstein and C. Murray, *The Bell Curve: Intelligence and Class Structure in American Life* (New York: Free Press, 1994).
69 S. Steinberg, 'America Again at the Crossroads', in Solomos and Back, *Theories of Race and Racism*, p. 567.
70 *Ibid.*, p. 568.
71 Cited in Goldberg 'Racial Knowledge', in Back and Solomos, *Theories of Race and Racism*, p. 169.
72 J. McLaughlin, *Travellers and Ireland: Whose Country, Whose History?* (Cork: Cork University Press, 1995), p. 76.
73 'Time for Travellers to move on', *Sunday Independent* (23 July 2000).
74 See E. Sheehan, *Travellers: Citizens of Ireland* (Dublin: Parish of the Travelling People, 2000).
75 Sir William Macpherson (1999) *The Stephen Lawrence Inquiry: Report of an Inquiry by Sir William Macpherson of Cluny* (London: HMSO).
76 I. O'Donnell, 'Imprisonment and Penal Policy in Ireland', *Howard Journal*, 43(1) (2004), pp. 253–66, pp. 262–3.
77 ESRI, 2006, p. 40.
78 C. Kelleher *et al.*, *Our Geels: All-Ireland Traveller Health Study* (Dublin University College Dublin/Department of Health and Children, 2010).
79 In particular see qualitative research undertaken as part of the above study. R. Moore, J. Turner, R. Nic Chártaigh *et al.*, *All-Ireland Traveller Health Study*, Qualitative Studies: Technical Report 3 (Dublin: University College Dublin/Department of Health and Children).

3

Nation-building and exclusion

This chapter examines dominant (and changing) conceptions of Irish national identity. It explores the development of exclusionary conceptions of identity homogeneity linked to nationalism and nation-building from the nineteenth century onwards with reference to the experiences of Protestant, Jewish and Traveller minority communities. Much of this chapter is concerned with the past; first, to demonstrate how, with regards to dominant understandings of 'Irishness', the goalposts of imagined community have moved before and are likely to move again. From the nineteenth century onwards, Irish nation-building has been characterised by the development of exclusionary conceptions of identity and a socio-genesis of homogeneity linked to nationalism. Nations might be defined as 'imagined communities' where claimed ties of common history and ancestry achieve a sense of belonging.[1] They involve imagined ties in so far as any individual member will only ever interact with a minute proportion of those embraced by the same sense of identity. Yet these ties may also be 'real' in so far they relate to economic and political interdependencies especially insofar as these relate to 'others' or 'outsiders'. A process of nation-building which has contributed to contemporary Irish society and the development of the Irish state has been accompanied by a politics of national identity within which claims of social membership of various minority groups were discounted through racialised discourses which distinguished these from the 'true' Irish.

The politics of Irish identity

Throughout the nineteenth century profound shifts occurred within Irish nationalism whereby one hegemonic construction of Irishness which emphasised the Irishness of the minority Protestant elite was gradually displaced by a new Catholic 'Irish-Ireland' nationalist hegemony. The comparatively early development of mass political organisations in Ireland long preceded a belated industrialisation. This fostered a religious–ethnic conceptualisation of nation bound up with kinship ties and peasant tribalisms – such as represented within secret societies, rather than one shaped by class politics and secular modernisation.[2] Yet the community basis of this nationalism rapidly changed. From the 1820s a leadership ideologically inspired by liberalism and utilitarianism led a grassroots peasant movement organised by a modernising Catholic Church. From the 1830s the introduction of mass education accompanied the rapid decline of the Gaelic cultural base. The religious component of the identity of the Catholic majority intensified as a result of a huge societal dislocation produced by the famine in the 1840s, which undermined traditional forms of cultural identity. Fervent devotion to the Church provided a viable substitute symbolic system for the dying world of Gaelic culture.[3] Around the same time the Catholic Church became the focus of a project of organisational and doctrinal modernisation through what became referred to as the devotional revolution. Although the majority of the population were Catholics the nature of their religiosity had gradually shifted from reflecting a society where religious orthodoxies coexisted with popular supernaturalism to a reformed ultramontane Catholicism (which emphasised the authority of the papacy) characterised by a mission of constrictive modernisation.[4] The coincidence of Protestant evangelical revival and renascent Catholicism contributed substantially to an increase of religious sectarianism whereby religious affiliation became more central to the construction of identities:

> As the religious experience of all sorts of Irishmen and women became more 'modern', so priests, parsons and ministers were increasingly seen by their flocks and increasingly saw themselves as the guardians of theologically formal and conscious sectarian attitudes.[5]

Catholicism became institutionalised in Irish nationalism within the mass movement seeking Catholic Emancipation and resolution of other Catholic grievances such as tithes, bias in the judiciary, and Protestant proselytisation. In 1823 the Catholic leader Daniel O'Connell formed 'the Catholic Association', which developed from the then usual form of political organisations with membership drawn from social elites into an innovative mass movement which sought to mobilise hitherto excluded social classes within constitutional politics. Mass participation in the Association, as in subsequent political and cultural movements, was dependent on the active support of the Church.[6] Catholic conceptions of nation were also fostered through the emergence of a strong national and regional Catholic press by the 1840s.[7]

Protestant nationalism was based upon cultural and historical claims of Irishness as well as upon religious identity. A new Irish-Ireland hegemony undermined these claims within an exclusivist ideology, which constructed Ireland as a Catholic nation with a Gaelic cultural base and the Protestant minority as an 'out-group'. Yet Protestant advocates of Gaelic culture such as Douglas Hyde played a pivotal role in leading the mass diffusion of cultural nationalism as its ideological ownership shifted from Protestant elites to a nationalist movement which was predominantly characterised by Catholicism. As cultural nationalism became extended within the mass movements of Catholic nationalism it became used to fostering claims of cultural distinctiveness at the expense of the Protestant minority. It envisaged an assimilationist and exclusionary project of fostering such distinctiveness.[8] This Irish-Ireland nationalism came symbolically to dominate the new state from the 1920s to at least the 1960s.[9]

The Gaelic revival was initially fostered by a Protestant elite anxious to reaffirm its place in Irish society at a time when it faced political marginalisation and when an increasingly strident political rhetoric identified Irishness with Catholicism.[10] The Protestant Young Irelander movement of the mid-nineteenth century began the revival of Gaelic at a time when Catholic nationalism professed a distaste for the Irish language on utilitarian grounds.[11] Its revival was initially fostered by Protestant movements:

> Prior to the rise of the Gaelic League, Catholic nationalism was characterised by a pragmatic acceptance of the fact of Anglicisation: O'Connell's repeals, the Fenians, Home Rulers under Parnell and after, all focused their attention on the attainment of a purely political autonomy, supported by arguments based on history, legal precedent, justice and practicality. By contrast it was the Protestant patriots of the late eighteenth century who had first linked the assertion of Irish constitutional rights to an exalted vision of the Gaelic past. The Young Irelanders further developed the notion of an Irish claim to independence, based on cultural identity as well as geography and legal title, and drew on Gaelic literary heritage as raw material for political symbolism and propaganda.[12]

The impetus for Protestant cultural nationalism was provided by threats of social and political modernisation which threatened its elite status within Irish society and was set in opposition to 'the contemporary reality of an unruly democratic politics and an upstart Catholic bourgeoisie'.[13] It provided a conservative ideology which drew upon idealisations of rural society and pastoral tranquillity as the authentic source of Irishness.[14] It also emphasised an 'elite harmony', which served a hegemonic role in perpetrating a hierarchical society where lord and peasant were bound by shared cultural values and mutual respect. This 'elite harmony' constructed the superior status of Protestant elites as natural within a broader colonial ideology which racialised the non-Protestant Irish as inferior:

> Nineteenth century English discourses on Ireland combined Victorian domestic ideology with pseudo-scientific ethnographic analyses of racial characteristics ... The supposedly Irish feminine characteristics of sentimentality, ineffectuality, nervous excitability and unworldliness rendered the Irish incapable of self-government; it was argued, and thus invited strong, dispassionate and rational Anglo-Saxon rule.[15]

Colonisation thus was depicted as a benevolent and natural co-joining of the races within a marriage which adhered to dominant Victorian under-standing of the natural relationship between patriarch and woman. The rhetoric of Catholic nationalism was in many ways a response to racism within Victorian representations of the Irish. The racial construct of the idealised Gael provided an ideological mechanism for the expression of anti-Protestant sectarianism within cultural movements. It served a similar nation building purpose as colonial racisms which depicted the Catholic Irish and other colonised peoples as inferior within Britishness.

There were important differences in how cultural nationalism was mobilised within Protestant and Catholic movements. The former occurred through an elite cultural movement which sought to revive Gaelic language and literature while resisting the very social changes which made the latter possible. The latter occurred within the mass cultural and sporting organisations – notably the Gaelic League, which led the mass revival of the Irish language, and through the Gaelic Athletics Associa-tion (GAA) – within which Catholic, Gaelic republicanism was promul-gated. GAA *cumman* (clubs) were organised along parish boundaries. Catholic priests played a pivotal role in the organisation of these as they had previously in the organisation of the mass political movements of the O'Connell and Parnell eras. GAA *cumman* incorporated the tribalism of rural secret societies and local factions and built upon the strong collec-tive identities fostered within localities during the land war of the 1880s.[16] Although the GAA was initially founded by 'a moderate combination of clergy, home rulers and republicans' it came to be dominated by the IRB (Irish Republican Brotherhood) from 1887. Republican control was accompanied by a 'ban' which prohibited GAA members from playing, or watching, allegedly foreign games such as football (which had been played in north county Dublin since the seventeenth century) rugby and hockey.[17] Codified versions of ancient Gaelic games such as hurling were introduced, along with Gaelic football, an entirely new sport, in their place. The new sporting 'traditions' fostered a republicanism which equated Irishness with Catholicism.

Douglas Hyde's inaugural speech as President of the newly organised National Literacy Society in 1892 was entitled 'The Necessity for De-Anglicising Ireland'. This called for a cultural revolution through the promotion of Irish literature, language and native sports. These goals also became embodied the following year within another new mass organisation, the Gaelic League, which was successful in institutionalising the Irish language within the educational system prior to independence. Irish-Ireland cultural nationalism owed much to Protestant formulations of Gaelic culture in its rejection of urban secularism and opposition to imported mass culture. It also evoked an idealised ruralism which embodied values which were seen as distinct from British culture. However this new hegemony was characterised by an anti-Protestantism bound up with an anti-British xenophobia. According to Garvin:

> From the 1890s to 1960s, nationalist and nativist themes were used to erect ideological and organisational defences against the cultural and political assaults seen to be emanating from the Anglo-Saxon world and elsewhere … In particular, the fear of secular individualism, seen as threatening Irish communal values, was often associated with a fear of the modern and an imperfectly camouflaged hatred of Protestant culture.[18]

Catholic nationalism became the bearer of a sectarian and exclusionary religious-ethnic conception of nation. It provided an ideological context within which various forms of exclusion and discrimination became institutionalised within Irish society.

The Irish Protestant minority

Protestant identity in independent Ireland

An ethnic group might be defined as a socially distinct community of people who share a common history and culture and often share a distinct language and religion.[19] Such a definition suggests that ethnicity is bound up with cultural separateness and that this separateness the consequence of being excluded from, or peripheral to the mainstream of society. As such, it can be particularly appropriate in conceptualising the marginality imposed by cultural distinctiveness within a nation state constructed around a different ethnic identity. Poole, in a study of Irish Protestant communities, argues that this relationship can change to the extent that it is no longer appropriate to categorise a group within a society as ethni-cally distinct.[20] He argues that shifts in ethnic labelling and even de-ethni-cisation can result from cultural assimilation.

The Protestant minority in Ireland at the time of independence consti-tuted a distinct ethnic group. This ethnicity consisted of a religious compo-nent – bound up with religious habitus, identity and expression – and a cultural component – consisting of disparate elements (stratified by social class) relating to a British heritage expressed symbolically, occupation-ally, and in terms of sports and pastimes. Prior to the formation of the state, and more so subsequently, Protestants cleaved to the necessity of separate educational and cultural institutions as a means of preventing religious assimilation. The dominant religious–ethnic hegemony gave rise to the need for a strong Protestant ethnic identity and to the conditions for its erosion through assimilation. This assimilation occurred initially though violence and exclusion and later through state intolerance of ethnic, though not religious, distinctiveness. After 1922 the preservation of religious distinctiveness was seen as a matter of communal survival. For example, the Church of Ireland espoused a policy of social segre-gation and isolation while at the same time pragmatically emphasising loyalty to the Irish state and the Irishness of the Protestant community.[21]

Protestantisms in Ireland, based upon a strong communal religiosity, were sustained through the separatist mechanisms of denominational education and social clubs. However, there were limits to the possibilities for cultural separatism within the new nation state. Rugby, hockey and cricket, and to some extent soccer, fostered a sense of cultural distinctive-ness much in the way that Gaelic Games fostered cultural identity among Catholics.[22] These forms of cultural expression were broadly accept-able within nationalist Ireland. Protestants were compelled, however, to de-emphasise other forms of cultural distinctiveness. Protestant cultural identity had been characterised by an attachment to public symbols and rituals associated by the dominant community with Britishness. The murder of a Protestant, Albert Armstrong, for giving evidence in court against men who had torn down a British flag from outside his place of work is cited by Bowen as an example of the problems faced by Protes-tants who insisted in publicly manifesting such an explicit cultural distinc-tiveness.[23] Identity had to be suppressed as part of the price of inclusion within the new state as a religious minority. Protestants were exhorted by their own religious leadership to recognise Irish nationality.

Protestant concerns about religious assimilation were justifiable given their marginality after Irish independence. Assimilationist aims, and fears in turn about being assimilated, existed within Catholic nationalism throughout the nineteenth century. While the Catholic leader, Daniel O'Connell, did not contemplate a political suppression of Protestants he could envisage their future assimilation within a post-Repeal Ireland. In 1842 he outlined such a possible future to Paul Cullen, then Rector of the Irish College in Rome and later the architect of the 'devotional revolution' which modernised Irish Catholicism:

> The Repeal of the union would be an event of the most magnificent importance to Catholicity, of an importance so great and so valuable that I am prevented from presenting it in its true colours to the British people … If the union were repealed and the exclusive system abolished, the great mass of the Protestant community would with little delay melt into the overwhelming majority of the Irish nation. Protestantism would not survive the Repeal ten years.[24]

Following Irish independence in 1922 the new state did not embark on a project of religious assimilation. In effect, toleration was extended to the Protestant minority as a religious minority but not as an ethnic group. The state, however, played a major role in hastening the disappearance of non-religious ethnic differences between the two communities.[25] The laws of the new state were not directed 'against Protestants' but the state came to embody the dominant construction that Ireland was fundamentally a Catholic society in how the moral teaching of the Catholic Church became institutionalised within the civil code through legislation on censorship, divorce, adoption and contraception. The Catholic hierarchy infrequently involved itself in legislative processes because there was little need to do so. The Catholic Church possessed a 'non-decisional' form of power. It had the capacity to mobilise politically in deference of its interests but rarely had to because these could be anticipated and addressed in a 'non-political' and uncontentious manner. As good Catholics, legislators and voters were deeply committed to expressing their faith in the laws and institutions of the country.

The state displaced cultural symbolism associated with the Protestant minority in favour of a symbolism which venerated Catholic nationalism. This was exemplified by how nationalist hostility to the commemoration of Armistice Day and Remembrance Sunday, which commemorated the dead of the Great War (including thousands of Irishmen), became, to some extent, institutionalised within the new state. In the decades after independence, parading veterans and the sellers of the poppies which they wore to mark their commemoration were heckled and assaulted.[26]

Commemoration parades were banned by the state during the Second World War on the basis that these violated Irish neutrality. State representation at Remembrance events vacillated. Avoidance of commemorations reflected the peaks of populist republicanism. A marked decline of state endorsement of the symbolism of Remembrance followed the Irish Republican Army (IRA) border campaign during the 1950s and the resurgence of violence in Northern Ireland after 1969 but was reversed in the wake of the public outrage which followed the bombing of Enniskillen on Remembrance Sunday 1987.[27] In 1993, the seventy fifth anniversary of the Armistice, an Irish head of state attended a Remembrance Sunday service for the first time.

The decline of the Protestant community

At the beginning of the twentieth century the number of Protestants in the twenty-six counties were only slightly less numerous than northern Catholics (though these constituted a smaller percentage of the total population). In 1901 Protestants comprised 10.7 per cent (343,552) of the total population of the twenty-six counties. By 1991 this number had declined to 3.2 per cent (111,699).[28] There were a number of reasons for this decline. Many Protestants were occupationally displaced within the new state. The Royal Irish Constabulary was disbanded. The British army withdrew from Irish barracks. Many teachers, civil servants and those in other ancillary professions transferred to England or Northern Ireland. The size of the Church of Ireland declined by 34 per cent between 1911 and 1926, from 250,000 to 146,000; a decline which was closely paralleled within the other Protestant Churches and which suggests considerable emigration though these figures also included deaths during the First World War.[29]

Protestant confidence in the ability of the new state to afford them protection was undermined – most visibly during the Truce and civil war periods (1921–23) – when agrarian unrest provoked a wave of mansion burning and attacks on Protestant homes.[30] About 200 'big houses' were burnt out in 1922 and 1923 and a number of Protestants were murdered.[31] The term 'ethnic cleansing' was first coined in the early 1990s in relation to forms of systematic ethnic exclusion in the former Yugoslavia. Hart[32] argues, in a study of the experiences of the Protestant community during and after the war of independence, that the term could be used to describe events in a number of counties. He notes that in County Cork the IRA deliberately shot over 200 civilians between 1920 and 1923 of which 70 (36 per cent) were Protestants. The percentage of Protestants killed was five times the overall percentage of Protestants within the civilian population. Murders and death threats against many individual Protestants were accompanied by the seizure of Protestant lands in some cases and more generally by a widespread pattern of harassment whereby Protestants became 'fair game' to angry or covetous neighbours. There were many attacks on churches, cemeteries, rectories, school buildings and masonic halls. According to Hart: 'murder, arson and death-treats were a very small part of a much wider pattern of harassment and persecution. For every such case, there were a hundred raids, robberies or other attacks. Most rural and small-town Protestants spent these years in a constant state of anxiety, waiting for the next knock on the door'.[33]

Hundreds of families fled temporarily but returned to their homes, land and businesses when it seemed safe. Many others emigrated permanently because of the threat of violence, and as a consequence of social and economic changes brought about by the Great War and due to uncertainty about their future within the new state. After the 1920s the Protestant community lost their distinct political identity within Irish politics. This political assimilation first occurred through the displacement of their pre-independence political leaders and later – when an initial settlement which gave them strong representation in the Senate was abandoned – through a decline of representation in Dáil Éireann as the mechanics of the electoral system were altered to their disadvantage.[34]

Studies of the Protestant community in Ireland after independence have noted practices aimed at obstructing their purchase of land and shops. Auctioneers would withdraw properties if a Protestant turned out to be the highest bidder. Protestants had to bid through intermediaries unknown in the locality.[35] Bowen describes cases where Catholics derived considerable satisfaction at hearing of a Catholic purchase of, or marriage into, a Protestant farm or business. For instance, in one rural parish the Catholic Priest acknowledged that, on a number of occasions, he had been taken aside by parishioners whose comment was 'tis grand we got it back'.[36]

Social policy and the Protestant minority

A dominant Gaelic, Catholic and agrarian construction of nation and citizenship precipitated the marginalisation of the Protestant minority in areas such as education and health. Welfare had an ideological role in the cultural reproduction of the nation rather than in its expansion. A post-colonial emphasis on economic and cultural isolation combined with underdevelopment combined with the persistence of nineteenth-century colonialist welfare practices. The resultant moribund welfare economy offered little scope for ideological innovation or development to the extent that even the Catholic social thinking which emerged in the 1930s had little impact upon this most Catholic of nations until the post-war period when an emphasis on economic expansion precipitated new debates on welfare. In the era after independence Catholic social thought was better at rejecting than at advocating change.[37]

Social policy was to some extent shaped by ideological aspirations for a Gaelic-Catholic Ireland. The newly independent Irish state was characterised, for its first few decades, by a concern with economic and cultural sovereignty.[38] The status of the Irish language was reflected within the new state particularly in education. Catholic ethos influenced the nature of welfare provision and the strength of the Church as a voluntaristic provider of welfare – particularly education and health – influenced how it continued to be organised.[39] As put by O'Tuathaigh; 'it is widely accepted that this exclusivist Irish-Ireland ideology was dominant, not only in the official rhetoric but more pervasively in the symbols and statutes of the Irish state from the 1920s to, perhaps, the 1960s'.[40]

During the nineteenth century separate Protestant and Catholic education and health systems developed in Ireland. The development of some Protestant evangelical schools from the eighteenth century was followed, after the repeal of the Penal Laws, by a fast-growing Catholic school system.[41] Concerns about the spread of proselytisation through Protestant charity schools in turn provided the impetus for the spread of Catholic free schools. These Catholic schools became integral to the development of a modernised Catholic Church and Catholic nationalism. Catholic and Protestant educational expansions were both fostered by processes of religious modernisation and deepening sectarianism. Catholic sectarianism constructed the Protestant minority as a threat within an explicitly racialised discourse. One account in 1927 of Catholic attendance at Protestant schools referred to this phenomena as a 'disease' that was 'especially virulent in Dublin'.[42] Protestants as such were constructed as a threat, which could contaminate Catholics.

Religious tolerance was constitutionally enshrined and, in practice, the state went out of its way to protect the minority's religious rights through special measures aimed at keeping small Protestant schools open and by insisting that no child could be required to take religious instruction without parental agreement.[43] In 1919 the Catholic hierarchy pronounced it unlawful under Canon Law for Catholic parents to send a child to any non-Catholic school or university without express permission. After independence, separate Protestant education was not threatened as it safeguarded Catholics from contamination. This protected the Protestant minority from religious assimilation but Catholic political supremacy allowed for discrimination in other areas. Catholic politicians supported discrimination in favour of Catholics in state positions to ensure that Catholic moral sensibilities were not endangered.[44]

The emergence of a nationalist school of Irish history was an important component in the building of the 'Irish nation'. The 'greening of
Irish history' placed heavy emphasis upon the struggle against British
imperialism and landlordism, the dignifying of Irish Gaelic culture, and
upon the positive and often heroic, representation of the key figures
of Irish nationalism and of nationalist struggle in general. It served to
contest Anglocentric and pejorative representations of Ireland and thus
foster national self-respect.[45] A chauvinistic emphasis on the sufferings
of Catholic Ireland at the hands of British oppressors replaced one aimed
at fostering loyalty to the crown and empire. This served to foster an
anti-Protestantism which constructed Irish Protestants as 'outsiders'. The
role of school curricula in ideologically disseminating dominant constructions of Irishness through subjects such as history was recognised and
contested by the Protestant minority. For instance, the introduction of
compulsory teaching of the Irish language in the 1920s was viewed with
apprehension by Protestants:

> It was felt that the literature available in Irish was on the whole, by
> implication and innuendo, if not explicitly anti-Protestant, hardly likely
> to present their faith and traditions to new generations of the Protestant
> community in an encouraging light.[46]

In health, as in education, the impetus for maintaining a dual system
was a sectarian concern with imposing a Catholic ethos on all health care
for Catholics. In this context there were few overt attempts to encroach
upon the institutions of the minority community. In 1949 political control
of the Protestant Meath Hospital was usurped by the Catholic Knights
of Columbanus who managed at the annual general meeting to vote out
the existing board and replace it with one of Catholic members. The coup
was contested unsuccessfully in the High Court but a private member's
bill, supported by a majority of the Dáil – with the support of the Catholic
Archbishop, Dr McQuaid – effectively restored the status quo.[47] At the
same time the hierarchy opposed Protestant involvement in health care
for Catholics. The Catholic hierarchy successfully opposed, for example,
the participation of Catholics in the proposed National Anti-Tuberculosis
League in 1942 because of alarm at the Protestant flavour of its leadership.
It proposed instead that the League be subsumed within the predominantly Catholic Irish Red Cross.[48] The difficulties of providing a separate
health system for Protestants exceeded those in education with the result
that the Protestant minority was dependent upon a system governed by
Catholic ethics and operational control.[49] A growth in state involvement
in health funding was accompanied by the supremacy of a Catholic ethos
in the system as a whole.[50]

This supremacy was compounded within adoption legislation where again presumptions of dualism effectively discriminated against the Protestant minority. Adoption legislation was introduced in Ireland for the first time in 1952. The Adoption Bill reflected the consultative input of the Catholic hierarchy in stating that adoptive parents must be of the same religion as the natural parents or of the mother if the child was born out of wedlock. The presumption of the bill reflected Catholic social teaching on inter-faith marriages. The 1952 Act prohibited adoption by couples of mixed religions. In 1974 this was found to be unconstitutional on the basis that it was religiously discriminatory.[51]

Nationalism and anti-Semitism

The Limerick 'pogrom'

A so-called pogrom in 1904 destroyed the viability of Limerick city's small Jewish community which had built up since the 1880s. By 1904 the community consisted of about twenty-five families who worked as shopkeepers and peddlers travelling around Limerick and the neighbouring counties selling merchandise, such as religious pictures, cheap jewellery and clothes from door to door on a weekly payment system. This small community came under periodic anti-Semitic attack from the 1880s. For example, on Easter Sunday 1884 the house of the family of Lieb Siev came under attack by a crowd of about one hundred people when it became known that they had slaughtered a chicken that morning, in accordance with Jewish law, to celebrate the end of the Feast of the Passover.[52] The attack was also fuelled by the knowledge that some Jewish traders had not closed their shops on St Patrick's day.[53] This date was not a public holiday at the time but was perhaps the date in the Irish Catholic religious calendar most closely associated with 'Irishness'.

The vulnerability of the local Jewish population to anti-Semitic violence at the time was noted in the *Limerick Chronicle* which on 3 May 1884 stated; 'it needed but the cry so often heard in other cities – that the presence of the Jews was a standing insult to Christians – to light the torch of persecution'. This concern about the potential eruption of latent anti-Semitism into overt hostility against the Jews was subsequently realised in 1896 in Killaloe Co Clare, about twenty miles from Limerick, when an anti-Semitic sermon on the Crucifixion led to attacks upon Jewish peddlers from Limerick. As reported in the *Limerick Chronicle* on 2 November 1892; 'the few Jews who came there as usual on business, instead of meeting with the customary friendly greetings, were in some instances, shunned like lepers, in others beset by a wild infuriated mob'.[54]

The 1904 campaign against the Jews in Limerick was mobilised by Fr Creagh, the leader of a Catholic organisation, the Arch-Confraternity of the Holy Family, which had significant power within the city. The Arch-Confraternity was a mass organisation of Limerick lay-Catholics – it had a membership of 6,000 in 1904 – established by the Redemptorists, a religious order of missionaries who played a key role in 'devotional revolution' which modernised Irish Catholicism along sectarian lines during the nineteenth century. Redemptorists were travelling revivalist missionaries, similar to Methodists, who staged religious events or 'missions' in the areas they visited designed to renew religious fervour and enthusiasm.[55] They promoted an emotional intensity in communities which could foster religious devotion but also intolerance, sectarianism and, in 1904, anti-Semitism.

As spiritual director of the Arch-Confraternity, Fr Creagh was in a powerful position of leadership in Limerick. However, this in itself cannot account for the pogrom in Limerick. Racism against Jews within Irish society, religious sectarianism, xenophobia and dominant nationalist constructions of social membership all contributed to events in Limerick. As well as Fr Creagh other Catholic clergy also engaged in hostility towards the Jews of Limerick during 1904.[56] Fr Creagh received no reprimand from his superiors within the Redemporist order for his campaign against the Jews. He was able to marshal a deep-rooted prejudice against the Jews.

Anti-Semitism, Catholicism and Irish nationalism

The campaign against the Limerick Jews drew ideologically from anti-Semitism in other European countries, notably France. Catholic nationalist newspapers such as the *United Irishman* reflected the anti-Semitism of the Catholic press in France during the Dreyfuss Affair. Anti-Semitism in Limerick was therefore an aspect of a broader Christian anti-Jewish racism. Fr Creagh's sermons were primarily an attack on the trading practices of Jews in Limerick. They also regurgitated many of the usual justifications for anti-Semitism – that the Jews had, at one time, engaged in the ritual murder of Christian children and that they had killed Christ. Furthermore, he blamed the Jews for anti-Catholicism in France.

Catholic anti-Semitism in Limerick was an expression of religious sectarianism. The Jews were constructed as a threat to Catholic Ireland and their expulsion was legitimised within a xenophobic discourse. Religious politics in Limerick were characterised by a sectarianism between Catholics and Protestants which had been heightened by the impact of the

devotional revolution and by evangelical Protestantism in the city. In
this context criticisms of the pogrom which came from Protestant leaders
and those criticisms which emerged at a national and international level
were seen as partisan expressions of anti-Catholicism within a Catholic
nationalist discourse which linked anti-Semitism and anti-Protestantism.
On 20 April, an article in the *Munster News* had accused the Church of
Ireland Bishop of Limerick, Bishop Bunbury, of slander. The Bishop had
spoken in opposition to the boycott and subsequently the Church of
Ireland general synod passed a resolution to draw the matter to the attention of the government. The article stated defiantly 'the days are gone
when a Papist, ridden over by a Protestant fox-hunter, should crawl, hat
in hand, to beg his honour's pardon for having been in the horse's way'.
Ten days later, the *Limerick Leader* published an article entitled 'The libel
of Limerick' which accused the Protestant press of bigotry in exaggerating
the persecution of Jews in Limerick. The article claimed that 'Ireland is, at
present, being drained of its Gaelic population by emigration, and Jewish
colonists are trooping in to fill up the place of the emigrants, and to turn
Ireland into a filthy Ghetto'.[57] Criticism of the Arch-Confraternity's anti-
Semitism by non-Catholics became understood as an expression of anti-
Catholic sectarian politics and a slight upon the good (Catholic) people of
Limerick. This 'anti-Catholicism' became a nationalist *cause célèbre*.

In one of his sermons Fr Creagh called for the Jews to be turned out of
Ireland as they had been turned out of other countries:

> Twenty years ago and less Jews were known only by name and evil
> repute in Limerick. They were sucking the blood of other nations, but
> those nations rose up and turned them out and they came to our land to
> fasten themselves on us like leeches, and to draw our blood when they
> had been forced away from other countries. They have, indeed, fastened
> themselves upon us, and now the question is whether or not we will
> allow them to fasten themselves still more upon us, until our children
> and we are helpless victims of their rapacity.[58]

The strategy for achieving the expulsion of the Jews from Limerick
was one of economic and social exclusion through the imposition of a
boycott. Fr Creagh successfully urged his congregation to avoid commercial dealings with the Jews.[59] The boycott originated as a form of 'moral
coventry' or ostracisation urged by Charles Stuart Parnell in a speech in
Ennis Co. Clare on 19 September 1880 as a tactic to prevent bids on farms
vacant as a result of evictions:

> You must show him on the roadside when you meet him, you must
> show him in the streets of the town, you must show him at the shop

counter, you must show him in the fair and the market place, and even in the place of worship, by leaving him severely alone – putting him into a kind of moral coventry – isolating him from his kind like the leper of old – you must show him your detestation of the crime he committed.[60]

Soon after, this practice took its name from the shunning of Captain Boycott, a landlord's agent in Mayo who had sent eviction notices to tenants demanding fair rents. The practice of boycotting emerged in the highly charged context of land agitation during the 1880s. Boycotting was constructed as an emancipatory practice within Irish nationalism. It was employed against landlords by the Land League in an attempt to protect vulnerable peasants from losing their homes and means of living. However, the boycott against the Jews in Limerick more than twenty years later aimed to deprive the Jews of their homes and livelihoods. The urging of a boycott against the Limerick Jewish community constructed these as oppressors of the Irish people. Anti-Semitism could, as such, be represented as contributing to the emancipation of the 'Irish'. The relationship between nationalism and anti-Semitism in 1904 was therefore characterised by a number of elements. The Jews were racialised as exploiters and enemies of the 'real' Catholic Irish. Anti-Semitism within Irish nationalism drew on the language of anti-colonialism which linked the emancipation of the peasantry with the removal of Protestant landowners. The place of Irish Jews within a narrowly imagined 'Irish' society became precarious following the institutionalisation of such nationalist hegemony within the new state. Chapter 4 examines the institutionalisation of anti-Semitism in the practices of the post-1922 Free State within the context of exclusionary conceptions of citizenship and immigration practices.

The socio-economic context of anti-Semitism

Boycotting was constructed within Catholic nationalism and the highly charged context of land agitation as an emancipatory practice. The boycott of the Limerick Jewish community was bound up with representations of these as exploiters of the 'Irish' within nationalist discourse. This discourse first emerged in the 1880s when Jewish traders who travelled rural areas from the 1880s were likened to the 'Gombeen Man', a derogatory term, of somewhat imprecise meaning, applied to exploitative shopkeeper-money lenders in rural society as exploiters of Irish people within the land politics which had dominated Irish nationalism.[61] The campaign against the Jews of Limerick occurred within a contemporary climate within which anti-Semitism was compatible with patriotic support of Irish trade. In Limerick the pogrom was endorsed at the time and retrospectively by members of two local trades union bodies: the Mechanics'

Institute and the Workman's Industrial Association. This was echoed by an advertisement by Irish tailors which urged the boycotting of Jewish competition and, in subsequent years, similar advertisements by Dublin cabinetmakers.[62]

The participation of Jewish immigrants within an expanding retail sector during the late nineteenth century became a focus of nationalist hostility. The Jews mostly settled in urban communities working predominantly, according to the 1891 census and the 1901 census, in retail trade as peddlers, drapers, commercial travellers and general traders. However, with the exception of the licensed victualler trade, Catholics were underrepresented in the retail sector. This underrepresentation became, along with economic subordination to Protestant landlords in agriculture, a focus of Catholic nationalism. Concerns about equity became intertwined with a xenophobic preoccupation with the exploitation of Irish workers by Jewish 'sweated labour' and traders.[63] Jews were vulnerable to representation, according to prevalent racist stereotyping, as the economic enemies of Catholics. They could be seen as exploiters of the dominant community. They became linked in the popular imagination with the problem of exploitative money lending in Irish society. The presence of a large class of indigenous moneylenders in the country towns during the nineteenth century and a corresponding absence of proper banking facilities came to be regarded as a serious problem within Irish society; one which attracted responses from the state and the Catholic voluntary sector.[64] An editorial responding to debates about Jewish immigration written by Fr Thomas Finlay, a Jesuit social reformer and promoter of the cooperative movement, justified the potential exclusion of Jews on economic grounds:

> Our first duty is to ourselves and to our own people and no sympathy with the suffering and persecuted Jews can avail to free us from this obligation. If the influx of the Jews into Ireland constitutes an economic danger to the industry of the wealth producing classes amongst us, then it would be a duty to resist – not out of hatred of the Jews, but out of concern for ourselves.[65]

The campaign against the Limerick Jews in 1904 employed similar justifications for their expulsion. Fr Creagh targeted nationalist opinion in Ireland in a second sermon, given a week later which was made available to the press in advance.[66] This depicted the Jews as enslavers of the Irish people akin to Cromwell, a symbol of religious oppression for Catholic nationalists. He stated that 'slavery to them is worse to the slavery to which Cromwell condemned the poor Irish who were shipped to the Barbados'. Fr Creagh then urged mobilisation against the Jews; 'Let us defend ourselves before their heels are too firmly placed upon our necks'.

Such action was legitimised as true to 'faith and fatherland'. He urged his congregation 'not to be false to Ireland, false to your country and false to your religion, by continuing to deal with the Jews'. The Jews therefore were depicted as enemies not just of Catholicism but of Ireland. An editorial in the *United Irishman* in 1904 by Arthur Griffith similarly identified the Jews as enemies of the nation:

> No thoughtful Irishman or woman can view without apprehension the continuous influx of Jews into Ireland ... strange people, alien to us in thought, alien to us in sympathy, from Russia, Poland, Germany and Austria – people who come to live amongst us, but who never become of us ... Our sympathy – insular as it may be – goes wholly to our countryman the artisan whom the Jew deprives of the means of livelihood, to our countryman the trader whom he ruins in business by unscrupulous methods, to our countryman the farmer whom he draws into his usurer's toils and drives to the workhouse across the water.[67]

This editorial was but one example of the explicit anti-Semitic tone of the Catholic nationalist press in and around the time of the 1904 Limerick pogrom. Griffith was the founder of the Sinn Féin movement which emerged as the dominant political party in southern Ireland in the 1918 elections and whose advocacy of cultural and economic protectionism shaped the character of the newly independent state in the first few decades after independence. The Jewish population was, as revealed by the Limerick pogrom, extremely vulnerable to economic and social exclusion perpetrated by the dominant community. Irish retail practices, within an economy where many customers had irregular access to cash and were thus in need of credit, were shaped by kinship networks, friendships and interdependence between shopkeepers and customers.[68] This interdependence gave the customer some degree of protection from exploitation but also accorded the shopkeeper both status and protection – for customers too had their good names to protect in their financial dealings – within a set of embedded practices. Jewish traders, as outsiders, were economically vulnerable because they could not draw on such protections.

Travellers

Social change and social closure

Helleiner argues that the precise origins of the Irish Traveller community are unclear. She notes that fragmentary accounts of Irish 'Tinkers' or 'Itinerants' pre-date the famine, which is often associated with the origins of the Travellers, by a number of centuries, to at least the Tudor era.

Accounts from that time suggest a colonial emphasis upon suppressing their mobility linked to the supplanting of Gaelic ways of life with Anglicised practices of land ownership.[69] In the years preceding the famine, Travellers comprised but one element of a large permanent and seasonally migrant population. Socio-economic changes throughout the nineteenth and twentieth centuries within Irish rural society increasingly exposed migratory populations, including Travellers, to real and symbolic marginalisation. Prior to the famine, the *First Report from His Majesty's Commissioners for Inquiring into the Conditions of the Poorer Classes in Ireland* (1835), which examined poverty in seventeen Irish counties, depicted a complex rural society, within which there were strong social bonds between sedentary and migratory ways of life. Small tenant farmers were part of a peasantry touched by the need for seasonal migration. They were obliged by customs of hospitality to give alms to those seasonal beggars unable to subsist for the entire year on their own conacre and to various other categories of dispossessed vagrants. Travellers were identifiable from accounts in the report as a specific class with distinct economic activities and social relations – notably mobile family-based households linked through ties of kinship – yet they remained relatively invisible within the larger migratory population.

The years preceding the famine were marked by a crisis in communal forms of support for seasonal migrants and vagrants due to extensive displacement within rural society. There is frequent reference in the 1835 report, for example, to the practice of older parents, having made over their land to their children in the expectation of being supported by them leaving home at times of shortage to go begging, and often not returning. The subsequent famine devastated this marginal peasantry. It led to the rationalisation of their smallholdings and combined with successful nationalist campaigns for land reform in the 1880s to produce a new rural class of Catholic landowners. Travellers survived as a landless class within rural society. They retained a distinct economic role within rural society until at least the 1950s when their skills and trades became obsolete. Gmelch and Gmelch, writing in 1974, described this next stage of displacement:

> In the last two decades, however, the Travellers' traditional rural way of life has been disrupted. Modernisation in Ireland has led to the introduction of new goods and machinery which made their traditional trades and services obsolete. Plastic containers and enamelware have eliminated the demand for tinware. Farm mechanisation has replaced much of the need for workhorses. And improved roads, the private automobile, and the expansion of bus service have all contributed to the demise

of peddling by making it easier for farm women to travel to provincial towns to shop.[70]

The social exclusion of Travellers, as such, deepened throughout the nineteenth and twentieth centuries and became embedded in the practices of the Irish state which came to pursue overt policies of assimilation from the 1960s when economic modernisation had all but dislodged the Travellers from rural society.

Racialisation of Travellers

This exclusion became justified through a racism, which constructed the Travellers as 'other' in relation to the dominant imagined community. Racialisation of Travellers preceded the emergence of modern Irish nationalism in so far as Travellers were linked to colonial racialisations of Gypsies and of the Irish. By the 1890s academic scholarship had identified the Travellers as distinct from the Gypsies. Their language was identified as a Gaelic tongue. Within the racial logic of late nineteenth-century Gypsyilogy this categorised them below 'true' Gypsies, whose nomadic way of life was racially determined and within the majority of travellers whose vagrancy was attributable to degeneracy.[71] This esoteric racialist categorisation combined with dominant nineteenth century 'Poor Law' conceptualisations of poverty which explained poverty in terms of moral failing.

In rural society the racialistion of Travellers in Ireland occurred within a rural lore which linked them to crop failure but also within a 'magical–traditional' Catholic religious folklore which spun tales of their transgressions against Christ or St Patrick hence explaining why they were fated to remain outside of society forever. Helleiner describes one tale which explained that the tinkers were cursed because they were the only ones who would agree to drive the nails into the feet and hands of Christ.[72] Nomadism was depicted as a punishment, which served, for example, to justify differences between the treatment of Traveller and sedentary artisans. Travellers were also marginalised within a Catholic nationalism which hegemonically constructed a social membership linked in rural society to place and land ownership:

> the push for modernity in twentieth-century Ireland caused nomadism and sedentarism to be presented in *positional*, rather than *complementary* terms. As elsewhere in Europe, nationalism in Ireland stressed the organic links between 'the people', or *volk*, and their homeland, or *heimat* … The whole idea of a *volk* conjured up images of people with a strong territorial imperative, a people linked to the national territory through a 'blood and soil' racism that fused a people with their homeland in one organic whole.[73]

The emergence of an ideological basis for the exclusion of non-sedentary groups such as Travellers coexisted with the invisibility of Travellers within nation-building discourses. The extent of ideological and social marginality of the Travellers within the emerging nation can be seen from near total lack of references to them in mainstream histories and studies of nineteenth- and twentieth-century Ireland. Travellers were, in essence, an invisible minority and a people 'without history' within the nation of the dominant imagination.

Traveller spatial exclusion

By the 1960s Travellers had become economically and socially displaced from rural society. The general movement of Travellers to urban centres was part of broader demographic changes in Irish society. However, the urbanisation of Travellers rendered them extremely venerable to hostility from the dominant community and to ongoing processes of spatial exclusion as the spaces within Irish society for non-sedentary ways of life diminished. In this context, Travellers were constructed as a social problem experienced by sedentary people. They were represented as a deviant underclass within racialised discourses which depicted Travellers as a deviant population. These provided the ideological context for overt policies of assimilation by the state. These processes of exclusion are examined in detail in Chapters 6 and 7.

Parallels between Protestant, Traveller and Jewish exclusions

Racialisation and closure

Protestants, Jewish people and Travellers became the focus of racialisations which, in each case, served as justification for their exclusion within Irish society. The concept of racialisation refers to political and ideological processes by which groups come to be defined with reference to real or imaginary characteristics and where 'race' or ethnicity is used to define boundaries between groups of people. It provides a mechanism for depicting non-assimilated groups as enemies of the dominant imagined community.

Belief in Jewish 'conspiracies' – produced by a racialisation of Jews based on theological underpinnings within Christianity and hostility to Jewish cultural distinctiveness – has been a common feature of anti-Semitism for centuries. In 1904, in Limerick, the campaign against the Jewish community was provoked by sermons of Fr Creagh which reiterated many of the usual 'justifications' for anti-Semitism. For example, the Jews were said, at one time, to have engaged in the ritual murder of Christian children and were said to have killed Christ. Prevalent racialisations of the Jews made it possible to construct the Jews, as a culturally distinct non-assimilated population, as enemies of the nation. The power of prevalent racialisations was such that even opposition to anti-Semitism became captured by a dominant discourse which constructed the exclusion of Jewish people within nationalism as natural. O'Riordan argues that an examination of the writings of Michael Davitt, a 'most vigorous opponent of anti-Semitism' who supported the Limerick Jewish community in 1904, shows the extent to which nationalism could legitimise anti-Semitism.[74] Davitt distinguished in his 1903 book, *Within the Pale: The True Story of Anti-Semitic Persecutions in Russia*, between justifiable and unjustifiable anti-Semitism. Anti-Semitism, Davitt stated, had produced odious crimes but yet might be justifiable in defence of a nation:

> Where anti-Semitism stands, in fair political combat, in opposition to the foes of nationality, or against the economic evils of unscrupulous capitalism anywhere, I am resolutely in line with its spirit and programme.[75]

Anti-Protestantism found expression within nationalist anti-British discourse which attributed blame for past sufferings and wrongs. For example, the conviction that England had inflicted famine on Ireland became an integral part of an Irish history which provided a simple, readily intelligible explanation of a vastly complex occurrence. It drew on the deepest of the hatreds bound up with anti-Protestant popular religious feeling:

> For, out of Irish folk tradition there emerges, clear and burning, fierce hatred of official charity, given through Protestant stores, by degrading methods, sometimes only in return for abjuring Catholicism. Meat soup was offered on Fridays to starving Catholics by Protestant 'soupers'. Some Protestants would provide relief to Catholics only if they attended Protestant churches, schools or lectures, denied the main tenets of Catholicism. Or offered insults to statues of the Blessed Virgin. The association of food with proselytism burnt anti-Protestantism even deeper into Irish minds.[76]

The myths of mass defection from the Catholic Church as a result of 'Protestant souperism' were unfounded. The 1861 census showed no marked increase in the number of Protestants even in areas where proselytisation was most prevalent.[77] Constructions of Protestants as exploiters of the Catholic Irish were also fostered within an anti-Protestant discourse about the threat of freemasonry which racialised the close communal bonds and interrelationships of this small minority. The Free and Accepted Masons of Ireland – a predominantly Protestant body – attracted much suspicion from the Catholic community. However, the shrill denunciations of freemason conspiracies far exceeded a reasonable suspicion of some degree of mutual preferment in trade among members.[78] Freemasons were often linked with the Jews as enemies of Catholicism. Catholic sermons and publications, from the turn of the century, frequently constructed them as plotting against Catholic morals – be it through the propagation of capitalism, communism or atheism – and as economic exploiters of Catholics. As such, denunciations of freemasons can be understood as a racialisation of Protestants and linked with hostility towards them as an economically relatively privileged minority. Catholic sectarianism constructed the Protestant minority as a threat within an explicitly racialised discourse. One account in 1927 of Catholic attendance at Protestant schools referred to this phenomenon as a 'disease' that was 'especially virulent' in Dublin'.[79] Protestants, as such, were portrayed as a threat that could contaminate Catholics.

Travellers, as will be seen in Chapters 6 and 7, remain a racialised minority. Historically they were constructed as an out-group within a folklore that explained and justified their marginalisation within Irish society as the result of imagined religious transgressions. Here there were striking parallels with Christian anti-Semitism. At the same time Travellers remained an invisible or discounted minority within the nation until they were dislodged from rural society in a later phase of economic modernisation and social change. Furthers parallels between past manifestations of anti-Semitism in Ireland and anti-Traveller racism might be noted. Travellers since the 1960s might be viewed as a non-assimilatable minority. They are highly visible and exceedingly marginal. Anti-Traveller racism has proved to be an ideological tool capable of physically displacing Traveller populations from Irish communities in the same way that anti-Semitism precipitated the destruction of the Limerick Jewish community.

As noted in Chapter 2, Irish nationalism imagined nation within a discourse of racial distinctiveness. Jews could be constructed as enemies of the nation within the racialised discourses which sometimes accompanied representations of 'self' and 'other' within nationalist discourses. Protestants were constructed as 'other' within similar discourses. A recurring theme within Protestant communities in the decades after independence was a need to mask their ethnic distinctiveness. Manifestations of difference were experienced as risks of risk of displacement and perhaps as a fear of racialisation. To some extent Protestant de-ethnicisation could be read as a coping strategy or as assimilation in the face of monoculturalism.

The state as an agent of closure

The exclusion of Protestants, Travellers and Jewish people found ideological justification within racialised discourses which portrayed the dominant population as victims of minorities and in turn represented the exclusion of minorities as legitimate. These perceived 'exploitations' justified spatial exclusions of one sort or another. Dominant constructions of Irishness were institutionalised in legislation and policy in a number of ways. The role of the state as an agent of closure varied in different cases. Although religious discrimination was not endorsed by the state, religious minorities were the focus of a range of exclusionary pressures. The Jewish minority became 'justifiably' the focus of overtly discriminatory practices as a non-assimilated population within a monocultural state. Prevalent racialisations of the Jews allowed their overt exclusions to be portrayed as 'natural' and in the 'national interest'. Simply put, the Jews were held to be 'naturally' the enemies of the nation. After independence official religious tolerance went hand in hand with a deep-rooted anti-Semitism within state practices. From the late 1930s, explicitly anti-Semitic immigration policies sought to prevent the enlargement of the Jewish community. These will be considered in Chapter 4. Finally, the Irishness of Travellers was not contested within the dominant ideology. Instead their very existence was denied. Their claims of distinctiveness were refuted. As they lost their 'place' in Irish society, they became increasingly vulnerable to racialisation and physical exclusion. Their subordination and assimilation became the price of any degree of social citizenship.

Conclusion

This chapter has discussed some of the exclusionary consequences of nation-building and social modernisation from the nineteenth century for minority communities in Ireland. First, it examined the emergence of a hegemonic religious–ethnic construction of social membership in the nineteenth century by which the Irish nation was constructed as a Catholic nation. This was bound up with shifts in economic and political power in Irish society, which combined to marginalise minority groups within Irish society. Ideological processes of nation-building were accompanied by processes of economic, social and institutional modernisation. A specific 'Irish-Ireland' project of modernisation was articulated within Catholic nationalism prior to independence. This became the political face of ideological and institutional monoculturalism in the decades following independence. Nation-building emerged, then, through processes of social closure which ideologically and materially displaced minorities from the 'nation'. Minorities experienced hegemonic constructions of national identity, in various ways, as ideological justifications for material, spatial or political exclusion.

Notes

1 B. Anderson, *Imagined Communities: Reflections on the Origins and Spread of Nationalism* (London Verso: 1983).
2 J. Hutchinson (1996), 'Irish Nationalism', in D. George Boyce and A. O'Day (eds), *The Making of Modern Irish History: Revisionism and the Revisionist Controversy* (London: Routledge, 1996), p. 114.
3 D. H. Akenson, *Small Differences: Irish Catholics and Protestants 1815–1922* (Dublin: Gill & Macmillan, 1991), p. 138.
4 K. T. Hoppen, *Ireland since 1800: Conflict and Conformity* (London: Longman, 1990), p. 68.
5 *Ibid.*, p. 76.
6 Catholic clergy, under the constitution of the Catholic Association, were ex officio members. Priests acted as organisers and canvassers for the Association. See D. Keogh, *Twentieth-Century Ireland: Nation and State* (Dublin: Gill & Macmillan, 1994), p. 73.
7 M. Kelly, 'The Media and National Identity in Ireland', in P. Clancy, M. Kelly, J. Wiatr and R. Zoltaniescki (eds), *Ireland and Poland: Comparative Perspectives* (Dublin: UCD Press, 1992), p. 75.
8 D. P. Moran in *The Philosophies of Irish-Ireland* (Dublin: James Duffy & Co., 1905) argued that the Irish nation was, de facto, a Catholic nation, its cultural base was Gaelic, and this culture should be promoted so as to able to absorb all other 'extraneous' elements which through the centuries had come to the land.
9 G. O'Tuathaigh, 'The Irish-Ireland Idea: Rationale and Relevance', in E. Longley (ed.), *Culture in Ireland* (ed.), *Division or Diversity* (Belfast: Institute of Irish Studies, 1991).
10 S. J. Connolly, 'Culture, Identity and Tradition', in B. Graham (ed.), *In Search of Ireland: A Cultural Geography* (London: Routledge, 1997), p. 59.
11 M. Howes, 'Lady Wilde and the Emergence of Irish Cultural Nationalism', in T. Foley and S. Ryder (eds), *Ideology and Ireland in the Nineteenth Century* (Dublin: Four Courts Press, 1998), pp. 155–6.
12 Connolly, 'Culture, Identity and Tradition', p. 56.
13 *Ibid.*
14 P. J. Duffy, 'Writing Ireland: Literature in the Representation of Irish Place', in Graham, *In Search of Ireland*, p. 68.
15 C. Nash, 'Embodied Irishness', in Graham, *In Search of Ireland*, p. 114.
16 T. Garvin, *The Evolution of Irish Nationalist Politics* (Dublin: Gill & Macmillan, 1983), pp. 66–7.
17 *Ibid.*
18 T. Garvin, 'Patriots and Republicans', in W. Crotty and D. E. Schmitt (eds), *Ireland and the Politics of Change* (London: Longman, 1998), p. 146.

19 K. Stillitoe and P. H White, 'Ethnic Groups and the British Census: The Search for a Question', *Journal of the Royal Statistical Society*, 155(1) (1992), p. 143.

20 M. Poole, 'In Search of Ethnicity in Ireland', in Graham, *In Search of Ireland*, p. 132.

21 K. Bowen, *Protestants in a Catholic State: Ireland's Privileged Minority* (Belfast: Queen's University Press, 1983), p. 116.

22 D. Caird, 'Protestantism and National Identity', in J. McLoone (ed.), *Being Protestant in Ireland* (Galway: Social Studies Conference, 1984), p. 61.

23 Bowen, *Protestants in a Catholic State*, p. 198.

24 A. Clifford (ed.), *'Godless Colleges' and Mixed Education in Ireland: Extracts from the Speeches and Writings of Thomas Wyse, Daniel O'Connell, Thomas Davis, Charles Gavin Duffy, Frank Hugh O'Donnell and Others* (Dublin: Athol Books, 1981), p. 91.

25 See Poole, 'In Search of Ethnicity'; Bowen, *Protestants in a Catholic State*.

26 L. Leonard, 'The Twinge of Memory: Armistice Day and Remembrance Sunday in Dublin since 1919', in G. Walker and R. English (eds), *Unionism in Modern Ireland* (Dublin: Gill & Macmillan, 1996), pp. 107–9.

27 *Ibid.*

28 J. Coakley, 'Religion, Ethnic Identity and the Protestant Minority in the Republic', in Crotty and Schmitt, *Ireland and the Politics of Change*, pp. 86–9.

29 Caird, 'Protestantism and National Identity', p. 56.

30 Coakley, 'Religion, Ethnic Identity', p. 92.

31 P. Somerville-Large, *The Irish Country House: A Social History* (London: Sinclair Stevenson, 1995), p. 353.

32 P. Hart, 'Class, Community and the Irish Republican Army in Cork, 1917–1923', in P. O'Flannagan and C. G. Buttimer (eds), *Cork: History and Society: Interdisciplinary Essays on the History of an Irish County* (Dublin: Geography Publications, 1993), p. 92.

33 *Ibid.*

34 Poole, 'In Search of Ethnicity', p. 139.

35 J. White, *Minority Report: The Protestant Community in the Irish Republic* (Dublin: Gill & Macmillan, 1975).

36 Bowen, *Protestants in a Catholic State*, p. 169.

37 T. Fahey, 'The Catholic Church and Social Policy', in S. Healy and B. Reynolds (eds), *Irish Social Policy in Ireland* (Dublin: Oak Tree Press, 1998), p. 206.

38 N. Hardiman, and C. Whelan, 'Changing Values', in Crotty and Schmitt, *Ireland and the Politics of Change*, pp. 66–85.

39 M. Pellion, *Contemporary Irish Society* (Dublin: Gill & Macmillan, 1982), p. 95.

40 O'Tuathaigh, 'The Irish-Ireland Idea', p. 58.

41 Keogh, *Twentieth-Century Ireland*, pp. 61–2.

42 *Catholic Bulletin* (1927), cited in White, *Minority Report*, p. 145.

43 C. McGuinness, 'Being Protestant in the Republic of Ireland', in J. McLoone (ed.), *Being Protestant in Ireland* (Galway: Social Studies Conference, 1984), p. 31.

44 Bowen, *Protestants in a Catholic State*, p. 36.

45 L. P. Curtis, 'The Greening of Irish History', *Eire-Ireland*, 26(2) (1994), pp. 23–5.

46 Protest by the Church of Ireland General Synod Board of Education resulted in the publication of a new history book for use in Protestant schools in 1945 (see Caird, 'Protestantism and National Identity', p. 63).

47 White, *Minority Report*, p. 165.
48 R. Barrington, *Health, Medicine and Politics in Ireland 1900–1970* (Dublin: Institute of Public Administration, 1987), p. 162.
49 Protestant women were concerned about being treated in Catholic and public hospitals due to the institutionalisation of Catholic ethics within the health system. See McGuinness, *Being Protestant in the Republic of Ireland*, p. 32.
50 Barrington, *Health, Medicine and Politics in Ireland*, p. 126.
51 Article 44.2 (iii) of the Irish Constitution, as amended by the Fifth Constitution Act (1972), states: 'The state shall not impose any disabilities or make any discrimination on the grounds of religious profession, belief or status'.
52 D. Ryan, 'The Jews of Limerick: Part One', *Old Limerick Journal*, 17 (1984), pp. 27–30.
53 G. Goldberg, 'Ireland is the only country…"Joyce and the Jewish Dimension"', *Crane Bag*, 6(1) (1982), pp. 5–11.
54 *Limerick Chronicle* (3 May 1884) and (2 November 1892).
55 L. J. Taylor, 'The Mission: An Anthropological View of an Irish Religious Occasion', in C. Curtin and T. M. Wilson (eds), *Ireland from Below: Social Change and Local Communities* (Galway: Galway University Press, 1987).
56 D. Keogh, *Jews in Twentieth-Century Ireland* (Cork: Cork University Press, 1998) p. 44.
57 *Munster News* (20 April 1904) and *Limerick Leader* (30 April 1904), cited in Keogh, *Jews in Twentieth-Century Ireland*, p. 49.
58 *Ibid.*, p. 28.
59 Fr Creagh encouraged customers of Jewish traders not to pay their debts and suppliers of milk not to sell to the Jewish community. See D. Ryan, 'The Jews of Limerick: Part Two', *Old Limerick Journal*, 18 (1985), pp. 36–40.
60 Cited in J. E. Dunleavy and G. W. Dunleavy, *Douglas Hyde: A Maker of Modern Ireland* (Oxford: University of California Press, 1991), p. 105.
61 The term derives from the Irish *gaimbin*, meaning interest or usury. The term 'gombeen man' tends to be used to mean a shopkeeper who combined retailing with moneylending or integrated usurious practices into retailing. The term became applied to Jewish moneylenders. See G. Moore, 'Socio-Economic Aspects of Anti-Semitism in Ireland: 1880–1905', *Economic and Social Review*, 12(3) (1981), p. 201.
62 See M. O'Riordan, 'Jewish Trade Unionism in Dublin', in P. Feely (ed.), *The Rise and Fall of Irish Anti-Semitism* (Dublin: Labour History Workshop, 1984), pp. 25–36.
63 *Ibid.*
64 Moore, 'Socio-Economic Aspects of Anti-Semitism in Ireland', p. 196.
65 *Lyceum* (July 1893), cited in Keogh, *Jews in Twentieth Century Ireland*, p. 20.
66 Cited, *ibid.*, p. 36.
67 *United Irishman* (13 January 1904), cited by M. O'Riordan, 'Anti-Semitism in Irish Politics', in Feely, *Rise and Fall of Irish Anti-Semitism*, p. 1.
68 C. Arnsberg, *The Irish Countryman: An Anthropological Study* (London: Macmillan, 1937).
69 See J. Helleiner, 'Gypsies, Celts and Tinkers: Colonial Antecedents of Anti-Traveller Racism in Ireland', *Ethnic and Racial Studies*, 18(3) (1995), pp. 532–5.
70 S. B. Gmelch and G. Gemlch, 'The Itinerant Settlement Movement: Its Policies and Effects on Irish Travellers', *Studies*, 63(249) (1974), pp. 1–16, p. 1.

71 Helleiner, 'Gypsies, Celts and Tinkers', pp. 534–6.
72 *Ibid*.
73 J. McLaughlin, 'Nation-Building, Social Closure and Anti-Traveller Racism in Ireland', *Sociology*, 33(1) (1999), p. 128.
74 M. O'Riordan, 'The Sinn Fein Tradition of Anti-Semitism: From Arthur Griffith to Sean South', in Feely, *Rise and Fall of Irish Anti-Semitism*, p. 19.
75 *Ibid*.
76 P. O'Farrell, *Ireland's English Question: Anglo-Irish Relations 1534–1970* (London: B. T. Batsford, 1971), p. 113.
77 T. Inglis, *Moral Monopoly* (Dublin: University College Dublin Press, 1998) p. 160.
78 White, *Minority Report*, p. 116.
79 *Catholic Bulletin* (1927) cited *ibid*., p. 145.

4

Ireland and the Holocaust

This chapter considers anti-Semitism in Irish society from independence in 1922 until the 1950s with a specific focus upon Ireland's response to Jewish refugees before, during and after the Holocaust. A number of historians have taken the view that while there was undoubtedly anti-Semitism in Irish society in the era after independence, it was of little consequence. Three arguments from this perspective will be examined. The first of these is that Irish anti-Semitism was inconsequential because it was latent and did not result in the persecution of Ireland's Jewish minority. The second argument is that the mainstream politics of post-independence Ireland never overtly embraced anti-Semitism because of the absence of a perceived 'Jewish problem' in Irish society. The third argument is that manifestations of anti-Semitism in Irish politics and religion were associated with marginal and even eccentric figures and as such were not to be taken seriously.

Such perspectives misrepresent anti-Semitism in Irish society before, during and after the Holocaust to a considerable extent. The evidence supporting this is to be found in the first instance in the immigration practices of the Irish state which were characterised by overt anti-Semitism from 1938 until Ireland's ratification of the UN Convention on the Status of Refugees (1951) in 1956. These practices suggest a degree of complicity with the persecution of Jews by the Nazis which was shared by a number of other countries. They also indicate *some* similarities between the goals of Nazi Germany and the Irish state of attaining and maintaining societies which were *judenfrei*, or 'without Jews'.

Some aspects of anti-Semitism in Ireland are illustrated by one of the characters in Joyce's *Ulysses*, set in 1904 – the year Jews from Limerick were driven from their homes – who states that Ireland is the only country which has never persecuted the Jews because she never let them in. The character, Mr Deasy, a Protestant, is an anti-Semite. He considers that England – her finance, her press – is in the hands of the Jews and that the Jews, wherever they are present, are to blame for the decline of nations.

Deasy makes the point that the Jews have ruined England and would, if let in, ruin Ireland also. His anti-Semitism is religiously justified for, as he puts it, they (the Jews) have sinned against the light. Joyce in this passage is writing about a number of distinct forms of anti-Semitism in turn. First, he refers to the moral or religious anti-Semitism which casts the Jews as the spiritual enemies of Christianity. Second, he alludes to the modern and secular forms of anti-Semitism that emerged during the nineteenth century. These, as will be noted, were distinct from, yet inter-twined with, the religious anti-Semitism characteristic of Christian society for centuries.

The argument made by Deasy, that Ireland did not yet have a Jewish problem because it never let them in, is patently erroneous both within the logic of *Ulysses*, whose main character is an Irish Jew, and in reality. There were Jewish communities in Dublin, Belfast Cork and, of course, Limerick. Yet it illustrates something important about anti-Semitism in general terms, noted by Goldhagen in *Hitler's Willing Executioners: Ordinary Germans and the Holocaust*, that applies to Ireland as much as Germany. It is that anti-Semitism in Ireland, as elsewhere, did not require the presence of a visible Jewish population. As explained by Goldhagen, European anti-Semitism from the Middle Ages onwards was often an 'anti-Semitism without Jews':

> Even when the Jews were permitted to live amongst Christians, few Christians knew Jews or had any opportunity to observe Jews at close range. Christians segregated Jews into Ghettos, and restricted their activ-ities through a host of oppressive laws and customs. Jews were isolated physically and socially from Christians. Christian antisemitism was not based on any familiarity with real Jews. It could not have been. Similarly, most virulent anti-Semites in Germany during Weimar and during the Nazi period probably had little or no contact with Jews. Entire areas of Germany were practically without Jews, since Jews formed less than 1 percent of the German population and 70 percent of Jews lived in large urban areas. The anti-Jewish beliefs and emotions of all such antisemites could not possibly have been based on any objective assessment of Jews, and must have been based only on what they *heard* about Jews, when listening to and partaking in the society's conversation, which itself was equally cavalier about representing the Jews faithfully, having a genesis, life and shape independent of the Jews whom it purportedly described.[1]

He argues that the religious nature of anti-Semitism made it possible for it to persist even in societies where there were no Jews. Britain, for example, expelled its Jewish population in the thirteenth century and was without Jews until the seventeenth century, yet a deep-rooted anti-

Semitism persisted in the popular imagination, whether in folk traditions or represented in the plays of the Elizabethan era.[2] Deasy, who considered that there were no Jews in Ireland, most certainly knew no Jews. His anti-Semitism was ideological rather than empirical. The anti-Semitism which found expression in Irish immigration practices from the 1930s to the 1950s was similarly grounded in prevalent racialisations and stereotypes. Immigration policy goals of keeping Jews out of Ireland can be understood as a response to an imagined Jewish problem rather than the consequence of some 'rational' calculation that the Jews, as a culturally distinct non-assimilated population, posed a distinct threat to the social order.

Anti-Semitisms and modernity

Some explanation of the shifting nature of anti-Semitism which accompanied processes of social modernisation in nineteenth-century Europe is necessary to account for the prevalent anti-Semitisms in Irish society in the era after independence. Processes of societal modernisation and secularisation during the nineteenth century augmented moral anti-Semitisms linked to Christian beliefs with new forms bound up with secular racial 'logic' and nationalism.

Racial anti-Semitism

In the nineteenth century religious 'proofs' of the legitimacy of racism and anti-Semitism were joined by 'scientific' proofs of the biological inferiority of black people to white people and of the perniciousness of the Jews. Nineteenth-century racial discourses conceived of nations in terms of lineage and genealogy. Within these discourses the existence of a German race or indeed an Irish race took on a political and social reality. Irish nationalism emerged through a process of social closure which culminated in an ethnic-religious formulation of Irishness. The ethnic component of this construction of national identity was bound up with genealogical and biological claims. In nineteenth-century Germany the Jews as a 'race' became represented as inferior to the German race. The idea of a Jewish race emerged as a counterpoint to that of a German race within German nationalist ideology. They were the 'other' against which the German nation defined itself. In France anti-Semitism also became the central mobilising theme in the construction of an ethnic homeland defined by culture and race.[3] Goldhagen argues that the concept of race profoundly shifted the nature of anti-Semitism in Germany. The idea that

Jews were the enemies of the German race was fundamental to a process of nation-building. Anti-Semitism in Germany acquires a new ideological coherence:

> Now, with race, a unifying, easily comprehended and metaphorically powerful concept at last appeared to integrate those various and inconsistent strands into a comprehensive, consistent explanation of Jewry and its relation to Germany.[4]

A new set of charges were superimposed upon those of Christian anti-Semitic tradition. These included claims that the Jews worked against national goals, that they constituted a danger to the social order of the nation state, and that they were to blame for undesirable economic and social changes. Race, as lineage, genealogy and biology, lay at the core of a modern or secular anti-Semitism which was fundamentally different from that which was informed by Christian doctrines. It shifted the imagined relationship with the Jewish 'other' from one informed by religious transgressions which could be forgiven and redeemed through religious conversion to ones which were racially immutable. Simply put, Jews could never become part of the biologically defined German race. They could never be assimilated. As explained by Goldhagen:

> Racist antisemites denied the dated Christian notion that all souls could be saved through baptism, and the notion that conversion would remove the only difference between Jewish Germans and Christian Germans...
> The conversion to Christianity could no more transfer the Jews into Germans than the skin of Blacks could be turned white.[5]

In this context religious conversion became seen as a deception. The resultant deepening of anti-Semitism became institutionalised in 1935 in the Nuremburg Laws which deprived German Jews of citizenship. Jewishness was defined both by racial and religious criteria with the result that persons with Jewish forebears as well as those who professed the Jewish religion were legally classified as Jewish. A distinction was made under the Nuremburg Laws between *Mischlinge*, or persons of mixed descent who had one or two grandparents who were Jewish by 'race' but who themselves were not Jewish by religion and those who had three or more Jewish grandparents. Those classified as *Mischlinge* faced widespread persecution within German society.

Goldhagen argues that the Christian churches in Germany sought to exclude Jewish converts from their congregations in response to widespread hostility among Protestants and Catholics to having to take the sacraments with them.[6] In this context the churches institutionalised racist anti-Semitism and internalised the racial categories imposed by the Nuremburg Laws. Blood won out over baptism. In 1933 the German bishops had made efforts to prevent the persecution of German Catholics who had converted from Judaism. These proved difficult under the proposed terms of the Reich Concordat, a yet to be ratified treaty between the Vatican and the Reich, whereby the Church promised loyalty to the German state and to not interfere in politics in return for various concessions from the state. The Catholic Church submitted a memorandum of complaint about the treatment of Catholics which mentioned the treatment of Jewish converts to Catholicism but this was not accepted by the German government under the terms of the Concordat. Subsequently, the Catholic authorities acknowledged the racial distinctions of the Nazis between Catholics and Catholics who were descended from Jews. Cornwell argues this willingness to make such distinctions was indicative of a collusion with the overall anti-Semitic policy of the Reich.[7] Irish refugee policies from 1938 until the end of the Second World War, it will be seen, similarly internalised the classifications of the Nuremburg Laws.

In Ireland Jews became understood as enemies of the nation within a nationalism which drew upon religious sectarianism. Irish-Ireland nationalism shared with German nationalism notions that nation was synonymous with race. Within Irish nationalism, as in German nationalism, identity was constructed in opposition to a specific non-national other. In the Irish case Jews were understood as enemies of the Church and by implication enemies of the nation, even if the sectarian 'other' against which the Catholic Irish nation was predominantly defined was Protestant rather than Jewish.[8] Twentieth-century expressions of anti-Semitism in Ireland depicted the Jews as enemies of Church and enemies of the nation; though perhaps here the distinction was a subtle and unnecessary one within the context of a hegemonically Catholic nation state.

Modernity and the Holocaust

The historiography of Holocaust studies can be broadly broken into two schools of thought on the question as to whether the Nazis sought to eliminate the Jews from the outset or not. An intentionalist school maintains that the former is the case. A functionalist school on the other hand maintains that the 'final solution' of genocide emerged through a rational process of attempting and then discarding other means to exclude Jews from the Reich. Bauman in *Modernity and the Holocaust* describes Nazi efforts to get rid of the Jews in functionalist terms; whereby the 'final solution' emerged not as a considered choice made at the start by ideologically motivated leaders.[9]

It did, rather emerge, inch by inch, pointing at each stage to a different destination, shifting in response to ever-new crises, and pressed forward with a 'we will cross that bridge once we come to it' philosophy.

The first of these efforts was the expulsion of Jews from Germany. Initial solutions of state-sanctioned violence, removal of citizenship and confiscation of property, all aimed at removing the Jews from German society, were accompanied by proposals to physically expel Jews from the Reich. Various plans for settling Jews outside Germany were considered (a 'Jewish principality' in Misko in Poland was envisaged and Eichmann spent a full year working on a project to ship the German Jews to Madagascar) but these were abandoned as unfeasible.[10] As the jurisdiction of the Reich grew, and the numbers of Jews in German 'territory' grew from an initial 600,000 to several millions, the possibilities for physical expulsion diminished. This, according to the 'functionalist' school, precipitated the final solution. As such, it followed a number of earlier efforts to make Germany and then German occupied Europe *judenfrei*. By comparison, in Ireland the solution to 'the Jewish problem' was principally a matter of restricting immigration.

Bauman argues that the Holocaust was the consequence of bureaucratic and rational characteristics of modern Western societies whereby modernity became a precondition for the expression of a particular genocidal form of racism. In simple terms, the Holocaust was produced through processes of mass production and bureaucratic organisation. Bauman quotes Weber by way of explanation. 'The honour of the civil servant is vested in his ability to execute conscientiously the order of superior authorities, exactly as if the order agreed with his own conviction. This holds even if the order seems wrong to him and if, despite the civil servant's remonstrances, the authority insists on the order.'[11]

Weber argues that bureaucratic processes remove the imperative for moral decisions in how organisational roles become defined.[12] As Bauman puts it, the human objects of bureaucratic tasks cease to be subjects of moral demands. Such bureaucratic rationality is evident within the administrative and decision making processes of Western societies where they affect groups such as refugees and welfare recipients as well as persecuted minorities. For example, refugees become dehumanised within the bureaucratic processes of states even in the era following the UN Convention on the Status of Refugees (1951) which obliges states to provide asylum to refugees from persecution. First, as applicants they are bureaucratically classified into the separate categories of asylum seekers (persons seeking asylum) and refugees (those who are officially recognised as 'genuine refugees' within the administrative criteria of individual states). The way in which they are classified determines whether they are seen to be part of society or whether they are, for administrative purposes, classified as outside that society even while they live within its jurisdiction. They can be denied all the rights of citizenship and can even be imprisoned. Under the logic of citizenship it becomes 'natural' that the non-citizen should not have social and economic rights.

German Jewish citizens became excluded when the rules of citizenship were redrawn according to the racist criteria of Nuremburg Laws. They were then excluded by other countries which may not have had racist citizenship laws but where the criteria for determining visa applications were bound up with exclusionary formulations of citizenship. In the Irish case Jewish refugees could be treated dispassionately according to the administrative criteria of responsible government departments. However, within the restrictive criteria governing the admittance of 'aliens' they were classified differently to other refugees. A policy of overt discrimination against Jewish refugees in the administration of visa criteria allowed all Jewish refugees to be classified as subversive. It became possible to institutionalise societal anti-Semitism within Irish bureaucratic processes.

Anti-Semitism in post-independence Ireland

Catholic anti-Semitism

Anti-Semitism in Irish society had much in common with that in other European societies, including Germany, during the 1920s and 1930s, where the Jews were a small minority of the overall population. In Ireland the Jewish population numbered just a few thousand. However, even in Germany, where there were more than half a million Jews, they comprised a comparatively small minority group. By comparison, in 1933 there were 23 million Catholics in Germany yet they too constituted a minority.[13] As such, German anti-Semitism was, to a considerable extent, an anti-Semitism without Jews.

Expressions of anti-Semitism in the writings and sermons of Irish Catholic clergy mirrored those in other countries in content during this period in how religious and secular justifications of anti-Semitism combined to portray the Jews as enemies of both church and nation. Anti-Semitic violence in 1904 was justified principally as a response to economic exploitation, which was likened to colonial exploitation, and by depictions of the Jews as enemies of Catholicism in France. The charge was also made that they killed Christ. In 1916 the *Catholic Bulletin*, a nationalist paper, published a series of anti-Semitic articles including one that restated age-old unfounded accusations of ritual murder. The series was accompanied by posters to advertise the paper which employed the headline 'Murder by Jews'.[14] The justification and character of anti-Semitism within Catholic and nationalist discourses changed little in the decades after the Limerick 'pogrom' except to periodically update the precise nature of the conspiracies of moral corruption against the Catholic nation of which Jews were accused. For example, in 1919 the Bishop of Limerick, Denis Hallinan, blamed Parisian Jews 'bitterly opposed to Christianity' for promoting indecent fashions in women's clothing. After 1922 Irish Catholicism became intertwined with an isolationist nationalism to generally oppose outside influences on Irish society. The promotion of conservative social values and hostility to social change at times became bound up with expressions of anti-Semitism whereby prevalent racialisations of the Jews were used to blame these for the promotion of unwelcome social change. During the 1930s a range of Catholic publications – *The Irish Catholic*, *The Catholic Bulletin*, *The Irish Mind*, *The Irish Rosary and the Cross* – depicted Jews as conspiring against the moral fabric of the nation and, along with communists and freemasons, plotting international conspiracies and revolution. Jewish conspiracies were, it was alleged, in control of the international press, international finance and cinema.[15]

Periodic anti-Semitic outbursts and some sustained campaigns by Catholic clergy met little censure within the Church hierarchy. Irish religious anti-Semitism before the Second World War reflected that of the Catholic Church as a whole. In Germany, for example, Catholic publications of all sorts disseminated an anti-Semitic litany during the early 1930s that was often indistinguishable from Nazi propaganda.[16] This continued during the war when, for example, a pastoral letter in 1941 which blamed the Jews for the death of Jesus implied that the 'self imposed curse of the Jews' justified their treatment by the Nazis. Such ongoing expressions remained religiously compatible with Church doctrine. In 1938 Pope Pius XI commissioned an encyclical on Nazi racism and anti-Semitism which was never issued.[17] This document on the unity of the human race, for all its good intentions, reflected traditional Catholic anti-Semitism. It stated on one hand that anti-Semitism was inadmissible but on the other hand implied that it was justifiable. It argued that God had chosen the Jews to make way for Christ's redemption but that they denied him and killed him. It stated that the Jews deserved the 'worldly and spiritual ruin' that they had brought down on themselves.

Opposition by some Catholics to anti-Semitism, prompted by growing awareness of the plight of the Jews in Germany and concern about anti-

Semitic agitation in Dublin during the Second World War, led to the foundation of a Catholic–Jewish ecumenical body which was suppressed by the Catholic hierarchy.[18] The Pillar of Fire Society, founded by members of the Legion of Mary, sought to engage in ecumenical dialogue with the Dublin Jewish community. However, this group was suppressed as were other ecumenical groups such as the Mercier Society which consisted of Catholics and Protestants. This suggests an explanation of sectarianism rather than anti-Semitism. Yet the repression of Catholic–Jewish ecumenicism was in keeping with Vatican policies on Church relationships with Jewish congregations in Germany during the quarter century prior to the Holocaust when these were the remit of Cardinal Pacelli who became Pope Pius XII in 1939.[19]

Anti-Semitism in Irish politics

It has been argued that anti-Semitism never became a major preoccupation within Irish party politics, even during the 1930s with the emergence of movements such as the National Guard – popularly known as the Blueshirts[20] – and the Irish Christian Front. A number of historians have argued that the Blueshirts did not engage in anti-Semitic politics,[21] or violence,[22] or have argued that expressions of anti-Semitism associated with the Blueshirts were not to be taken seriously because they were part of a general climate of xenophobia rather than motivated by anti-Semitism per se.[23] According to Lee the Blueshirts were simply traditional conservatives with few of the essential characteristics of Fascism 'decked out in fashionable but ill-fitting continental garb'.[24] Other writers are similarly disparaging of the Blueshirts in comparing them to continental or British Fascist movements both as a political force and as the bearer of anti-Semitic politics.[25] Such arguments claim that Irish anti-Semitism was of a different and lesser order to that in other countries. They hinge on a comparison of the manifestations of anti-Semitism in Ireland and elsewhere and conclude that since an overtly anti-Jewish politics did not emerge that somehow anti-Semitism in Ireland existed to a lesser degree also.

Goldhagen argues that one should resist the temptation to think about anti-Semitism in terms of a simple dichotomy between latent and manifest racism.[26] This simply measures how preoccupied an anti-Semite is with Jews at the moment rather than the nature of the beliefs about Jews which are prevalent. There is a big difference between intergroup antipathy which amounts to a dislike of some other group and holding religious or racial beliefs that such a group embodies evil. The issue is not whether anti-Semitism is latent or manifest but rather the nature of the anti-Semitism itself. The key issue for Goldhagen, in seeking to explain the role of ordinary Germans in the Holocaust, is the extent to which anti-Semitism is woven into the moral order of society. He argues that Christian anti-Semitism held that the Jews violated the moral order of the world. By their existence they defiled all that was sacred. As such the Jews came symbolically and discursively to represent much of what was evil in the world and not just represent it but become synonymous with it as self-willed agents of evil.[27] Although anti-Semitism was never a major preoccupation of Irish party politics this by no means discounted the possibility of institutionalised anti-Semitic beliefs within politics and bureaucracy. It will be seen that presumptions that Jews constituted a threat and an evil shaped political and administrative responses to Jewish refugees.

The National Guard or 'Blueshirts' articulated an exclusionary conception of Irishness which sought to recast the dominant exclusionary Catholic nationalism within a movement that borrowed some of the rhetoric of Fascism. Lee argues that they did so with less success on both counts than Fianna Fáil, the dominant nationalist party.[28] Their inability to command the heights of mainstream Irish politics had to do with an inability to mobilise myths of Irishness and speak for faith and fatherland with the efficacy of Fianna Fáil. Lee argues that Fianna Fáil possessed, more so than the Blueshirts, a number of Fascist organisational characteristics; a charismatic leader, the political pageantry of torch-light parades, an ideological emphasis on agrarian utopianism, communal identity, adeptness with the rhetoric of nationalism and a virtual monopoly on historical mythology.

Nevertheless the Blueshirts sought at times to apply the xenophobic and racist formulae of continental Fascist movements within an Irish context. The constitution of the National Guard restricted membership to 'citizens of Irish birth or parentage who professed the Christian Faith'. The cause was consciously endorsed and enforced to the exclusion of Ireland's Jewish community not just when the National Guard was established but after its merger with Cumann na nGaedheal in 1933. As explained by O'Regan: 'When the Christian Clause was introduced into the National Guard and later in the constitutions of the Young Ireland Association and League of Youth Blueshirts, Cumann na nGaedhealers, and for that matter Centre party deputies, were prepared to look the other way, if, that is they took any notice at all'.[29]

The Blueshirts did not explicitly engage in hostility against Ireland's Jewish minority but they discriminated against the Jews where they could. The ideological basis for this discrimination was, at face value, xenophobia which did not distinguish between one outgroup and another. The movement itself professed ideological opposition to 'communism and alien control and influence in national affairs'.[30] However, these 'evils' were attributed to the Jews within an anti-Semitic racism. The leader of the Blueshirts, Eoin O'Duffy, remained preoccupied with anti-Semitism after the demise of the organisation. Subsequently, he depicted the role of his Irish Brigade in the Spanish civil war as being against 'Communism, Jews and Freemasonry'.[31] In November 1938, O'Duffy wrote that Hitler's annexation of the Sudetenland was an inspiration for Catholic Ireland's own anti-partition campaign. In an appeal to the dominant nationalist imagination, he threatened minorities with the consequences of disloyalty to the Catholic state:

> The members of the Southern minority, the ex-Unionists, Protestants, Jews and others... must declare themselves and show whether or not they have gratitude. This is a testing time and we will inevitably form judgements of the sincerity and national usefulness of the various groups living in this nation by their actions now.[32]

A small number of politicians were vocal exponents of anti-Semitism in subsequent years. Some others were involved in anti-Semitic group behind the scenes.[33] During the 1940s Oliver J. Flannagan, an independent member of parliament (TD), and Paddy Belton TD, the leader of the by then defunct Irish Christian Front used their positions in the Dáil to make pronouncements against Jews without reproach or censure.[34] Flannagan, who in the 1943 general election topped the poll in the Laois–Offaly constituency, advocated a Nazi-style repression of the Jews in Ireland in his maiden speech in the Dáil in July 1943; 'There is one thing that Germany did, and that was to rout the Jews out of their country. Until we rout the Jews out of this country it does not matter a hair's breadth what orders you make'. At one level this was an uncharacteristic expression of anti-Semitism in the Dáil. However, it should not be dismissed as eccentric. It was arguably representative of a broader political opinion which had to be taken into consideration in refugee policy. There is some evidence, as will be discussed later in the chapter, that Flannagan's opposition to Jewish refugees influenced Irish refugee policy.

The persistence of anti-Semitism

Between the late 1930s and the late 1950s a number of anti-Semitic pamphlets were published by Fr Dennis Fahy of the Holy Ghost Missionary Order. Fr Fahy was an influential figure among Irish Republicans such as Sean South, who established a branch of Fr Fahy's organisation, Maria Duce, in Limerick in 1954, following the priest's death, and disseminated his writings.[35] South, who was killed while leading an IRA attack on a police barracks in Northern Ireland, was a charismatic figure within

Irish nationalism. His funeral procession from Fermanagh to Limerick attracted a massive display of Catholic nationalist fervour. South can be seen to exemplify how sectarian anti-Semitism persisted in Limerick within devotional and nationalist movements half a century after the 1904 pogrom. In 1970 the Mayor of Limerick, Stephen Coughlan TD, gave a speech defending the Limerick pogrom:

> I remember the problem of the Jews in Limerick. Fr Creagh in his coura-
> geous way declared war on the Jews at Colooney Street, which is now
> Wolfe Tone Street. The Jews at that time, who are gone now, were extor-
> tionists, he had the backing of everybody in the City of Limerick... He
> had set the match to light the fire against the Jewish extortionists.[36]

In 1979 another Limerick mayor demanded the cancellation of a radio documentary on the 1904 pogrom stating that it was the kind of pro-gramme which Limerick must be protected against.[37] In the following decade defences of Fr Creagh's reputation were contested by some local historians and local politicians, notably Jim Kemmy, who had resigned from the Labour Party after Stephen Coughlan's speech in 1970 and was subsequently elected as an independent socialist TD for the city. In 1984, revisionist accounts of the pogrom by Limerick local historians were criti-cised by a Redemptorist Priest, Fr Baily, in the *Irish Times* who described the use of the word 'pogrom' as emotive and as a misnomer for minor disturbances which had occurred in the city in 1904.[38] He argued that Fr Creagh, his 'regrettable sectarian pulpit oratory notwithstanding', was predominantly concerned with the protection of the illiterate poor from exploitation; to this end he set up a savings bank and a clothing bank. He also argued that Fr Creagh's 'naive pulpiteering' played into the hands of Rabbi Levin, the leader of the Limerick community, whom he described as a master of public relations who secured worldwide exposure of his version of events in the media:

> I urge that the historian should take account of Rabbi Levin's influence
> on the coverage of the affair. For with great skill he peddled his version
> of events to the world press and national leaders. In particular he turned
> the spotlight away from the trading methods denounced by Creagh and
> onto the sectarian shots that the latter fired from his pulpit. I give Levin
> full marks for his tactical skill.

Although the Jews had been absent from the city for decades they continued to be constructed as exploiters of the dominant community. Any contestation of this tended to be perceived, within chauvinistic folk memory, as an attack on Limerick.[39] An attitudinal study undertaken in 1972 and 1973 on prejudice and tolerance in Ireland found that 20 per cent of respondents believed that the Jewish people were responsible for the crucifixion of Christ. The persistence in Irish society of a moral basis for anti-Semitism meant that the Jews could still be depicted as enemies of the community from which they had been expelled.[40]

Anti-Semitism and the state

The Irish response to Jewish refugees from 1938, when distinct responses to the Nuremberg Laws emerged in Ireland, to 1956, when Ireland ratified the UN Convention on the Status of Refugees (1951), was marked by an overt discrimination within the official policy of the state. However, anti-Jewish discrimination which resulted in the rejection of visa applications emerged at a political level, in the voluntary sector apparatus of refugee aid, in the actions of at least one importantly placed official as well as in the administrative criteria which governed the consideration of visa applications.

Immigration processes

Irish administrative responses to refugees emerged through the interaction of three different government departments. Each had a role in determining refugee applications according to their own ethos and priorities in what Goldstone describes as a 'three handed reel'.[41] Applications for visas from refugees were first vetted by officials of the Department of External Affairs abroad or by British officials in countries where Ireland did not have an embassy. This initial vetting role continued until Ireland's ratification in 1956 of the UN Convention (1951). The Department of Industry and Commerce had a pivotal role in the determination of applications where a work permit was needed to ensure that the applicant would not be a burden on the state. Sometimes the ability of applicants to provide investment, specialist skills and employment were factors in determining whether a person should be allowed residency. The determinations of Industry and Commerce were to a considerable extent shaped by 'zero sum' conceptions of the threats to the jobs of Irish citizens posed by foreign labour. Furthermore the criteria that refugees not constitute a burden upon the state required that most refugees were dependent upon being able to obtain financial sponsorship during their stay. Finally, under the Aliens Act (1935), the Department of Justice had the overall authority to determine visa applications.

The Department of Justice

In 1999 a Supreme Court judgment on the use of ministerial discretion in relation to deportations upheld a ruling of the High Court that the Alien Act (1935) was unconstitutional on the basis that it gave the minister of justice authority a power to deport without setting out the basis on which decisions to deport should be made. The ruling explained how, in the absence of established criteria that set out the basis on which refugee applications should be determined, decisions were vulnerable to prevailing political pressures as well as to prejudices of various institutional actors within the Department of Justice:

> The case turned on whether the legislature could in the terms of Section 5.1e of the Aliens Act (1935) delegate to the Minister power to deport aliens, or whether it was an impermissible delegation of legislation contrary to Article 15.2 of the Constitution (which states the sole and exclusive power for making laws for the state is vested in the Oireachtas)... Analysed in accordance with Article 15.2 of the Constitution, as must be done, the Act was an abdication of the legislature's duty to set policies and principles... Article 15.2 set out in emphatic language the exclusive law-making role of the national parliament which was an 'essential component of the tripartite separation of powers which is the most important part of our constitutional architecture'. The Aliens Act, 'not the slightest degree unclear or unambiguous' empowered the Minister of Justice to exclude and deport not merely particular aliens but whole categories of aliens determined by their nationality or class. When the Act was enacted, the power of Saorstát Eireann to expel or deport aliens was, in the absence of legislation, vested in the Crown acting on the advice of the Executive Council. The change effected in the law by Section 5.1e of the Act was not a conferring on the State of an absolute power to deport aliens. It already had that power. But it was now to be exercised by the Minister.

> The objective of Section 5.1e was to enable the Minister to exercise at his absolute and uncontrolled discretion, the power of deporting individual aliens or categories of them subject only to the some restrictions regarding diplomats and aliens resident here for five years. The effect was that the Minister, not the Oireachtas, was to determine what aliens and classes of aliens could be deported and what modifications there should be of an exercise of that power. The Oireachtas had effectively determined that policy in the area should be the Minister's responsibility.[42]

The implementation of the Aliens Act (1935) was, as such, open to abuse in terms of allowing ministerial discretion for the variable treatment of different racial and ethnic groups and allowed for a ministerial discrimination against Jewish refugees which, at times, augmented discriminations against Jewish refugees in determining visa applications for Jews. Some of the criteria applied by Justice officials in determining visa applications related to considerations of national security with an emphasis on keeping out political undesirables.[43] Discrimination against Jewish applicants went beyond evaluations by officials that individual Jews constituted a threat to Irish society. It became state policy to formally classify all Jews as such a threat.

The Department of External Affairs

The Department of External Affairs was perhaps the most open and progressive of the three departments involved in the consideration of visa applications. One would expect diplomats to be less xenophobic in temperament to officials whose main brief was the protection of national security and native industry and employment. This was arguably the case, in relative terms, in the formulation of diplomatic responses to requests for asylum from Jewish refugees and others. In 1938, for example, the department urged Irish participation in a conference at Evian-les-Bains which was called by President Roosevelt to respond to the refugee situation following the annexation of Austria by Germany in 1938.[44] During and after the war the department took the lead role in some initiatives to take in Jewish refugees from Vichy France and Italy and survivors from the Belsen-Bergen concentration camp.

However, responses to Jewish refugees from Nazi Germany were for a time influenced to some extent by the anti-Semitism of Charles Bewley who was the senior official at the Irish Legation in Germany from 1933 to 1939. Bewley was an anti-Semite who became increasingly intoxicated with the Nazi project during his stay in Berlin from 1933 to 1939.[45] During this time he came to support at first the oppression, then the exclusion and subsequently the murder of German Jews as necessary from the perspective of the Reich in a series of shifts which mirrored changes within German society and within the apparatus of the Nazi state. By 1935 he had come to accept Nazi racial justifications of the treatment of the Jews.[46]

Bewley's anti-Semitism was well known to his superiors in the Department of External Affairs. In 1922 Gavan Duffy, Dáil Éireann minister for foreign affairs wrote that he had known Bewley for several years and had a high regard for him, adding that 'I know he is mad on the Jewish question'.[47] In making the decision about Bewley's suitability for a diplomatic post (as a trade representative) Duffy took into account reports of an incident in Berlin where Bewley had stated publicly about Robert Briscoe that it was 'not likely that a Jew of his type would be appointed by the Irish government as its representative' (Bewley's own account of the incident), using 'a string of the most abusive and filthy language' (Briscoe's account in a letter to Duffy at the time). Duffy considered that Bewley's anti-Semitic convictions were 'so pronounced' that he would have difficulty in dealing with all persons and questions within the scope of an envoy to Berlin, where the Jewish element was very strong. The problem was not anti-Semitism per se but, as Andreas Roth put it, 'Bewley's openly sported mad variant.'[48]

Bewley served in Berlin in the early 1920s and returned to head of the Irish legation between 1933 and 1939 to succeed Daniel Binchy, an unambiguous critic of National Socialism.[49] Bewley's support of Nazi persecution of the Jews influenced his own role in the initial vetting of visa applications from Jewish refugees on behalf of the Irish state.[50] There were indications that he also sought to prevent Jews for obtaining Irish visas which they had been granted. Keogh in *Jews in Twentieth Century Ireland* has argued that the response to a Viennese Jew, George Clare, in 1938 provides evidence of this.[51] He describes how Bewley held back visas for the Clare family which had already been granted and were, in fact, 'awaiting collection' at the Irish Legation in Berlin. On arrival in Berlin they were told by an official that the visas had not arrived. The official implied that the Minister, Bewley, would be unwilling to help them to resolve the matter. She advised them to contact Dublin again and to return a week later to the Legation at which time she told one of the family that a policy decision rather than a distaste for speedy action had been responsible for the delay in issuing the visa. The Clares were required to wait in Berlin for a further six weeks, until the machinery for the factory they were setting up in Ireland (the reason they obtained their visas) had actually arrived in the country. During this time they lived through the *Kristallnacht* (night of broken glass) of which Bewley had expressed overt approval.[52] This resulted in the murder of about 100 Jews and the destruction of several thousand Jewish businesses. Subsequently, the Clares received their visas and only then, they believed, due to the courageous persistence of Frau Kamberg, the official they had dealt with at the Legation.

The Nazification of an Irish anti-Semite

Bewley has acquired a similar status to Fr Creagh, the Redemptorist who played a pivotal role in anti-Semitism in Limerick, as a unique and untypical aberration, rather than someone who embodied widely felt beliefs and attitudes. Critiques of Bewley have tended to focus on his role as a diplomat but the figure of Bewley offers potential to examine the anti-Semitism as a phenomenon in Irish society more generally. Michael Kennedy suggests that Bewley's affinity with the Nazi project might be understood, in part, by his own nationalist and Catholic ideological preoccupations. Bewley, he states, possessed an Irish nationalism which was virulently anti-British. As such he represented a strain of pro-German sentiment of the 'my enemies enemy is my friend' kind which emerged during the struggle for independence during the First World War and persisted among many Irish republicans during the Second World War.[53] Second, he describes Bewley's enthusiasm for Nazism as an authoritarian project of national renewal and for a 'miracle in the purification of the stage, literature and general life in German cities' which was close to the aspirations of the pastoral letters of Irish bishops and those embodied within Irish censorship legislation.

These affinities may account for Bewley's pro-German sentiments but they do not necessarily either explain his anti-Semitism per se or his adherence to the racial anti-Semitism which was embodied in Nazism. They might be explained however by the presence of anti-Semitism within exclusionary formulations of Irish nationalism and by the ideological nature of this anti-Semitism. Bewley's brand of exclusionary nationalism was closest perhaps to that of the Christian Front which itself drew upon continental Fascism. As noted earlier, arguments that the Blueshirts were a poor vehicle for anti-Semitic politics at an ideological level are problematic given the nature of Irish anti-Semitism as a discourse which understood Jews to be a profound threat to the religious and social order. Bewley's personal journey as a fellow traveller in the creation of the Holocaust from 1933 to 1939 was not one shared by many other Irish people though perhaps this was in some cases, at least, for want of opportunity. Bewley was recalled to Dublin in 1939. However, he remained in Germany during the Second World War and worked as a sometime journalist, penning anti-English propaganda. During the war he submitted a number of confidential reports to the German government on Irish affairs aimed at supporting the German war effort. After the war he was arrested and interrogated by the Allies in Italy. He remained an apologist for the Nazi regime and wrote a sympathetic biography of Herman Goering, to whom he was close during his time in Berlin.[54]

Discriminatory immigration practices

An overt policy of discrimination against Jews emerged in Ireland in 1938. It lasted throughout the Second World War and the aftermath of the Holocaust. The Department of Justice routinely advised against the admittance of Jews until 1956 when Ireland ratified the UN Convention (1951). Discrimination within state practices took the form of subjecting Jewish applications for visas to specifically stringent interpretation within an overall illiberal immigration policy. Overt discrimination against Jews can be dated from the government's devolution of refugee policy to a voluntary body in November 1938. In the run-up to the Second World War, officials were receptive to requests from Irish and foreign Catholic organisations for visas on behalf of Catholics abroad. The result of the lobbying of such groups was the institutionalisation of a voluntary group – the Irish Co-ordinating Committee for the Relief of Christian Refugees – within immigration policy.[55] The reason for such a devolvement of refugee policy was related to the unwillingness of the state to become involved in providing for the welfare of asylum seekers. The committee was given responsibility for vetting refugee applications; and was expected to provide for the maintenance of those whose admittance they recommended.

A Department of Justice memorandum on 16 November 1938 endorsed the views of the committee that the state should admit Catholic refugees who had converted from Judaism but not Jewish refugees. These views became institutionalised within state policy when the Minister of Justice devolved the vetting of prospective refugees to the committee:

> These proposals relate only to Christians with Jewish blood. The Co-ordinating committee are of an opinion that this country should confine its efforts to such persons as there are adequate funds subscribed by the Jewish communities in other countries to deal with the cases of practising Jews. The Co-ordinating Committee are, it is understood, prepared to undertake the responsibility of sifting applications for permission to settle here and putting forward names only of persons whom they are satisfied will be suitable in every way. It is thought that the Committee's offer should be accepted.[56]

Discrimination against Jewish refugees was justified in an article by T. W. T. Dillon, Secretary to the Committee, in an article in the Irish journal *Studies* in 1939 entitled 'The Refugee Problem'. The article advocated a policy of admitting Christian refugees considered as non-Aryan 'hybrids' (those with Jewish ancestry who had converted to Christianity) under the Nuremburg Laws. It argued that the plight of these 'Christian Jews', a term used frequently in the article, exceeded that of the unconverted Jews. The term 'Christian Jew' was also used interchangeably with the term 'Catholic' to denote to a large body of Catholics 'some thousands – who are to-day treated as pariahs in Germany and Austria'.[57] These, it was argued, suffered worse than the unconverted Jews. Their employment, homes and property were forfeit but, it was argued, they were not able to turn to the American Jewish community for help:

The story is told that Goering came to Vienna and confiscated the whole funds of the Jewish community. They wired to America asking for help. The next day their funds were replaced to the last cent in dollars safe in American hands, where Goering could not touch them. But the Jewish Catholics had no claim to those funds.[58]

The article made a case for focusing Irish refugee policy upon the plight of Christian (Catholic) Jews by arguing that Catholics were doubly oppressed; first by the Nazis and second because the 'ordinary refugee... who has nothing to recommend him except his Christianity' was excluded by the international Jewish community.[59] The Jews were represented (the story is told) as comprising an international conspiracy according to prevailing anti-Semitic racialisations. Dillon goes to considerable lengths to argue that Jews who have converted to Christianity are genuine Christians. This argument is used to represent the convert refugees as morally deserving of assistance from Catholic Ireland within a dualism which constructs the unconverted Jew as a less deserving 'other':

> The great majority of Hybrids are Christians. They are the offspring of Christian marriages in which one or both of the consorts were themselves Christians and in which the children were baptised at birth. Others have been converted later in life. Since the beginning of the nineteenth century there has been a steady stream of conversion to Christianity. No doubt many of these conversions had no great religious significance, but were rather a sign of assimilation to German society. But there is no reason to doubt that the children of these converted Jews were brought up as sincere Christians. Indeed it would not have been easy, in 19th century Germany, to neglect the religious upbringing of children, since religion was taught in all the state schools. We may take it, therefore, that a large proportion of the Hybrids are genuine Christians who have received the same religious education as their 'Aryan' fellow countrymen.[60]

> It is stated that there were an unusual number of Jewish converts in or about the time that Hitler came to power. It is difficult to understand what motive, other than genuine conviction, could have induced a Jew to become a Christian just at that time. By doing so he sacrificed the not inconsiderable advantages attached to his membership of the Jewish community, and he had been forewarned by Hitler that Creed would make no difference to his fate... It is certainly worse to be a Christian Jew in Germany to-day than to be a Jew *tout court*. The Jew has a better chance of emigration and is sure of a good reception in any foreign country from the local Jewish Community.[61]

Writing from Berlin in an effort to undermine the admission of some ninety refugees into Ireland by the Co-ordinating Committee Bewley argued that there was 'no safeguard that non-Aryan Christians were not Jews who had baptised out of convenience'.[62]

By means of the distinctions promoted by Dillon and exploited by Bewley Irish refugee practices internalised the racist 'logic' of the Nuremburg Laws. It was undoubtedly the case that Austrian 'Jewish Catholics' faced persecution from the state and that the Irish committee sought to help this group at the behest of the Austrian Catholic Church. However, it was also the case that Catholic charities in Austria had agreed not to help non-Aryans and as such accepted the primacy of race laws over their own rite of baptism.[63] This was in contrast to the Society of Friends in Vienna who sought to help all categories of non-Aryan during this period.[64] The decision of the Irish Co-ordinating Committee and the Department of Justice to admit only Jewish Catholics was inevitably a complicit with the distinctions within the Nuremberg Laws between Aryans, Hybrids or *Mischlinge*, and Jews in so far as discrimination against Jews fell within this racist hierarchy.

The workings of Irish refugee policy and the interpretations of the governing legislation, the Aliens Act (1935), within this context can be illustrated by the response of the Department of Justice to attempts by Lily Briscoe, wife of the Jewish Fianna Fáil TD Robert Briscoe in April 1939 to secure permits for two distant relatives. She was informed that 'the only refugees who are admitted to this country are persons whose cases are recommended to the Minister by the Irish Co-ordinating Committee for Refugees'. This was a fairly typical response to representations to the Department of Justice on behalf of Jewish refugees throughout late 1938 and early 1939.[65]

Irish politics and the Holocaust

Even where there was a willingness to accept Jewish refugees – which certainly increased as the war advanced – it was not deemed to be politically feasible to admit to commitments to accept Jewish refugees. Initiatives to admit Jews had to be accompanied by a degree of subterfuge. On 5 April 1943 deValera had agreed 'in principle' to accept 500 Jewish refugee children from Vichy, France. The Irish Red Cross – who agreed to organise the care of these refugees – sought permission to publish details of the initiative on the basis that when doing so the word 'Jewish' would be omitted. A letter from the secretary of the Irish Red Cross to the Department of External Affairs put this as follows:

> At yesterday's meeting of the Executive Committee the Chairman told the members of his telephone conversation with you when he agreed on behalf of the Society to take 500 Jewish refugee children here. The

meeting endorsed the Chairman's action and it was decided to ask your Department for permission to publish this. When publishing it we shall omit the word 'Jewish'. When we receive your permission we shall get in touch with the Jewish Community here in order to make arrangements for the reception and housing of the children. [66]

A question on the matter was put to deValera in the Dáil by Oliver J. Flannagan in 1944. DeValera replied, disingenuously in terms which omitted any reference to Jews; 'A proposal for the reception of refugee children was made and accepted. I cannot, however, at this stage give further information'.[67] Flannagan accused deValera of lying (i.e. not 'giving the reply he had been given' by officials) but this was not the case. The response adhered to the text of a written brief prepared by the Department of External Affairs which also omitted any reference to Jews.[68]

Arguably, the perceived necessity to advance initiatives to admit Jews by stealth and subterfuge indicates their vulnerability to prevalent anti-Semitism in Irish politics. deValera was supportive of efforts to admit Jewish refugees into Ireland and would have been regarded as a friend to the Jewish community.[69] He ensured that the 1937 constitution protected the religious freedom of the Jews.[70] However, politicians such as Flannagan represented the dominant political perspective on whether Jews should be admitted into the country.

Anti-Semitism as state policy

Official government reports contained overt expressions of anti-Semitism for a number of years after the war. A draft memorandum dated 24 September 1945 set out the official anti-Semitic perspective of the Department of Justice policy in unequivocal terms:

> It is the policy of the Department of Justice to restrict the immigration of Jews. The wealth and influence of the Jewish community in this country, and the murmurs against Jewish wealth and influence are frequently heard. As Jews do not become assimilated with the native population, like other immigrants, there is a danger that any big increase in their numbers might create a social problem.[71]

This statement was reiterated with an amendment to the opening sentence which read, 'The immigration of Jews is generally discouraged', in a number of subsequent reports on refugees and immigration issues from 1938 until 1956 when Ireland ratified the United Nations Convention on Human Rights. A Department of Justice memorandum, dated 28 February 1953, argued that its 'policy' of excluding Jews was supported by other government departments:

In the administration of the alien laws it has always been recognised in the Departments of Justice, Industry and Commerce and External Affairs that the question of the admission of aliens of Jewish blood presents a special problem and the alien laws have been administered less liberally in their case.[72]

Whatever the veracity of the first part of this claim, the second part was certainly true. Keogh argues that Irish refugee policy on the admission of refugee children was generally liberal; though not in the case of Jewish children.[73] For example, efforts to secure admission for 100 orphan Jewish survivors of Bergen-Belsen, soon after the end of the Second World War, had met with resistance from the Department of Justice even though arrangements to provide for their care had been put in place by the Irish and British Jewish communities at no cost to the state. In August 1946 the Minister of Justice refused permission to admit the children on the grounds that it had always been policy to restrict the admission of Jewish aliens. This decision was overturned after the Chief Rabbi approached deValera and the children were admitted on a temporary basis. They were subsequently relocated to Canada, the United States, Israel and Britain.[74] A reply by the Irish government to a questionnaire issued by the Consultative Assembly of the Council of Europe in 1952 recorded that close on 1,000 refugee children had been admitted since 1947. These were all Christian with the exception of the 100 Jewish children from Belsen-Bergen.

The forms of religious discrimination institutionalised before the Second World War, through official recognition of the Irish Co-ordinating Committee for the Relief of Christian Refugees, persisted during the immediate post-war era. The memorandum of 23 February 1953 proposed a new system for vetting refugees on a similar basis to that 'adopted for the admission of non-Aryan refugees' in 1938 and 1939. This was to be administered by a new committee with a similar remit to the pre-war committee. The memorandum contrasted 'refugees of good character of Catholic and Christian religions' with Jewish refugees. Jews from eastern European countries were depicted as a political danger to the Irish state:

There is a strong anti-Jewish feeling in this State which is particularly evident to the Alien Section of the Department of Justice. Sympathy for the Jews has not been particularly excited at the recent news that some thousands are fleeing westwards because of the recent round-up of communist Jews who had been prominent in Governments and Government service in eastern European countries.[75]

The author of the memorandum and several others opposed to the admittance of Jewish refugees was a Department of Justice official named Peter

Berry who, like Charles Bewley, in External Affairs was ardently anti-Semitic.[76] The context was an application to allow ten Jewish families to enter the state. However, the applicants were described as attempting to buy preferential treatment for themselves. The memorandum went on to state: 'I particularly don't like the bait that ample money will be forthcoming for the maintenance of these Jewish families if they are allowed to take their place at the head of queue of thousands who have been waiting in fear and misery for an opportunity to start life anew in another country'. There were disparaging references to the Jewish Fianna Fáil TD, Robert Briscoe, who supported the application. The memorandum stated that 'our experience is that they will stand up for each other'. Outrage was professed that such an application should even be advanced. Following a lecture based on this chapter in 2003 at the Reform Synagogue in Terenure, Dublin, Ben Briscoe, son of Robert, remarked that Berry had been treated as a family friend by his father, and had given no indication of the ardent anti-Semitism he practised behind the scenes as a civil servant.

Conclusion

There has been a tendency within Irish historiography to depict anti-Semitic outbursts within national politics or within Catholic discourse as atypical. Figures such as Fr Creagh, Eoin O'Duffy, Charles Bewley, Oliver J. Flannagan, Fr Fahy, Peter Berry or Stephen Coughlan can be portrayed as unrepresentative, yet they articulated anti-Semitisms shared by some key decision-makers and, arguably, within Irish society more generally. This chapter points to a legacy of overt racial discrimination within Irish refugee policy. Anti-Semitism within official practices and within politics was sanctioned by pervasive racialised constructions of the Jews as enemies of Irish society. Such prejudices prevailed in the absence of ideological contestations of anti-Semitism within Irish society.

In particular, the Department of Justice identified the Jews as enemies of the nation and portrayed their exclusion as a mission of national defence. This defensive role was shaped, first, by the very remit of the department to enforce exclusionary immigration policies. However, prevailing anti-Semitism led to the Jews being identified as enemies of faith and fatherland. Discrimination against Jews, even within the context of illiberal immigration policies, was perceived to be in the public interest. This was all too possible within a context where no legal obligation to accept refugees was acknowledged by the state and where no challenges to the discretionary use of ministerial power had been forthcoming.

A striking feature of Irish anti-Semitic discourses, as articulated by civil servants, was the extent to which these remained unchanged after the Holocaust. These discourses became sanitised from the late 1950s after Ireland ratified the UN Convention on the Status of Refugees (1951). They dissipated without discussion or retraction. It may be stating the obvious to point out that the purpose of including anti-Semitic statements in civil service reports was to further policy goals of excluding Jews. For their authors, such pronouncements legitimised and furthered such objectives. Ratification of the Convention in 1956 shifted the goals of Irish refugee policy. Overt policies of discrimination became unfeasible within the context of an obligation to admit all those who sought refugee status. Yet, it may also be stating the obvious that ratification of the Convention did not remove anti-Semitism from Irish society. A degree of ongoing justification of past actions, notably the attacks in Limerick in 1904, has drawn upon unreconstructed anti-Semitism. Racisms, including anti-Semitism, do not have to be formally articulated to have an exclusionary impact. Institutional racism is the outcome of both stated and unstated racialised perspectives. Notwithstanding the ratification in 1956 of the 1951 Convention, Irish refugee practices were not significantly reformulated until the 1990s. In the decades after 1950s these remained ad hoc and were guided, to a considerable extent, by pre-Convention thinking. This chapter reveals a legacy of racism within political and administrative processes with potential consequences for other groups of refugees and immigrants. This legacy is explored in the next chapter.

Notes

1 D. Goldhagen, *Hitler's Willing Executioners: Ordinary Germans and the Holocaust* (London: Abacus, 1996), p. 41.

2 D. Cohn-Sherbok, *The Crucified Jew: Twenty Centuries of Christian Anti-Semitism* (London: HarperCollins, 1992), p. 118.

3 B. Jenkins and N. Copsey, 'Nation, Nationalism and National Identity in France', in B. Jenkins and S. A. Sofos, (eds), *Nation and Identity in Contemporary Europe* (London: Routledge, 1996).

4 Goldhagen, *Hitler's Willing Executioners*, p. 66.

5 *Ibid.*, p. 68.

6 *Ibid.*, p. 105.

7 J. Cornwell, *Hitler's Pope: the Secret History of Pius XII* (London: Penguin, 2000), p. 159.

8 J. Sugden and A. Barnier, *Sport, Sectarianism and Society in a Divided Ireland* (Leicester: Leicester University Press), p. 29.

9 Z. Bauman, *Modernity and the Holocaust* (London: Sage, 1996), p. 15.

10 *Ibid.*, p. 16.

11 M. Weber, cited by Bauman, *ibid.*, p. 22.

12 M. Weber, cited in G. Ritzer, *Sociological Theory* (London: McGraw-Hill, 1996), p. 129.

13 Cornwell, *Hitler's Pope*, p. 133.

14 Keogh, *Jews in Twentieth-Century Ireland* (Cork: Cork University Press), p. 70.

15 *Ibid.*, p. 80.

16 Goldhagen, *Hitler's Willing Executioners*, p. 109.

17 Pius XI was seriously ill and had only weeks to live and did not instruct publication of the encyclical, entitled *Humani generis unitas* ('The Unity of the Human Race') before he died. It was subsequently quashed (see Cornwell, *Hitler's Pope*, p. 191).

18 L. O'Broin, *Just Like Yesterday: An Autobiography* (Dublin: Gill & Macmillan, 1986), pp. 147–50.

19 Cornwell, *Hitler's Pope*, p. 70, pp. 295–7.

20 The 'Blueshirts' copied the appearances of continental Fascist movements but never proclaimed themselves as a Fascists movement. They maintained a support for democracy. Their commitment to corporatism and vocational organisation was shaped by the Catholic social teachings of Pope Pius XI and was shared with other political parties in Ireland. See M. Manning, *The Blueshirts* (Dublin: Gill & Macmillan, 1987), p. 242 and J. A Murphy, *Ireland in the Twentieth Century* (Dublin: Gill & Macmillan, 1975), p. 82.

21 J. J. Lee, *Ireland 1912–1985: Politics and Society* (Cambridge: Cambridge University Press, 1989), pp. 181–2. Also see See Manning, *Blueshirts*, pp. 75, 240.

22 J. O'Regan, *The Irish Counter-Revolution 1921-1936* (London: Gill & Macmillan, 1999), p. 334.

23 *Ibid.*

24 Lee, *Ireland 1912–1985*, pp. 181–2.

25 In a chapter entitled 'Bring on the Dancing Blueshirts' (O'Regan, *Irish Counter-Revolution*, pp. 324–40).

26 Goldhagen, *Hitler's Willing Executioners*, p. 37.

27 *Ibid.*, p. 38.

28 Lee, *Ireland 1912–1985*, pp. 182–3.

29 O'Regan, *Irish Counter-Revolution*, p. 334.

30 M. Cronin, *The Blueshirts and Irish Politics* (Dublin: Four Courts Press, 1997), p. 34.

31 *Hibernia* (April 1938).

32 *Irish Independent* (31 October 1938).

33 A Garda undercover officer reported that some members of Fianna Fáil were members of an anti-Semitic organisation which also included O'Duffy and some members of the Gardaí in its membership. See R. Fisk, *In Time of War* (London: Paladin, 1985), p. 433.

34 M. O'Riordan, 'The Sinn Fein Tradition of Anti-Semitism: From Arthur Griffith to Sean South', in P. Feely (ed.), *The Rise and Fall of Irish Anti-Semitism* (Dublin: Labour History Workshop, 1984), p. 22.

35 *Ibid.*, p. 24.

36 Cited in P. Feely, 'Introduction', *ibid.*, p. 1.

37 *Irish Times* (24 February 1979).

38 *Irish Times* (3 August 1984), *Irish Times* (6 September 1984).

39 There are some commonalties between this defensiveness and the response during the 1990s to Frank McCourt's *Angela's Ashes* which perceived the book as an attack on Limerick.

40 A survey undertaken in 1972 and 1973 found that 20 per cent of respondents believed that the Jews as a people are to blame for the Crucifixion of Christ. See M. McGreill *Prejudice in Ireland Revisited* (Maynooth: Survey and Research Unit, 1996).

41 K. Goldstone, '"Benevolent Helpfulness?" Ireland and the International Reaction to Jewish Refugees, 1933–9', in M. Kennedy and J. M. Skelly (eds), *Irish Foreign Policy 1919–1966: From Independence to Internationalism* (Dublin: Four Courts Press, 2000), pp. 122–3.

42 *Irish Times* (21 May 1999).

43 For example, socialists were considered as subversive. Irish officials regularly consulted their British counterparts about visa applications. They had access to the British 'black list' (the suspects index). See Goldstone, '"Benevolent Helpfulness?"', p. 123.

44 *Ibid.*, p. 127.

45 See M. Kennedy, 'Our Men in Berlin: Some Thoughts on Irish Diplomats in Germany 1929–39', *Irish Journal of International Affairs*', 10 (1999), pp. 53–70.

46 Bewley described the Jewish laws as one of the highlights of the 1935 Nuremberg Rally (*ibid.*, p. 65).

47 Letter 22 March 1922, cited in A. Roth, *Mr Bewley in Berlin: Aspects of the Career of an Irish Diplomat* (Dublin: Four Courts Press, 2000), p. 13.

48 *Ibid.*, p. 15.

49 In 1933 Binchy wrote a prescient essay on Adolph Hitler. Reprinted as D. Binchy, 'Adolph Hitler', in B. Fanning (ed.) *An Irish Century: Studies 1912–2012* (Dublin: University College Dublin Press, 2012).

50 In contrast a British official in Berlin, Captain Foley, saved many lives by dispensing visas as liberally as possible. See Goldstone, '"Benevolent Helpfulness?", p. 132.

51 Keogh, *Jews in Twentieth-Century Ireland*, p. 136.

52 As Kennedy puts it, he was not misled by Nazi propaganda, he agreed with Nazi tactics ('Our Men in Berlin', p. 68).

53 Fisk, for instance, recounts how one 'violently anti-British civil servant' would hoist the Irish Tricolour up the flag post at Killiney Castle, an Irish army base, every time the Germans announced a military victory. He also cites similar but more muted responses by J. J. Walsh, Minister of Posts and Telegraphs, in conversations with a military intelligence officer (*In Time of War*, p. 433).

54 See Roth, *Bewley in Berlin*, p. 57; Goldstone, '"Benevolent Helpfulness?", p. 132; M. O'Driscoll, 'Inter-war Irish–German Diplomacy: Continuity, Ambiguity and Appeasement in Irish Foreign Policy', in Kennedy and Skelly, *Irish Foreign Policy*, p. 83.

55 National Archives of Ireland, Dublin (hereafter NAI), Department of An Taoiseach (hereafter DT), 16 November 1938.

56 *Ibid.*

57 T. W. T. Dillon (1939) 'The Refugee Problem' *Studies*, 28(111) (1939), pp. 402–14.

58 *Ibid.*, pp. 409–10.

59 *Ibid.*, p. 412.
60 *Ibid.*, p. 407.
61 *Ibid.*, pp. 407–8.
62 Report from Charles Bewley to Joseph P. Walshe from Berlin, 21 January 1939, NAI DFA, 243/9.
63 For the broader context, see Cornwell who discusses at length how the Concordat between the Vatican and the Reich resulted in this (*Hitler's Pope*).
64 Dillon, 'Refugee Problem', p. 410.
65 Keogh, *Jews in Twentieth-Century Ireland*, p. 143.
66 NAI, Department of Foreign Affairs (hereafter DFA), 419/44 (Dublin: National Archives, 1944).
67 Dáil Éireann debates vol. 94 cols.1649–50, 1944.
68 NAI, DFA, 417/39/65/1, 1944.
69 See Keogh, *Jews in Twentieth-Century Ireland*.
70 Article 44 recognised the special position of the Holy Catholic Apostolic and Roman Church and the guardian of the faith professed by the majority of the citizens in Ireland but it also recognised the Church of Ireland, Jewish Congregations and other religious denominations.
71 NAI, DT, 69/8027, 24 September 1945.
72 NAI, DT, S11007, 23 September 1953.
73 Keogh, *Jews in Twentieth-Century Ireland*, p. 210.
74 *Ibid.*, p. 216.
75 NAI, DT, S11007, 23 February 1953.
76 Keogh, *Jews in Twentieth Century Ireland*, pp. 200–1.

5

Refugees and asylum seekers: UN Convention Relating to the Status of Refugees

This chapter examines how contemporary responses to refugees and asylum seekers in Ireland have been shaped by a legacy of exclusionary state practices and racism. As noted in the last chapter, this legacy included overt anti-Semitism within refugee and immigration practices from the late 1930s prior to Ireland's ratification in 1956 of the UN Convention Relating to the Status of Refugees (1951). The arrival of increasing numbers of asylum seekers in recent years was met by expressions of racism and intolerance within Irish political and public discourse. These have been characterised by racialisation of asylum seekers as a threat to Irish society and, in turn, the mobilisation of racist fears within policy debates. This chapter locates responses to asylum seekers from the late 1990s within a history of past responses to refugees. It begins with an examination of responses to Hungarian refugees admitted soon after Ireland ratified the UN Convention (1951). These were the first of a number of groups of programme refugees (groups granted refugee status on arrival) admitted between the 1950s and the 1990s. It is argued that responses to the Hungarians were characterised by an exclusionary pre-Convention ethos with much in common with the problematic responses to Jewish refugees noted in the previous chapter. The chapter compares responses to asylum seekers from the late 1990s, when for the first time these began to arrive in Ireland in substantial numbers, to responses to Hungarian, Chilean, Vietnamese and Bosnian programme refugees during the previous four decades. The chapter presents an overview of responses to asylum seekers by the Irish state during the first decade of the twenty-first century. It examines how restrictive responses to asylum seekers, aimed at reducing the numbers of persons who exercised their rights under the United Nations Charter on the Rights of Refugees, might be understood as part of a repertoire of exclusionary state responses to immigration. Specifically, it considers the racialisation of asylum seekers as an impetus for the 2004 Referendum on Citizenship which removed the existing constitutional birthright to citizenship to the Irish-born children of asylum seekers and other migrants.

The Hungarian refugees (1956–58)

Ratification of the UN Convention on Status of Refugees (1951)

The ratification of the UN Convention (1951) by the Irish state in 1956 was accompanied by a pronounced enthusiasm to admit refugees from Hungary. On 13 November 1956, just over two weeks before the UN Convention was ratified, the government agreed to grant asylum to 250 refugees from Hungary. Soon after, this number was increased to 1,000. The minister of defence, who was in charge of refugee reception, stated at the time that 'the number could be further increased if necessary to the maximum number possible given the resources of the country'.[1] Ward explains this enthusiasm in terms of foreign policy goals of representing Ireland as a paid-up member of the international community.[2] Popular support for the admittance of refugees also owed much to Catholic solidarity. Catholic sermons at the time, often reprinted in local newspapers, referred to the plight of anti-Communist Catholic martyrs in Hungary. For example, in County Clare, where they were accommodated, the Catholic Bishop gave such a sermon that was reported on the front page of the local newspaper three days before the decision to admit refugees. This spoke of the 'ancient Catholic nation of Hungary', of 'the heroic men and women in Budapest with no weapons save faith and courage'. They were described as 'brave soldiers of the Church now prostrate in a Gethsemane of anguish and suffering'.[3] A groundswell of public support of admitting Hungarian refugees was evident in the success of a church gate collection by the Irish Red Cross, which raised £170,000 for their care.[4] The money was used to pay the Department of Defence for the accommodation of the refugees in a former army camp in County Clare and to pay allowances to individual refugees who were not allowed social welfare payments by the state.[5]

Another article gave a fanciful account of the arrival of the refugees at the army camp at Knockalisheen in County Clare from Shannon Airport.[6] It began with a description of tired but cheerful refugees arriving at 'the old camp in the valley'. The article then imagined the gratitude of the refugees to the Irish people:

> Then they looked at the camp – this was to be their home. Then they followed the Red Cross members into warmly lit rooms. It was good to have a home, a home where you could live in peace, in freedom. It was good to have kindly people about you, saying soft things in a language you did not understand. It was wonderful to feel that here you could talk freely, you could laugh or sing if the mood caught hold of you, you could sit in the quietness and smoke.

> Out of wonder came admiration – and gratitude. They would pray for these boys and girls, men and women, bishops and priests and ministers, who were making it possible for them to live again. When you're thrown on the roads of the world such kindness goes very deep into your heart.

The article ended with an imaginary account of one refugee's experiences following the Hungarian uprising of the oppression of Catholicism which reflected the tenor of a number of sermons which had been printed in the same newspaper during the preceding months:

> He had gone into a Church once, to pray, but there were army officers in the building and it was a Church no longer … There was a photograph in his mind – it hung over a poor mantel, the first Communion picture of one who had received a Confirmation of fire. His mind did not grapple with problems any more. He was thankful for the great kindness and he was silent.

The Hungarians were represented as grateful and deserving and there is evidence that they were welcomed by Irish society and the local communities in the area to which they were sent.

A brief welcome

This positive initial response soon unravelled at an institutional level. The response that emerged was shaped by pre-Convention expectations that refugees should not be a burden to the state, yet at the same time should be subject to strict state control. As previously, responsibility for the care of the refugees was devolved to the voluntary sector. As previously, there was an expectation that the actual selection of refugees could be controlled. A selection policy was agreed and was entrusted to officials from the Department of External Affairs based in Austria. This aimed to restrict the perceived detrimental impact of the refugees by excluding those deemed to be incompatible with Irish society. As put in a Department of Defence memorandum on 10 November 1956:

> By selecting suitable families it is hoped (a) to maintain the basic Christian ideals of family life in a way ensure to that the best possible care and attention will be given to the moral, spiritual, educational and physical welfare of the family as a unit and (b) that the problems of subsequent re-settlement and employment would be reduced if they can be limited to the bread-winner in each family.[7]

The policy was rigorously implemented. For example, one official telegraphed his superiors in Dublin requesting permission to accept extended families; citing the example of a widower, his five children and a female cousin as typical of the Hungarian family group seeking asylum. The request was turned down. At face value, the government's policy of seeking families was less about moral or religious suitability than about restricting the entry of refugees into the Irish job market. That said, it was also bound up with a specific construction of family – one where only men engaged in paid employment – that was reflected in the Irish Constitution and a definition of family that drew directly from Catholic social teaching.[8] This policy was restated when Irish officials in Vienna sought some flexibility in its interpretation in a number of cases.[9] For example, one official telegraphed his superiors in Dublin requesting authorisation to accept extended families; citing the example of a widower, his five children and a female cousin as typical of the Hungarian family groups seeking asylum. The request was turned down. Expectations of religious affinity, within a popular discourse of Catholic solidarity, were accompanied by expectations that the Hungarians would fit in without placing demands upon Irish institutions. Conversely, it was expected that those who did not fit in should not be allowed into the country. When such demands emerged the refugee issue became perceived as an insoluble crisis. This response reflected an institutional monoculturalism which identified difference as a threat.

Control, containment and conflict

The experience of the Hungarians between 1956 and 1958 highlights the sorts of difficulties which can result from a regime ill-equipped conceptually or physically to address the needs of present-day asylum seekers. From the outset it was envisaged that the care of the refugees could be devolved to the voluntary sector. Their accommodation in an army barracks at Knockalisheen County Clare was funded entirely by the Red Cross. The refugees received meals and small cash allowance out of voluntary funds. Although Article 17 of the UN Convention (1951), which Ireland had just ratified, conferred upon the refugees a right to work, considerable efforts were made to prevent the Hungarians seeking employment. In effect, there was a policy of containment from the outset. Refugees were confined to the camp by the use of quarantine periods. When these elapsed, efforts were made to use the Gardaí to illegally restrict their movements.[10] In essence the refugees were locked up pending various decisions on policy being worked out by government officials. They were less than two months in Ireland before an emphasis on control and containment gave way to a resolve to remove them altogether. Commitments to accept more Hungarian refugees were abandoned.

Restrictions on the movement of refugees combined with authoritarian management practices to produce conflicts that culminated in a hunger strike on 29 April 1957 by most of the adults in the camp. Responses to the demands of the refugees were characterised by defensiveness and sensitivity to criticism within a discourse that suggested that the only possible alternatives to paternalistic and authoritarian forms of control providing for the refugees were those of repression and exclusion.

The refugees were treated, almost from the outset, by the state and by the voluntary agencies responsible for their reception and accommodation as disruptive and subversive. Initial difficulties in responding to the needs of the first groups which arrived led to a restriction in the number being accepted, within a month of the first arrivals, to the amount admitted already by that date (517 people). A commitment, in principle, to taking 1,000 refugees was abandoned and Irish officials in Vienna were instructed to enter into no commitments in respect of an additional 300 refugees who had already been selected. It was also decided to investigate the possibility, in suitable cases, of arranging employment for the refugees in Britain. The refugees were less than two months in Ireland before it was resolved to remove them altogether. As put in a Department of Defence memorandum in January 1957; 'The only solution to our problems is emigration for the main bulk of the refugees. Accordingly, my Minister is anxious that every effort be made to have the refugees accepted into Canada, or some such country of immigration.'[11]

Conflicts quickly emerged between the authorities and the refugees at the Knockalisheen army camp. From the outset the refugees were vocal in seeking a role in the administration of the camp. They elected a camp committee that found itself in conflict with the Red Cross. The Red Cross sought to suppress the committee. The Red Cross attempted to control the camp by contesting the legitimacy of the camp committee elected by the refugees. On 16 January 1957, officials posted a bulletin giving notice that 'the existing camp council is hereby dissolved' and the following day submitted a report to the government interdepartmental committee on refugees with details of twelve 'agitators' who they demanded be removed from the camp. This was not agreed due to a concern about 'undesirable press publicity'.[12] The Red Cross then sought to convince the government to remove Lazlo Pesthy, the elected leader of the refugees. A letter to the Department of an Taoiseach on 13 January from the secretary general of the Irish Red Cross accused Mr Pesthy of being single-handedly responsible for the conflicts at the camp and of intimidating the other refugees. It also argued that he should be removed from the camp for reasons of personal immorality:

Through the machinations of this man discipline at the Camp is at a standstill. He has intimidated the remainder of the refugees, has threatened the camp staff and recently brought into his hut in the Camp an undesirable woman for the night and refused to have her placed out of bounds.[13]

The accusations against Mr Pesthy were unfounded in a number of respects. A report from the local Garda Superintendent to the interdepartmental committee stated that any threats made by the refugees 'were not to be taken seriously', that Mr Pesthy had been re-elected as refugee leader by a massive majority in a secret ballot (he received 174 out of 193 votes cast) and that the 'lady of the night', as he put it, was in fact a woman from Limerick seeking refugee musicians to play in a band in the city.[14] She was turned away from the camp on a later visit but was eventually allowed in to collect musical instruments she had allowed the refugees to borrow. Although the accusations against the refugee leader were not taken seriously by government officials, he was still considered as a problem. It was agreed that Department of External Affairs officials in London should help him find a job in England 'as he had previously indicated some interest in moving there'.[15] It was noted that the 'problem' of the rest of the refugees would be resolved through 'onward migrations' to Canada, though this would not happen until April 1957.[16] The Hungarians made complaints about various restrictions on their movements – including (illegal) restrictions on their movements outside the camp – as well as conditions within the camp. As put in a statement issued in January 1957:

However great the material generosity of the Irish people may be, a community of 500 people living in partial confinement without information as to their future, can be overcome by a sense of frustration, which grows as this time of uncertainty goes on. Under such conditions, nervous tensions arise; smaller frustrations seem larger, major frustrations unbearable.[17]

They complained that the huts in the camp were cold, damp and unhealthy and that, as a result many women and children had become ill'.[18] These complaints, although denied by officials at the time, were substantiated in government and Red Cross reports.[19] A disparaging Department of Defence report on conditions at Knockalisheen likened conditions to those in an internment camp.[20] In the ensuing months the frustrations of the refugees deepened as no changes were made to the administration of the camp and relations with the camp administrators remained poor. This culminated in a hunger strike on 29 April 1957 by most of the adults in the camp. The hunger strikers refused to receive food from the authorities for their children who were fed from a stockpile of food put aside for this purpose.[21]

The hunger strike was abandoned following a long-sought visit from senior officials from the departments of External Affairs and of Justice to the camp. Subsequently it was agreed that the camp should be closed and that the refugees be moved, if necessary, to a more suitable facility. Most of the refugees willingly relocated to Canada in 1957 when the authorities there agreed to accept them. They argued that officials in Austria had encouraged their acceptance of relocation to Ireland on the basis that they would be later relocated to the United States.[22] By the beginning of 1959 some 438 of a total of 538 had left the country.[23] The last of the refugees was moved from the camp in January 1959, though not without difficulties. One woman, Mrs Palocz, and her daughter had been moved out of the camp in December 1958 to a hostel in Dublin. However, they returned to the camp in protest about the unsuitability of this accommodation. They barricaded themselves into their hut in Knockalisheen without food, light or fuel. Their protest ended with the offer of accommodation in Limerick.[24]

In part, the conflicts between Irish officials at the camp and the refugees can be explained by the lack of deference of the Hungarians. Government reports and correspondence of the era depict them as 'vociferous' in demanding their rights, in seeking to participate in decision-making about their fate and in the administration of the camp. Their willingness to mobilise and seek participation was countered by a very different indigenous Irish culture where those in authority expected deference, where notions of rights and of entitlements to welfare goods and services were undeveloped. Many of the refugees had previous experiences of contesting state oppression. For example, Laszlo Pesty the 35-year-old engineer, who was dismissed as camp leader of the refugees by the officials running the camp had been a political prisoner in Siberia for twenty-nine months and was subsequently imprisoned in Hungary. He was reported to have taken part in the original demonstrations against the Hungarian Communist regime with students of the Polytechnic University in Budapest and in the fighting that followed.[25] He escaped, leaving his wife and 3-and-a-half-year-old son behind. This biography may or may not have been typical of the Hungarian refugees who came to Ireland. However, it is one which was closer to the media depictions of the refugees as 'heroic men and women in Budapest with no weapons save faith and courage' than the criteria for pliant bread-winners, dependent women and children set out in the instructions of the Irish government to officials in Austria. As noted in an article in the *Irish Times*:

It is one thing to admit some hundreds of refugees within our shores. It is quite another to get down to the hard thinking on the question of their future, here or elsewhere ... The problem, however, cannot be regarded as solved until we have dealt with it in a way that will leave nobody – ourselves or others – with cause to regret our initial impulse of generosity.[26]

The regrets followed all too quickly. The response of the state was to endeavour to remove the refugees rather than address the shortcomings indicated by their complaints. Within one month of the arrival of the first refugees it was decided that they should be removed.

Programme refugees 1956–99

After 1956 many discriminatory or exclusionary practices remained unchanged, or changed gradually and informally, particularly with respect to asylum seekers. The total number of programme refugees admitted in the forty years following Ireland's ratification of the UN Convention in 1956 was fewer than 1,500. This was actually fewer than the number of refugees (more than 2,000) that had been accepted into the country in the two decades prior to 1956.

Prior to 1956, refugees had to satisfy officials that they were in a position to support themselves and their dependants and they would not enter the Irish labour market at a future date. Decisions to admit refugees were often dependent upon commitments by the voluntary sector that any refugees admitted would not become a burden on the state. To a considerable extent, this was to be expected within a 'mixed economy of welfare' within which the voluntary sector had a large role. This is a term that can be used to describe the balance of welfare provision between the public, private, informal and voluntary sectors. In Ireland it was characterised by resistance to state control of some areas of social policy such as health and education as a result of the influence of Catholic social teaching. However, in other areas, such as income maintenance and public housing, there was no resistance to state provision.[27] The role of the state in Ireland as a provider and regulator of welfare developed in a piecemeal manner after 1922 with a tendency to introduce schemes as an ad hoc response to social problems rather than through coherent and systematic planning.[28]

In this context, coordination of the reception and resettlement of refugees from the 1930s until the 1990s was largely left to interested parties in the voluntary sector. After 1956 the devolution of responsibility for refugees to the voluntary sector persisted while official recognition of the 'rights' of refugees expanded in a piecemeal fashion. Refugees, accepted under the UN Convention on the Status of Refugees (1951), became legally entitled

Table 5.1 'Rights' of programme refugees

Year, country of origin; number	Right to work	State-funded reception	Access to social welfare and social housing	Extent of resettlement programme
1956 Hungary (517 persons)	Limited. E.g.; 'Right to work' subject to consultation with trades unions in individual cases.	No. Army paid to accommodate refugees by voluntary sector. Reception organised Red Cross entirely funded by church gate collection (£170,000).	No. Allowances paid to refugees by Red Cross in lieu of benefits. Rents of those subsequently housed in Dublin paid by Red Cross.	None. Refugees accommodated in an army camp for more than a year. Language training not provided.
1973 Chile (120 persons)	Yes	No	Right to social welfare and public housing. No specific state refugee housing policy.	Minimal. Resettlement principally organised by a voluntary group, the Committee for Chilean refugees in Ireland, with the help of religious groups. No language class provision for adults until 1977, no special provision for children. Some access to state-run employment training (metalwork).
From 1979 Vietnam (582 persons by 1998)	Yes	Reception organised by Red Cross largely funded by church gate collection (£120,000). State contributed £18,296.	Right to social welfare and public housing. Refugees mainly accommodated by local authorities. No specific state refugee housing policy.	Initially accommodated at a reception centre in Dublin then dispersed around the country. No educational support for children after refugees were dispersed. No language support after initial reception period. Catholic Church coordinated access to housing etc. outside Dublin.
1985 Iran (25 persons)	Yes	No	Right to social welfare and public housing. No specific state refugee housing policy.	None. Flights to Ireland paid for by Dept of Foreign Affairs. Refugees assisted by Irish Baha'i community.

Year, country of origin; number	Right to work	State-funded reception	Access to social welfare and social housing	Extent of resettlement programme
From 1991 Bosnia (1,089 persons by 1999)	Yes	Yes	Right to social welfare and public housing. Refugees mainly housed in private rented sector. No specific state refugee housing policy.	Comprehensive programme coordinated by state (the Refugee Agency).

to welfare provision such as benefits, public housing, education and state training. Yet their 'entitlements' were extended in a piecemeal fashion (Table 5.1).

Refugees obtained rights to work and welfare but support from the state in accessing employment through education and training was minimal. In other areas such as housing and English-language education they remained largely dependent upon voluntary provision. For example, the state played a minimal role in the reception of Chilean programme refugees admitted in 1973 and 1974. Their resettlement was principally organised by a voluntary group formed for the purpose, the Committee for Chilean Refugees in Ireland, with the help of religious groups who lobbied state agencies to address the needs of the refugees. The Committee provided direct support to the refugees for about two years. The refugees were settled in local authority accommodation in Galway, Shannon and Waterford and some were placed on metalwork training schemes.[29] However, even after a number of years many refugees had found it difficult to secure employment. No provision was made to provide English-language classes for adult refugees until 1977 and then for only two hours per week.[30]

In 1979, the Irish government agreed to accept 212 Vietnamese refugees. As previously, responses to their needs emerged through the voluntary sector. The Irish Red Cross oversaw their reception. Their accommodation and settlement was largely funded by church charities. A Vietnamese Refugee Resettlement Committee was established by the government but, as previously, the state effectively devolved responsibility for the refugees to civil society. Following an initial period of accommodation in reception centres in Dublin, during which they received English classes, the refugees were dispersed around the country. Although only two of the initial 212 Vietnamese refugees had any knowledge of English they had to depend on untrained volunteers for English-language training following an initial reception period. In 1982 the Department of Education introduced a pilot scheme to teach English as a second language (ESL) in one area. Some of the refugees had to wait until 1988 to gain access to the scheme.[31]

The dispersal policy was not accompanied by any measures to ensure the successful resettlement of the refugees. Once housed, the Vietnamese children were placed in mainstream classes, in up to ninety-six schools by 1987, with no special support for them or their teachers. The Department of Education did not monitor Vietnamese children in schools and by 1989 had no idea of which schools they were at, or how they were doing.[32] The Vietnamese children suffered disproportionate education failure. The majority was between 13 and 16 years of age on leaving primary education. Many subsequently dropped out of school. The failure of the dispersal policy was marked by a pattern of secondary migration whereby most of the Vietnamese moved to the Dublin area so as to be able to provide each other with mutual support.

It was not until the late 1980s that the state began to move towards responsible participation in international regimes pertaining to both refugees and asylum seekers.[33] The pressure for change to a considerable extent came from the European Union (EU); notably as a result of the Schengen Agreement which set out a common EU policy on migrants and the Dublin Convention which established arrangements for determining responsibility for asylum seekers who had migrated within the EU. In 1991 a Refugee Agency was established and funded by the government to coordinate the admission, reception and resettlement of Convention refugees. The Bosnians who arrived in 1992 were the first group of refugees to benefit from a reception and resettlement programme organised and funded by the state. However, this resettlement programme met with limited success in some areas. For example, the Bosnians have continued to experience, along with the Vietnamese, disproportionately high rates of unemployment.[34]

At the same time, experience in responding to these groups provided the basis for developing good practices. The Refugee Agency drew upon past experiences of responding to the Bosnian programme refugees in their response to Kosovar refugees. The Kosovars were not granted the status of programme refugees but they were granted a leave to remain status, which was accompanied by a right to work and entitlements to training and support. The Refugee Agency executed an effective regional reception programme that contrasted with the dispersal of the Vietnamese. Agency officials visited local communities in advance to pave the way for the refugees. They coordinated the efforts of local groups, schools health boards to plan for the integration of the Kosovars into local communities from the outset. However, this emphasis upon good practice was sidelined within the histrionic response to the arrival of increased numbers of asylum seekers from the late 1990s.

From crisis to crisis

From 1994 the numbers of asylum seekers arriving independently began to rise rapidly from what had been a very small number each year. The growing population of asylum seekers in Ireland was soon portrayed as a crisis by politicians and officials and within the media. Ireland was being 'swamped'. Yet, as noted in Chapter 1, by the end of the decade the total number of asylum seekers in Ireland was fewer than 10,000. Asylum seekers comprised only a small proportion of migrants. Depictions of the presence of these asylum seekers as a 'crisis' mirrored the earlier response to the Hungarians in a number of respects. This 'crisis' seemed to be an administrative one but it was also the product of long-standing exclusionary perspectives and practices that made it difficult for the Irish authorities to get their heads around the problem. As before, administrative frustrations hardened into a resolve to impose barriers on asylum seekers. The decision to delay implementation of the Refugee Act (1996), which provided statutory protections for asylum seekers, mirrored the response to Hungarian refugees which the Irish government had agreed to admit just over two weeks prior to ratifying the UN Convention in 1956. In both cases decisions, in principle, to extend the rights of refugees and the responsibilities of the state unravelled when legislative reforms were found to be 'unworkable' in the absence of adequate infrastructure. Enthusiasm for progressive measures was quickly replaced by exclusionary measures that reflected the ethos of pre-Convention legislation.

The Refugee Act (1996) was a progressive piece of legislation that drew, to a considerable extent, on international good practice. It broadened the legal definition of a refugee to include persecution on grounds of gender and sexual orientation but did not set out a right to legal aid or – in keeping with past 'aliens' legislation – grant a right to work to asylum seekers. The Dáil passed it with all-party support, yet it remained unimplemented by the end of the decade. The Act was drafted at a time when Ireland received few and infrequent applications for asylum. However, it was enacted at a time when the number of asylum seekers began to noticeably rise. The number of applications in 1996 (1,179) was almost three times the number received the previous year. The following year the number of applications (3,883) was more than three times the number received in

1996. The rapid rise in the number of asylum seekers was used to justify non-implementation of much of the Act. As reported by the Department of Justice, Equality and Law Reform (DJELR) to the Joint Committee on Family, Community and Social Affairs (22 September 1998):

> An order has been made commencing sections 1, 2, 5, 22 and 25 of the Act but due to the large numbers of applications being made and the backlog thus generated the Minister came to the view that the procedures of the Refugee Act are unworkable and that the remaining sections of the Act should not be implemented at present.

Those portions of the Act that were implemented principally ensured the continuation of existing legislation and agreements namely: (1) the Dublin Convention (an agreement between EU states that refugees be required to seek asylum in the first state they enter and which allowed for the deportation of asylum seekers to that state from other EU states); (2) the principle of non-refoulment (that refugees admitted under the UN Convention (1951) not be sent back to their country of origin); and (3) existing legislation on extraditions. Interim procedures for processing asylum claims were based on administrative guidelines drawn up by the DJELR – as set out in a letter to the UNHCR – rather than having a statutory basis. Under these interim procedures, officials considered cases in camera.

Amendments to the Aliens Act (1935) were introduced on 29 June 1997 (the last day in office of the outgoing government). These increased the powers of immigration officers to determine whether 'aliens' should be allowed to enter the country. These emerged in a climate of political panic about the increase in numbers seeking asylum and as such constituted an effort to exclude those entitled to seek asylum from entering the country. Cullen describes their implementation in a distinctly racist manner:

> The word is that Gardai at immigration are on the lookout for blacks and gypsies, and checks on other passengers are either perfunctory or non-existent. Accent is a big determinant in whether you make it past the plain-clothes police or not.[35]

Although the amendment to the Aliens Act (1935) expressly did not apply to persons entering the state from Northern Ireland or Great Britain, the climate within which the measures were implemented fostered overt racism against black and ethnic minorities travelling legitimately from the UK. Six hundred foreign nationals were refused entry into the country from the UK in the first two months. About twenty of these had applied for asylum but were not permitted to enter the country by officials.[36] Black citizens of the UK were deported from time to time over subsequent years. Foreign nationals on legitimate trips to Ireland were arrested from time to time by immigration officials. For example, in November 2000 six Pakistani businessmen travelling on valid passports (stamped by the Irish consulate in Karachi) were imprisoned for a weekend in Mountjoy jail.[37]

A preoccupation with discouraging asylum seekers from coming to Ireland persisted within subsequent legislation introduced in response to the perceived crisis. A new Deportations Bill was quickly introduced to allow deportations to resume after deportations under the Aliens Act were found to be unconstitutional in 1999. The Illegal Immigrants (Trafficking) Bill (1999) made it harder to apply for asylum. The Bill proposed sanctions against those who aided asylum seekers to enter the state without recognising that many refugees were forced to use illegal means in order to flee persecution. It defined a 'trafficker' as a person who 'organises or knowingly facilitates the entry into the State of a person who he or she knows or has reasonable cause to believe to be an illegal immigrant'. An 'illegal immigrant' in turn was defined as a 'non-national who enters or who seeks to enter the State unlawfully'. As such, the Bill proposed the criminalisation of asylum seekers without proper papers and those who assisted them for humanitarian motives as well as financial gain. In essence, it placed responsibly for deciding who should be allowed to enter the state on the airlines and shipping companies making it harder for asylum seekers to seek protection under the UN Convention (1951).

The imagery of crisis was, to an extent, fostered by officials and political leaders with responsibility for asylum seekers. Asylum seekers were depicted as welfare scroungers, in competition with indigenous groups for welfare resources. This state discourse was widely echoed in the media with the consequence that an administrative 'crisis' was represented as a crisis for Irish society. This set up an equation whereby criticisms of infrastructural failure were countered with statements by politicians and officials that portrayed asylum seekers as deviant and dangerous. In this way racism in Irish society was mobilised for political and administrative purposes.

This was in marked contrast with state responses to programme refugees from 1956 onwards. For example, initial media accounts of the Hungarian refugees were welcoming. The shrill headlines which often accompanied accounts of asylum seekers in the late 1990s had been absent in media accounts of the Hungarians. The media discourse that greeted asylum seekers from the late 1990s could, in part, be explained by a requirement to conduct policy arguments about asylum seekers in the public domain. The Hungarians had been sequestered away from Irish society in Knockalisheen. Efforts to contain them were, by and large, successful. The debate that led to their exclusion occurred in camera. Asylum seekers on the other hand were a visible presence within Irish society. They could be seen, during 1999, on television queuing overnight outside the 'one stop shop' on Mount Street established to process their claims. An ensuing political furore, sparked by criticisms by Progressive Democrat Junior Minister Liz O' Donnell that the government's asylum policy was a 'shambles', prompted new restrictions on asylum seekers. As in the case of the Hungarians, problems in responding to asylum seekers provided an impetus for various exclusionary and emergency measures. Unlike then, measures were justified within a public discourse which drew upon and was shaped by racism against asylum seekers. For instance, a new dispersal policy was heralded by the temporary refusal of the Eastern Health Board to take responsibility for new arrivals and a statement by the chairman of the health board that called for 'bogus asylum seekers to be thrown out of the State'. In making a public case for punitive welfare policies, politicians and officials played to anti-asylum seeker feeling and racism. In this context, it proved difficult to acknowledge the lessons of past experiences in responding to refugees.

The total number of 7,724 applications received in 1999 was almost twice the total of 3,883 received in 1998. In 1999 the DJELR estimated that between 12,000 and 15,000 further applications for asylum would be received during 2000. The actual number of applications for 2000 was 10,938. The total number for 2001 was 10,325. In 2002 some 11,634 new applications for asylum were received. This fell to 7,483 for 2003, to 4,265 for 2004, to 4,323, for 2005, to 4,323 for 2006, to 3,985 for 2007, 3,866 for 2008 to 2,689 for 2010.[38] Many asylum seekers had to wait years to have their applications addressed and an exceedingly high percentage had their applications refused; this resulted in appeals that could drag out determination periods for years.

Twenty per cent of applications received in 1996 were approved. By 1999, of a total of 18,198 applications received between 1994 and 1999 some 920, or just over 5 per cent, were granted refugee status and 6346 or just under 35 per cent were refused. That left a backlog of over 60 per cent of all applications which continued to increase throughout 2000. By August 2000 there were 12,975 cases 'on hand'. By November 2000 this had increased to 13,000. In subsequent years the backlog of unprocessed applications began to decline – 11,124 by December 2001; 9,708 by February 2002; 8,081 by June 2002; 7,883 by August 2003; 4,738 by April 2004; and 3,340 by February 2005. By June 2005 the backlog stood at 2,425 cases but 1,101 of these were appeals against refusals of initial decisions. Exceedingly high turn-down rates for asylum applications inevitably produced appeals and of these a high percentage were successful. Of 1,046 appeal cases heard in January and February 2002 192 (18 per cent) were upheld. In May and June 2002 some 231 (28 per cent) of a total of 987 appeal cases were granted; 187 (22 per cent) of 846 appeals processed in January and February 2003 were granted. Over time, the percentage of appeals granted lessened. Of 918 appeals heard in March and April 2004, some 128 (just under 14 per cent) were granted. Between July and August 2004 some 93 (under 10 per cent) out of 1,061 appeals were granted.[39]

Of the 3,910 first-stage applications for asylum considered in 2009 just 97 (2.4 per cent) were granted. By 2010 Irish acceptance of asylum claims was the lowest in the EU at 1.3 per cent. This contrasted with 24 per cent for the UK, 46 per cent for the Netherlands and 70 per cent positive decisions on applications for asylum in Malta.[40]

Asylum seeker segregation

Welfare discriminations

Successive Irish governments have advocated the exclusion of asylum seekers from participation in Irish society. The Fine Gael Minister of Justice, Equality and Law Reform, Nora Owen TD who ushered in the Refugee Act (1996), opposed including a right to work for asylum seekers in the Act, lest it enable them to become established in Irish society before the state had determined whether not they would be allowed to stay. As she put it:

> It must be borne in mind that asylum seekers are allowed to remain in the State pending determination of their applications... I do not consider it appropriate to allow people, with temporary permission to remain in the State, to work and put down roots.[41]

The case for punitive welfare policies aimed at discouraging asylum seekers from coming to Ireland was set out by the next, Fianna Fáil, Minister of Justice, Equality and Law Reform, John O'Donoghue TD, in a speech to the Irish Business and Employers Confederation on 30 September 1999. This speech described asylum seekers as illegal immigrants and as exploiters of the Irish welfare system. Later that year the minister announced that from April 2000 asylum seekers arriving in Ireland would no longer be entitled to supplementary assistance and rent allowances. Existing welfare entitlements were replaced by a system of 'direct provision' that limited support for asylum seekers to basic accommodation, meals and cash allowances of £15 weekly for adults and £7.50 for children. These rates were considerably below benefit levels for indigenous welfare recipients in emergency accommodation. They most closely resembled a welfare scheme for hospitalised welfare recipients. As put by a trade union representative of community welfare officers, the rates were just about enough to 'buy a bottle of Lucozade and a few biscuits'.[42] The modelling of a welfare regime for asylum seekers upon a benefit scheme for those confined to hospital suggested an ethos of excluding them from life within the communities within which they lived. Asylum seekers accommodated under direct provision were subject to a state-fostered exclusion from Irish society.

A study published in 2001 found that asylum seeker children living in direct provision experienced extreme material deprivation.[43] They lived in households below the 20 per cent poverty line. Extreme income poverty combined with an inadequate reception and accommodation programme. The study found that an overwhelming majority of respondents on direct provision (92 per cent) stated that they considered it necessary to buy extra food to supplement the food provided in the hostels for themselves and their children. However, most (69 per cent) stated that they were unable to afford to purchase extra food. The report argued that the welfare discrimi-nations experienced by asylum seeker children on 'direct provision' were unambiguously contrary to Ireland's obligations under the UN Conven-tion on the Rights of the Child (1989). They were also contrary to a range of existing commitments addressing child social exclusion as set out in the National Children's Strategy (2001), the Programme for Prosperity and Fairness (2000) and the National Anti-Poverty Strategy (1997).

The research also found that the deprivation experienced by asylum seekers in direct provision was, in part, a result of administrative inflex-ibilities within reception centres. A number of respondents reported the imposition of arbitrary restrictions by hostel staff that made their day-to-day lives more difficult. A picture emerged, in some cases, of needless repression and even intimidation of asylum seekers by hostel staff. This had arguably been fostered by the guidelines provided to private sector hostel managers by the DJELR.[44] These set out a procedure for disciplining hostel residents without any corresponding emphasis on a procedure for dealing with the grievances of asylum seekers. This allowed private sector hostel and hotel staff to define what might be deemed unacceptable behaviour. It encouraged the use of verbal warnings to asylum seekers who were deemed by managers and staff to misbehave. The language used to describe asylum seekers within the guidelines – 'perpetrator' and 'offending party' – contributed to an expectation that asylum seekers had no rights to be heard. Nowhere was it mentioned that asylum seekers had a right to redress in the case of mistreatment in hostels.[45] At the beginning of the twenty-first century asylum seekers in direct provision accommodation experienced many of the frustrations and difficulties of the Hungarians nearly half a century earlier.

State-fostered segregation

The dispersal of newly arrived asylum seekers outside of Dublin, where most of those who arrived in the late 1990s had settled, met with objections from community groups in a number of instances. Such objections resembled objections to the accommodation of Travellers in some respects. The principal difference however was that such objections were almost all unsuccessful due perhaps to the lack of power of local elected authorities to veto accommodation plans. In a number of cases, local campaigns to prevent the arrival of asylum seekers attracted media attention. Much of the media commentary focused upon anti-asylum seeker racism in such host communities, but it is worth noting that the one successful objection to the development of an asylum seeker hostel emerged from Dublin 4, an affluent area where the RTE radio and television stations are located. Expressions of hostility to asylum seekers in places such as Kildare   town, Clogheen, County Tipperary and Corifin, County Clare, combined with a more general frustration about the acquisition of local hostels upon which local tourism depended and expectations that asylum seekers could be cared for in the local community without the provision of infrastructure or specific support. These expressions of hostility included an arson attack on the hotel designated for asylum seekers in Clogheen. A discourse of anxiety about the arrival of asylum seekers included demands that they be screened for AIDS and statements that linked asylum seekers to the threat of crime. At the same time local people in a number of communities expressed concern that asylum seekers would be isolated and marginalised.[46]

The broader context within which a wave of protests by residents made headline news, for a few weeks in May 2000, was one where asylum seekers were depicted as criminal racketeers in the media and as welfare scroungers by the government. Expressions of hostility within such communities were, in essence, sanctioned by the state. The asylum seeker dispersal programme was represented as an emergency response to an infrastructural failure in Dublin. The political discourse was, to an extent, one that represented asylum seekers as a burden to be dispersed. The implicit message was that host communities outside of Dublin would have to deal with problems which others had found it impossible to cope with. However, an alternative to the dispersal programme that emerged was to be found in the coordinated reception policy for Kosovar refugees that had been quickly and successfully implemented some months previously by the Refugee Agency. Other models of good practice were proposed by non-governmental organisations (NGOs) before dispersal commenced.[47]

However, the constraints imposed upon asylum seeker policies by a determination to limit their rights and entitlements made such experiences difficult to acknowledge. The differences between both responses included less support for host communities as well for asylum seekers. The asylum seeker dispersal programme amounted to a form of social dumping within which the state took little responsibility for the needs of asylum seekers and host communities. By contrast, the response to the Kosovar refugees had included preparatory work to coordinate the response of host communities and the putting in place of an infrastructure of support.

The DJELR increasingly shaped social policy responses to asylum seekers. In 2000 the Department's Directorate of Asylum Seeker Services (DASS) took over much of the remit of the Refugee Agency (established initially under the aegis of the Department of Foreign Affairs). It also acquired many of the welfare roles of the Department of Social, Community, and Family Affairs and the health boards following the introduction of direct provision and asylum seeker dispersal. This centralisation was preceded by official and unofficial edicts that sought to circumscribe the access of asylum seekers to various welfare goods and services provided by other departments and agencies. In 1999 a Department of Education official was advised 'unofficially' by the DJELR that asylum seekers should be charged for access to adult education. As reported in the *Irish Times*:

> Asylum seekers 'are not supposed to work, and I have been told in writing that they should have no access to education'. The letter accompanied an 'information note' sent to school and college principals in the Dublin area, instructing them that asylum-seekers must pay more than £2000 a year to take Post Leaving Certificate courses.[48]

The DJELR continued to press other government departments and agencies to exclude asylum seekers from provision for which they deemed they should not be entitled both behind the scenes and on a day-to-day basis. The rationale for such efforts was outlined by a DJELR official in 1998 who stated when asked whether the state had any intention of providing language training and integration for asylum seekers:

> There is an argument that if you assist in training them that (1) you will be giving them hope that they will be staying (2) you are helping them to integrate into the country which will make it much more difficult to remove them at the end of the whole procedure.[49]

The argument that asylum seekers should be excluded from state support persisted even when the minister of justice made a 'one off' decision in 1999 which allowed more than 3,000 asylum seekers the right to work. In 2000, FAS (the Irish industrial training authority) established an Asylum Seekers Unit to facilitate the employment of asylum seekers with the right to work. However, FAS was not permitted to provide asylum seekers with employment training. The Asylum Seeker Unit piloted a scheme that matched asylum seekers job vacancies for which they were deemed to be qualified. Participants in these schemes could also avail themselves of a job club to aid them to obtain employment for a limited period. The scheme was advanced on the principle that most asylum seekers with the right to work were 'job ready'. This analysis did not take into account barriers to employment due to racism and non-recognition of qualifications and employment experience obtained in their countries of origin.[50] It was in contrast with assumptions that most indigenous FAS clients were not 'job ready' and would therefore require training and other forms of support.[51] Such differential analysis of the needs of asylum seekers and indigenous marginal groups, where such needs were in essence the same, was a product of the restrictions imposed upon asylum seekers.

The subordination of social policy to goals of exclusion was perhaps most exemplified by the exclusion of asylum seekers from the remit of policies aimed at promoting the inclusion of new black and minority ethnic communities into Irish society. The remit of Minister of Justice, Equality and Law Reform includes responsibility for anti-racism initiatives, the implementation of equality legislation and measures to promote the integration of black and ethnic minorities into Irish society. In December 1998 the minister established an Interdepartmental Working Group to formulate a strategy for implementing the government's policy 'of responding positively to the needs of persons granted refugee status or leave to remain'. In January 2000 the Minister endorsed the report of this Working Group *Integration: A Two Way Process*.[52] The report emphasised the need to promote the integration of refugees and immigrants into Irish society. It defined integration as the ability to participate to the extent that the person needs and wishes in all the major components of society, without having to relinquish his or her cultural identity.[53] It argued for the removal of barriers that affected the ability of refugees to access mainstream services and employment.[54] It also emphasised the need to address barriers to employment through education and training, language support, recognition of the skills and qualifications of refugees and by improving their access to the labour market.[55] The report argued that the integration of refugees was unlikely to be achieved unless those who need it were given access to employment training, education, language training, and other forms of support. However, within the exclusionary logic of asylum policy, the social exclusion faced by asylum seekers was not acknowledged. Policies aimed at promoting inclusiveness and at contesting racism faced by the new black and ethnic minority communities in Ireland coexisted with policies aimed at promoting the exclusion of asylum seekers from Irish society.

The persistence of segregation

The asylum seeker issue became most intensively politicised during the years when the numbers of asylum seekers arriving in Ireland were rising rapidly. Various measures, including 'direct provision' and legislation aimed at impeding applications for asylum were introduced in response to this politicisation. These apparently succeeded in so far as numbers of applications reduced significantly on an ongoing basis. In 2000, when direct provision was being proposed and in the years that followed NGOs, churches and some community groups campaigned against direct provision with little success. The system became routinised. From time to time new studies reconfirmed the detrimental effects of the 'direct provision' system of the lives of asylum seekers.

In effect, the system had bedded down; a state-fostered system of deliberately marginalising asylum seekers had become routinised, and the asylum problem was deemed to have been solved by the Irish political system. The focus of the Department of Justice, through its Reception and Integration Agency (RIA), was upon the more effective management of this system rather than upon change or reform. NGOs such as the Irish Refugee Council, for their part, continued to criticise 'direct provision' but also focused on improving the management of the system in the absence of any political opportunities to achieve this.

Direct provision fostered internal barriers in two ways. First, punitively low levels of benefit (held to the same low level, year after year from 2000 to 2011) served to materially isolate asylum seekers from wider Irish society. Second, the creation of a parallel 'direct provision' welfare system for asylum seekers (operated by the DJELR, an entity with hitherto no track record in the provision of welfare goods and services and one charged with advocating the deliberate exclusion of asylum seekers from Irish society) administratively isolated these from the wider social policy system. For example, in areas such as child protection, although asylum seeker children were covered by the same legislation as other children, those in the case of the state received different (lesser) standards of care and protection. Administrative distinctions between the treatment of asylum seekers in some areas (lesser entitlements to social protection) contributed to institutional barriers in other domains where their rights were the same as Irish citizens. The direct provision rates introduced in 2000 were considerably lower than the entitlements of citizens and became even more so over time.

In some domains asylum seekers retained the same rights and entitlements as Irish citizens; examples here include rights to health care, to primary and secondary education (up to 18 years of age) and the right to vote in local government elections. In other domains they clearly had lesser rights and entitlements; examples include the absence of a right to work and the lower rates of benefits they received under 'direct provision'. In yet other domains asylum seekers were normatively treated by the state *as if* they had lesser rights than Irish citizens when under Irish law this was not the case. A key example here has been the treatment of asylum seeker children in care (unaccompanied minors). The Refugee Act (1996) specifically extended the provisions of the Child Care Act (1991) to refugees and asylum seekers. Under the Child Care Act, the Health Service Executive is required to 'promote the welfare of children in its area who are not receiving adequate care and protection'. However what has emerged is a distinctly two-tiered system of child protection.[56] The International Organization on Migration (IOM) has concluded that unaccompanied minors in Ireland are not being afforded the same child protection rights as Irish children.[57]

A 2004 study funded by the Combat Poverty agency identified food poverty among asylum seekers in reception centres in Sligo, Leitrim and Donegal owing to the low level of cash transfers under 'direct provision' and inability to address cultural issues affecting diet.[58] Even though this corroborated the findings of earlier studies, it had little or no effect upon asylum policy. In 2004, new asylum seekers lost their entitlement to child benefits, a significant part of their family incomes, under the Social Welfare (Miscellaneous Provisions) Act (2004). This legislation imposed a two-year period of non-entitlement to benefits upon migrants from outside the EU. Levels of payment to asylum seekers in 'direct provision' remained unchanged year on year, whereas other categories of benefit recipients received year-on-year increases in the levels of payment to which they were entitled. The cold resolve to ensure that there was no increase year after year to the tiny sums of money that asylum seekers received, in a society that was then awash with money, suggests a deliberate goal of fostering segregation from life in Irish society.

Many asylum seekers came to live in reception centres that resembled Knockalisheen during the 1950s, Knockalisheen itself was reopened as an asylum reception centre. In such centres asylum seekers were kept in place not by barred windows or barbed wire but by an inability to afford bus fares, newspapers, cups of coffee, subscriptions for clubs and leisure activities. In January 2007 the 270 asylum seekers at Knockalisheen went on hunger strike for two days because they were unhappy with living conditions at the former barracks. One asylum seeker was quoted as saying: 'People outside the walls of Knockalisheen don't know how we live. It's a prison. Animals should live here not humans.' A letter signed by the hunger strikers complained about the food ('in meals we find foreign objects such as hair strands, broken plastic shards, rough particles of shells, especially in the bean porridge served') and hygiene conditions ('Only one toilet roll is given out once a week, which is not enough').[59] A 2007 study corroborated these conditions and other twenty-first century equivalents to the kinds of petty coercion which confronted refugees in Knockalisheen during the 1950s.[60] Residents were not allowed to invite visitors to their rooms unless these were escorted by a security officer. Residents were prohibited from keeping cooking utensils or crockery in their rooms, nor could they keep food in their rooms. Several participants in the 2007 study referred to a 'food raid' the previous year in which all the rooms in the Reception Centre were searched for food supplies. The study identified similar kinds of issues arising from overcrowding as identified in earlier such studies:

Generally residents live in partitioned rooms, sharing a toilet and shower cabinet with one other family, two families to a room with a partition between them. If full families are accommodated, that is families with a father present, then they occupy a full (double) room but the family must be a four-member family to qualify.[61]

Various other studies, complaints from residents and some further hunger strikes made similar complaints about routine coercion. In July 2010 asylum seekers at the Mosney Accommodation Centre began a hunger strike in response to a decision by the RIA to relocate 111 of them to another centre in Dublin. Those identified for removal included 74 'single men' and 34 'single women'. They were given just one week's notice of the move and their protest began a day before the the designated removal date. The rationale for the move was that, because of the declining numbers of people seeking asylum, centres were being reorganised to save money. The protests triggered by the proposed move clearly had much to do with ongoing frustrations experienced by asylum seekers in 'direct provision'. One hunger striker, a Kurdish man, who was to be moved to Dublin stated that he had lived in Mosney for seven years, while waiting for his case to be resolved. Although considered single, he had a girlfriend at Mosney who was pregnant. They were to be separated. He stated that he had been moved five times during his seven years as an asylum seeker in Ireland but 'never by choice'.[62]

In December 2010 the Irish Refugee Council issued a press release timed to coincide with the government's annual budget deliberations. It emphasised that the 'direct provision' rate of €19.10 per adult per week has never increased since its introduction a decade earlier. The statement also reiterated earlier criticisms of asylum seeker reception centres:

> We are all now aware of the terrible consequences of institutional care on Irish children we must not let this happen again to children living in Direct Provision. We hear daily of the agony some parents experience living in this system: not allowed to cook for their family, not allowed to study and not allowed to work takes an enormous toll on individual lives. Many wait years for a decision on their asylum application.
>
> An asylum seeker from Sudan recently spoke to the IRC about his sadness and despair: because there is not enough space in the tiny room he lives in with his baby and his wife, for his child to crawl. This father said he feared for his son's development.[63]

Such press releases and various research reports exposing the living conditions faced by asylum seekers and their children have had very little impact on asylum policy. Once the key decisions were made and a system of reception centres put in place, the plight of asylum seekers died as a political issue.

Asylum, racism and citizenship

Responses to asylum seekers by the Irish state, notably the introduction of 'direct provision' and legislation against trafficking can be located in a broader sequence of state responses to immigration aimed at asserting Irish sovereignty, control of external borders and the maintenance of internal borders impeding the full participation of some migrants within Irish society. Asylum policy along with citizenship and naturalisation policy both came under the remit of the DJELR. The first phase consisted of efforts to defend Irish sovereignty against asylum seekers, through the ramping up of border controls by means of carrier liability legislation and the introduction of direct provision to deter applications for asylum (represented by the then Minister of Justice as welfare tourism).

For the first few years of the twenty-first century Irish immigration debates continued to be preoccupied by asylum seekers. A raft of legislation did much to criminalise and make dangerous the act of seeking asylum. Michael McDowell, as Minister for Justice, Equality and Law Reform, sought to undermine and then remove the constitutional right of Irish-born children of immigrants to citizenship, interpreted by the High Court in 1987 as a right to remain in the state with their families.[64] The ruling allowed for the regularisation of a significant number of asylum seekers and other immigrants with Irish-born children.[65] A 'policy decision' was made to begin to refuse leave to remain to asylum seeker families in the knowledge that this would trigger a further test case in the Supreme Court.[66] In April 2002 the 1987 ruling was overturned in the High Court (*Lobe* v. *Minister of Justice*). On 23 January 2003 the Supreme Court upheld this ruling. In essence the Supreme Court ruled that the Irish citizen child of non-citizens could be deported with its parents unless the non-citizen parent agreed to be deported without their child.[67] After *Lobe* v. *Minister of Justice* (2003) Irish-born children entitled to citizenship and their families could be deported. At the time some 17,500 applications for residence from parents with Irish citizen children were pending. Most were from Africans and former asylum seekers.[68] Deportations made possible by the 2003 ruling proved controversial; media accounts emphasised the plight of 'Irish children' and their families. Some expressions of Irish solidarity with Africans achieved a high profile, particularly in the case of Elukanlo Olakunle a 20-year-old student living in Palmerstown, who was deported to Nigeria in his school uniform.[69] A campaign by fellow students secured his return. The 2003 *Lobe* ruling was effectively superseded by the June 2004 Referendum on Citizenship that removed the existing birthright to citizenship from the Irish-born children of non-citizens. The Referendum outcome delegitimised such solidarity; those deported were no longer portrayed as Irish.

The case for the Citizenship Referendum made by Michael McDowell, the then Minister of Justice, Equality and Law Reform centred on claims about the exploitation of Irish maternity health services by asylum seeker mothers seeking Irish citizenship for their children. In essence, the minister claimed that a crisis in maternity hospitals had been precipitated by the exploitation by 'non-national' mothers of 'loopholes' in the Constitution that allowed them to claim citizenship for their Irish-born children. Minister McDowell argued that in the thirteen months or so since the Supreme Court ruling that there has been 'no diminution in the numbers of non-nationals arriving heavily pregnant'.[70] As he put it when the Referendum was first mooted in March 2004:

> Our maternity services come under pressure because they have to deal at short notice with women who may have communications difficulties, about whom no previous history of the pregnancy or the mother's health

is known, and who in about half the cases of first arrival (according to the Master of the Rotunda, Dr Michael Geary, as interviewed on RTE during the week) are already at or near labour.[71]

The essence of what the media referred to as the 'baby-tourism' argument was that immigrants stereotyped as asylum seekers were exploiting the Irish health system to gain access to Irish citizenship.[72] The Masters of the Rotunda and the Coombe, two maternity hospitals in Dublin, sought to distance themselves from claims repeated on a number of occasions by McDowell 'that they had pleaded with him to deal with the problem' arguing that a lack of funding for maternity services should not be used to introduce a referendum.[73] Claims by the minister that 'non-nationals' were exploiting maternity services emerged in a context where health service problems had already become highly politicised. As put by a prominent Irish political commentator: 'It is clear that the deliberate unsubstantiated stereotyping of immigrant mothers as exploiting the health services was stage managed to build political support for the idea of the referendum'.[74]

Conclusion

The ratification of the Convention (1951) resulted in only a partial break with the past. No legal or administrative infrastructure to fulfil Ireland's obligations under the Convention was put in place until the 1990s. Institutional responses to refugees and asylum seekers (a distinction created by the UN Convention) continued to be framed by pre-Convention legislation, notably the Aliens Act (1935). These responses continued to be shaped by pre-Convention expectations that refugees should not be a burden upon the state. Such expectations persisted even as rights and entitlements to refugees were extended over time on a piecemeal basis. Slow shifts in state practices relating to refugees occurred over several decades within a framework designed to exclude certain categories of non-nationals.

However, at the end of the twentieth century the marginalisation of asylum seekers resembled the treatment of refugees prior to 1956 to a considerable extent. Similarities were to be noted not just in terms of welfare restrictions and exclusions from employment but in how asylum seekers, as a vulnerable population, became the focus of racism which was legitimised by the state. Ireland might be described as a reluctant host to asylum seekers and refugees. The experiences of the Hungarians can hardly be explained by racism in the same way as experiences of Jewish refugees in the preceding two decades. Instead, they encountered institutional barriers that culminated in a determination to remove them from the country. State and voluntary sector responses to the Hungarians were characterised by a monoculturalism which, when challenged, provided an impetus for exclusion. The vehemence with which they were spurned demonstrated the exclusionary potential of monocultural organisational practices. It is argued that responses to asylum seekers at the end of the twentieth century mirrored earlier exclusionary practices. Here, again, an apparent inability of institutions to cope with relatively small numbers of asylum seekers provided the impetus for punitive measures aimed at discouraging the use of the right to claim asylum.

In both cases the impetus for exclusion has been driven by the state. Perceptions of a refugee crisis among officials during late 1950s were not reflected within Irish society. Media accounts of Hungarian refugees were generally welcoming or, on occasion, critical of the inadequacies of provision for refugees put in place by the state. In contrast, recent histrionic media accounts depicted a threat of the country being swamped by asylum seekers. In part, this panic was fuelled by representations of the asylum issue by ministers, politicians and public officials, as insoluble. Arguably, racism within Irish society continues to be mobilised for administrative purposes.

Asylum seekers, drawn from many different countries and origins and ethnic groups, but including many of Ireland's black population became a racialised group within Irish politics. A significant proportion of Ireland's twenty-first century immigrant population and much of its black population were at one stage asylum seekers, or believed to be such. Asylum seekers became in Ireland and elsewhere in 'Fortress Europe' a despised group of unwanted immigrants. They were often not allowed to work for several years and many spent years in conditions of enforced poverty and segregation from wider Irish society, denied access to state-funded English-language training and employment training courses. Africans, in particular, have run a gauntlet of racialised exclusion. At a time when the Irish state encouraged large-scale immigration they were in effect portrayed by the state as pariah migrants. Direct provision and the Referendum on Citizenship were specifically directed against black asylum seekers and their children. It would be difficult to fully understand high rates of social exclusion experienced by many black people in Ireland without considering the legacies of such state-fostered exclusion.[75]

Notes

1 *Irish Independent* (30 November 1956).
2 E. Ward '"A Big Show-off to Show What We Could Do": Ireland and the Hungarian Refugee Crisis of 1956', *Irish Studies in International Affairs*, 8 (1996), pp. 131–41.
3 *Clare Champion* (10 November 1956).
4 *Irish Times* (18 January 1957).
5 National Archives of Ireland, Dublin (hereafter NAI), Department of An Taoiseach (hereafter DT) S11007 (18 January 1957).
6 *Clare Champion* (1 December 1956).
7 NAI, DT, S11007 (10 November 1956).
8 See Article 41.2, *Bunreacht na hÉireann* (1937). 'In particular, the State recognises that by her life in the home, woman gives to the State a support without which the common good cannot be achieved. The State shall, therefore, endeavour to ensure that mothers shall not be obliged by economic necessity to engage in labour to the neglect of their duties in the home.'
9 NAI, DT, S11007 (27 November 1956).
10 The advice of the Department of Justice was that the police had no authority in law over the movement of any refugees unless the minister made an order under the Aliens Act (1935). The making of such orders – which it was noted had been advocated by the police – could result in those who contravened them being deported. This raised the unanswered question of what would happen to a refugee who left the camp. Could they be arrested or not? A meeting of an interdepartmental committee and the Red Cross 'to consider problems relating to the Hungarian refugees' agreed (a) to serve a notice on each refugee to require him or her to register as an 'alien' under section 18 of the Aliens Act (1935) and (b) not to leave Knockalisheen camp without the permission of the Irish red Cross Society officer in charge. It was agreed that Red Cross officials would discourage refugees from leaving the camp. Those who left without permission were to be arrested, as a last resort after efforts at persuasion (NAI, DT, S11007 (10 December 1956)).
11 NAI, DT, S11007 (19 January 1957).
12 *Ibid.*
13 *Ibid.*
14 NAI, DT, S11007 (21 January 1957).
15 *Ibid.*
16 Memorandum from Department of Justice to Department of an Taoiseach. NAI, DT, S11007 (19 January 1957).
17 *Irish Times* (14 January 1957).
18 *Irish Independent* (11 January 1957).
19 The Red Cross complained about the unsuitability of conditions for expectant mothers and children in a letter to the minister for defence (NAI, DT, S11007 (10 January 1957)).
20 Memo from Department of Defence to Department of an Taoiseach (NAI, DT, S11007 (4 December 1956)).
21 *Irish Times* (30 April 1957)
22 A memorandum from the UNHCR to the Department of External Affairs confirms that some refugees who agreed to Ireland on the expectation that

they would later be relocated to the United States (NAI, DT, S11007 (13 May 1957)).

23 *Irish Press* (3 January 1959).

24 *Irish Times* (20 December 1958).

25 *Irish Independent* (17 January 1957).

26 *Irish Times* (14 January 1957).

27 B. Fanning, 'The Mixed Economy of Welfare', in (eds), G. Keily, A. O'Donnell, P. Kennedy and S. Quin, *Irish Social Policy in Context* (Dublin: University College Dublin Press, 1999), p. 67.

28 C. Carney, *Selectivity Issues in Irish Social Services* (Dublin: Family Studies Centre, 1991), p. 6.

29 T. Ward, 'Journeys in asylum space: a comparison of the socio-spatial production of asylum space in Norway and Ireland', M.Phil. thesis (Cork: Department of Geography and European Studies, 1999), p. 43.

30 G. Nolan, 'The education of refugee children: a review of Irish educational provision for refugee children in the light of international experience', M.Ed. thesis (Dublin: University College Dublin, 1997), p. 90.

31 *Ibid.*, pp. 92–5.

32 *Ibid.*, p. 95.

33 Ward, 'Asylum space', p. 45.

34 C. O'Regan, *Report of a Survey of the Vietnamese and Bosnian Refugee Communities in Ireland* (Dublin: Refugee Agency, 1998), p. 123. S. Bradley, *From Bosnia to Ireland's Private Sector* (Dublin: Clann Housing Association, 1999) p. 26.

35 P. Cullen, 'Refugees, Asylum and Race on the Borders', in E. Crowley and J. Mac Laughlin (eds), *Under the Belly of the Celtic Tiger: Class, Race, Identity and Culture in the 'Global Ireland'* (Dublin, Irish Reporter Publications, 1997), p. 105.

36 *Ibid.*, p. 104.

37 They had flown to Dublin from Karachi to examine equipment at an Irish block making firm. *The Examiner* (28 November 2000).

38 Figures from various issues of *Sanctuary*, a bimonthly newsletter on asylum and migrant matters. Refugee and Migrant Project of the Irish Bishops' conference, 'Sanctuary' (Maynooth: Irish Bishops' Conference, 1999–2010, various).

39 *Ibid.*

40 Eurostat asylum applications and first-instance decisions in third quarter of 2000.

41 Nora Owen TD, Dáil Debates, col. 835, 28 February 1996.

42 Vice-chair of the Eastern Health Board branch of IMPACT (*Irish Times* (27 May 2000)).

43 B. Fanning, A. Veale, and D. O'Connor, *Beyond the Pale: Asylum Seeking Children and Social Exclusion in Ireland* (Dublin: Irish Refugee Council, 2001).

44 Memorandum of Understanding (sample contract document) prepared by Directorate for Refugee and Asylum Support Services (cited in *ibid.*, p. 48).

45 *Ibid.*, p. 47.

46 *Irish Times* (29 April 2000).

47 B. Fanning and P. Mac Einri, *Regional Resettlement of Asylum Seekers: A Strategic Approach* (Cork: Irish Centre for Migration Studies, 1999).

48 *Irish Times* (6 April 1999).

49 Interview March 1998, cited in Ward, 'Asylum space', p. 128.

50 B. Fanning, S. Loyal and C. Staunton, *Asylum Seekers and the Right to Work in Ireland* (Dublin: Irish Refugee Council, 2000), p. 5.

51 *Ibid.*, p. 48.
52 Department of Justice Equality and Law Reform, *Integration: A Two Way Process* (Dublin: Official Publications, 2000).
53 Fanning *et al.*, *Asylum Seekers*, p. 9.
54 *Ibid.*, p. 29.
55 *Ibid.*, p. 45.
56 M. Corbett, 'Hidden Children: The Story of State Care for Separated Children', *Working Notes: Facts and Analysis of Social and Economic Issues* 59 (Dublin: Jesuit Centre for Faith and Justice, 2009) p. 20.
57 Pauline Conroy, *Trafficking in Unaccompanied Minors in Dublin* (Dublin: International Organization of Migration, 2003).
58 S. Manandhar, S. Friel, M. Share, F. Hardy and O. Walsh, *Food, Nutrition and Poverty amongst Asylum Seekers in North West Ireland* (Dublin: Combat Poverty, 2004).
59 *Limerick* leader 9 January 2007, cited in E. Ni Shé, T. Lodge and M. Adshead, *Getting to Know You: A Local Study of the Needs of Migrants, Refugees and Asylum Seekers in County Clare* (Limerick: University of Limerick, 2007), p. 48.
60 *Ibid.*
61 *Ibid.*, p. 49.
62 'Mosney refugees end their hunger strike', *Meath Chronicle* (7 July 2010).
63 'System needs reform – direct provision is not working', Irish Refugee Council, December 2010 (at: wwwirishrefugeecouncil.ie).
64 The Fajujonus, a Moroccan-Nigerian married couple with two Irish-born children, had successfully contested a deportation order under the Aliens Order (1946) on the basis that their children were Irish citizens. The Fajujonus argued successfully that their children, as Irish citizens, had a right to family life, in accordance with the rights of the child under Articles 41 and 42 of the Irish Constitution.
65 For example, some 4,071 people were granted 'leave to remain' in 2002; some 75 per cent of these (3,123) had initially applied for asylum.
66 D. O'Connell and C. Smith, 'Citizenship and the Irish Constitution', in U. Fraser and C. Harvey (eds), *Sanctuary in Ireland: Perspectives on Asylum Law and Policy* (Dublin: Institute of Public Administration, 2003), p. 265.
67 The Supreme Court ruling in *Lobe* v. *Minister of Justice, Equality and Law Reform* (2003) effectively limited the residency rights of the Irish-born children entitled to citizenship whose parents are neither Irish nor EU country citizens.
68 S. Mullally, 'Children, Citizenship and Constitutional Change', in B. Fanning, *Immigration and Social Cohesion in the Republic of Ireland* (Manchester: Manchester University Press, 2011), p. 28.
69 *Irish Times* (15 March 2005).
70 Michael McDowell, *Sunday Independent* (14 March 2004).
71 *Ibid.*
72 Referendum to deal with 'baby tourists' (11 March 2004; at: www.Irishhealth.com).
73 'Two of the masters have contested the minister's claims that they pressed for measures to stem the arrival of non-national women as distinct from asking for more resources', *Irish Times* (13 March 2004).
74 Alan Ruddock, *Sunday Independent* (11 April 2004); editorial, *Irish Times* (18 April 2004).
75 Fanning, *Immigration and Social Cohesion*, p. 144.

6

The politics of Traveller exclusion

Travellers in Ireland have faced deepening hostility from settled communities opposed to their presence since the 1960s when efforts to assimilate them into such communities began. Accounts of such opposition have been a staple of the Irish media on an ongoing basis over the last four decades yet no studies have been undertaken of the nature and extent of the spatial exclusion experienced by Travellers. Indeed, there has been little or no detailed research on discrimination against Travellers in social policy with the notable exception of one study on health in the late 1980s.[1] This has been subsequently cited as evidence of institutional racism encountered by Travellers.[2] This chapter seeks to provide a detailed case study of the politics of Traveller exclusion from 1963, when with the publication of the *Report of the Commission on Itinerancy*, the Travelling people became the focus of social policy for the first time, to the end of the twentieth century. The study examined responses to Travellers in County Clare. It principally consisted of an examination of all accounts of Travellers, which appeared in the main county newspaper, The *Clare Champion*, on a weekly basis, between 1963 and the end of 1999. Most of the newspaper articles examined were detailed accounts of the proceedings of meetings of Clare County Council and the Ennis Urban District Council. Other articles related to court proceedings, accounts of resident's campaigns, meetings of voluntary sector organisations and letters to the newspaper.[3] Other records in the public domain were also examined.

The Traveller problem (though rarely the problems experienced by Travellers) became the focus of a considerable number of local authority meetings in Clare from 1964 onwards. During the 1960s the local authorities were remote from the problem and could share in fairly abstract discussions of the need to assimilate Travellers through housing and education. With the emergence of hostility by residents to nigh on all proposals to accommodate Travellers any interest in the benefits of assimilation evaporated. A small number of councillors were consumed with anti-Traveller hostility throughout long careers in local politics. Some councillors felt the need, for electoral purposes, to establish anti-Traveller credentials or, at least, not be seen as supporters of Travellers. The Traveller problem remained an election issue in the minds of councillors.[4] It was 'something that came up time and again on the doorsteps'. At best there was little political impetus to address the needs of Travellers.

From assimilation to exclusion

The ideal of assimilation

Initial responses to Travellers in Clare were predominantly driven by the voluntary sector rather than by the local authorities. These included the development of education provision for Travellers and the development of a proposal for a large-scale 'camping site' on the outskirts of Ennis. The emergence of a plan for a specific site in 1969 followed some years of discussion of a solution to the 'itinerant problem' in the county. This discussion, which emerged as a response to the *Report of the Commission on Itinerancy* (1963), was initially fixated on achieving a once-and-for-all solution. The main focus of discussions of the report were upon the possibility of using the army camp at Knockalisheen, which had been used as a refugee camp some years earlier, to accommodate all the Travellers in the region.[5] Clare County Council, in conjunction with the local authorities in neighbouring counties, sought to develop the camp as accommodation for all Travellers living within a twenty- or thirty-mile radius of Limerick city.[6] Some councillors considered that such a scheme would facilitate assimilation. They could be educated, in one place, about how 'the settled way of life was better than the nomadic one':

> The chairman said that the regional camp would be an experiment. It was a first step. He felt that there was not much point in talking about the elderly itinerants. They would have to concentrate on the children and see that they were educated. He felt that education was the kernel of the problem and they would have a far better chance of educating the children if they were in a central camp.[7]

The second advantage, in the view of some councillors, was that it would remove the need to provided 'camping sites' around the county. As put by one councillor; 'If they provide camps in other places they would have people objecting'.[8] However, proposals to develop the camp were found to be impractical. As put by one councillor, who was also a senator and had served on the Commission on Itinerancy, they: 'could set up a regional camp but there would be no question of herding the itinerants into it. The itinerants had to get a living where they could find it and it would be unrealistic putting them into a big camp unless they were provided for.'[9] He advocated, instead, the development of a number of small camping sites at places frequented by Travellers on an ongoing basis. The Knockalisheen proposal proved unfeasible on a number of grounds. It would have required an unprecedented level of cooperation between local authorities and the army would have had to agree to release it. Nevertheless, the Knockalisheen plan was mooted from time to time by councillors and objectors to subsequently proposed sites in the years and decades which followed.[10]

The local political debate on the 'itinerant problem' remained somewhat abstract for much of the 1960s. Plans to settle the Travellers first emerged through the voluntary sector. The Ennis Itinerant Settlement Committee, established in 1967, began to work on plans to find a site where the 'large number of itinerants who frequent this area and in many instances make it their headquarters can be trained to become citizens able to live in a community'.[11] This committee adhered to the assimilationist approach of the Commission on Itinerancy in its emphasis upon the 'rehabilitation' of Travellers.[12] The efforts of the Ennis committee were modelled on those of a national movement of 'Itinerant' settlement committees that federated in 1967 as the National Resettlement Committee. This movement communicated its main focus of settlement in its emblem: 'A new symbol for the itinerant settlement movement which everyone will soon get to know is a road in the shape of an "S" (for settlement) leading to a little house'.[13]

It is easy in retrospect to disparage the goals of the committee and other such bodies around the country. However, its members were strongly motivated by a desire to alleviate the chronic poverty experienced by Travellers who lived on the roadsides of Clare and to stop what was seen to be the terrible consequences of hounding them from place to place.[14] The committee initially worked to provide new tents and caravans for those who were living in ramshackle tents or under upturned carts covered with tarpaulin. Their efforts principally focused upon a group of almost one hundred Travellers who were permanently camped on the Lees Road on the outskirts of Ennis. Their living conditions were described as 'worse than those of animals'.[15]

By 1969 the committee had devised a specific proposal for a 'camping site'. The site was to include grazing land for Traveller horses and to meet the needs of the community living on the Lees Road as a group. The Travellers were to be accommodated in 'tigins' on the site.[16] However, assimilation was thwarted by the emergence of a political unwillingness to provide sites. The political problems inherent in providing sites for Travellers had been anticipated by some of the supporters of Knockalisheen camp proposal and indeed objections emerged to almost all proposals to provide sites for Travellers in the years and decades which followed.[17] Within a short period of time this undermined the commitment of local authorities to the project of assimilation. The proposals, which were advanced by local authorities from the 1970s onwards, were sufficient to accommodate only a fraction of the Travellers in the county. They were built to take account of the objections of residents rather than to meet the needs of Travellers. This resulted in a significant proportion of the local Traveller population having no option but to remain on the roadside in the decades which followed.

Much of the initial impetus to develop designated sites for Travellers in Clare emerged from the voluntary sector rather than the local authorities. The settlement committee had a few isolated successes in settling Travellers in rural areas.[18] However, plans to develop a large-scale site for Travellers in the vicinity of Ennis failed as a result of objections from residents of the area in which the site was to be located.[19] In 1969 the County Council considered an ambitious proposal for a large-scale site at Lees Road to accommodate fifteen families. The County Council agreed to acquire the land for such a site but objections from local farmers, which were supported by some councillors, were sufficient to undermine support for the proposal. Within a very short period the possibilities for such a site receded and not one member of the Council expressed support for the proposal.[20] Some councillors had earlier supported an alternative site in a move to prevent a motion to develop a site on the Lees Road site from being put forward. However, the proposal to develop this site, on convent-owned land within the town, was never considered seriously. The *Clare Champion* reported that the proposal provoked laughter from councillors.[21] The Council had, according to the settlement committee, 'passed the buck'.[22]

This effectively ended any real hope of settling the Traveller community as a whole. A brief attempt to develop an alternative large scheme, on land offered by the Catholic Bishop, Dr Harty, for the entire community camped at Lees Road was abandoned at a very early stage in the face of a well-organised residents' protests.[23] Subsequently, proposals were devised for the development of four small sites, which would accommodate four families each in caravans, with a paddock for horses on a fifth site.[24] Horses would not be allowed under any circumstances on the residential sites although the paddock was several miles from some of these. Places on the sites were to be offered to families who had lived in the Ennis area for a number of years. The Council maintained from the outset that these were to be temporary sites.

Residents, in each case, sought either to prevent the sites being established or to reduce the number of Travellers allowed. As put by a spokesman for the various residents groups, they wanted 'time to discuss the matter between themselves and come up with a final solution'. The 'right' of residents to veto plans to accommodate Travellers became a factor in these and subsequent negotiations. A number of the proposed 'temporary' sites were eventually developed. These were, in some cases, reduced in scale, in response to objections by residents about the numbers of families to be accommodated. They were ill-equipped to meet the needs of the Travellers. A number had to be subsequently rebuilt because of the temporary and unsuitable nature of the facilities that were put in place.[25]

Insufficient levels of accommodation resulted in the ongoing presence of Travellers on roadsides in the Ennis area. The miserable conditions they faced on the Lees Road were replicated elsewhere when they were displaced by residents' protests to the 'aptly named Watery Road'.[26] The settlement committee subsequently campaigned vigorously for the development of a comprehensive site on the Watery Road. They publicised the 'sub-human' living conditions experienced by Travellers.[27] They lobbied the government to put pressure upon the local authorities.[28] Subsequently, the County Council proposed a scheme along the lines envisaged by the settlement committee. However, objections from residents of nearby housing estates led to these proposals for twelve houses, a community centre and a paddock being pared back to just six houses with no ancillary facilities.[29]

By 1970 there was a clear separation between the understandings and approaches of local authorities and the Itinerant Settlement movement of the Traveller problem. Both understood 'itinerancy' itself as the problem. Assimilationism, as a solution to this problem, seemed hegemonic. For example, in 1970 the Catholic hierarchy issued a statement calling for prayers for the welfare of the Travellers. It concluded: 'on next Sunday let us pray that we may be generous in our acceptance of the travelling people and untiring in our efforts to help them settle'. [30] However, commitments to pursuing the assimilation of Travellers unravelled in the face of political opposition all attempts at settlement. Councillors regarded the settlement committee as 'a bunch of fanatics' and as an unrepresentative clique, while members of the committee criticised council inaction as unjust.[31]

The reality of exclusion

After an initial burst of activity in the late 1960s and early 1970s little new specific accommodation for Travellers was developed until the mid-1980s. In 1972 there were forty-two families in the Ennis area. The proposals that had been developed to provide Traveller-specific accommodation could cater for, at most, just twenty-two of these.[32] There was a political unwillingness to commit to accommodating the rest of the Travellers. As put by one councillor: 'it would be too much for any town to house 42 itinerant families'.[33] The approach of the local authorities was summed up succinctly in a statement by the Ennis Itinerant Settlement Committee:

1 The council never plans for all of the families.
2 Each proposal to help the Travellers is balanced by a restricting promise to the objectors.
3 Decisions are deferred and deferred and deferred.[34]

The settlement committee argued that such an approach would prevent the assimilation of Travellers and that the sites that were being developed would not meet the needs of Travellers:

It has to be itinerant settlement without qualification... not allowing travellers to have horses, not providing a community hall or guaranteeing that no extensions of site will take place ever are blind rash promises. Sites built to please objectors and not suit Travellers and social workers are doomed.[35]

The local authorities pursued a minimalist policy of maintaining existing sites and, at the same time, sought to evict unsettled Travellers. Councillors spoke of sending some of the Ennis Travellers to other parts of the county.[36] Assimilationist arguments were used to reject the need for any further sites for Travellers. Suggestions were frequently made by councillors and residents groups that each village in the county should take one family. It was argued that the Travellers could be 'settled and absorbed into normal living conditions... but letting them live together, they would still continue their own ways'.[37]

Traveller exclusion in Ennis

Efforts to settle Travellers on the outskirts of Ennis in the late 1960s were thwarted, among other things, by the competing pressures of suburban development. Where suburban residential development had yet to occur, it was argued that Traveller accommodation should not be allowed because it would lead to a potential loss of future rates to the local authorities.[38] Rural areas on the outskirts of the town, that had been long-standing unofficial halting sites, became suburbanised and the new settlers were quick to cast the Travellers as interlopers. This can be seen from the changing nature of opposition between 1969 and 1978 to sites for Travellers that emerged in the Lees Road area. The objections which emerged to the initial proposed development principally came from farmers.

Objections by farmers to a second proposal, just a few years later in 1971, were accompanied by those of a residents' association. The solicitor representing the residents described the people in the area as middle class and expressed concern that the value of their bungalows would fall if itinerant families were settled in the area.[39]

From the early 1970s the local authorities increasingly prosecuted Travellers living in the town under public health legislation and for illegal parking. Those living in or around the town were fined and evicted on an ongoing basis throughout the 1970s and 1980s.[40] Plans to develop accommodation went hand in hand with efforts to fine and evict even those designated to receive accommodation. For example, in 1971 six Traveller families awaiting accommodation on the Watery Road were fined IR£2 each for obstruction. Their fines were paid by the Ennis Itinerant Settlement Committee who considered that they had been put in an invidious position through inaction by the local authorities in developing the site for their use.[41] Unaccommodated Travellers on the roadsides near Ennis area lived precarious lives. A storm in January 1974 destroyed or damaged most of their homes.[42] A group of 30 families consisting of 54 adults and 42 children had been living in ten huts, six caravans, six barrel-wagons and seven canvas or plastic shelters. A second storm later that month caused further damage to their homes.

Travellers who lived in the Ennis area faced considerable hostility on a day-to-day basis from residents, traders, councillors and the authorities. This found expression in punitive measures against those who allowed their horses to wander, in the prohibition of Travellers from public spaces, such as public houses and dancehalls, and in ongoing efforts aimed at discouraging Travellers from halting in or near the town.[43] From the 1960s until the 1980s the Gardaí sought custodial sentences for begging offences by Traveller women. For example, in 1980, two women were jailed for seven days each for begging in Ennis. The local Garda superintendent pressed the court for stiff punishment. He said that this type of offence was prevalent in Ennis and that several complaints from visitors had been received by the Gardaí. By the 1980s many of the unaccommodated Travellers living in the Ennis area had been born or had grown up in the town.[44] The size of this 'indigenous' community grew from an estimated fifteen families and some single people in 1976 to twenty families in 1984.[45] From time to time they were displaced by the local authorities following protests by residents and councillors but the use of the courts for such purposes became increasingly recognised as ineffective. Once evicted, they moved elsewhere in the town, 'playing' what one councillor referred to as 'musical chairs with the council, Gardai and the public at large'.[46] Yet, the use of such orders to placate anti-Traveller feeling persisted.[47] In 1970 residents of the market area objected to the construction of a public toilet on the grounds that Travellers might make use of it.[48] In 1977 a group of Ennis residents threatened a rent strike unless the Urban District Council agreed to 'rid their area of itinerants'.[49] In 1982 businesses at the Ennis shopping centre similarly threatened to withhold their rates.[50] These and a number of other protests against Travellers resulted in an ongoing political impetus to exclude Travellers from the town.

Councillors spoke in terms of making a stand against the Travellers. This became increasingly seen as the need to oppose not just unauthorised halting but the presence of Travellers in the town as such. A number of Traveller families had been allocated council housing. By 1974 eighteen families lived in houses in the town. Councillors increasingly spoke of not allowing anymore Travellers to be housed.[51] During the 1980s efforts to remove unaccommodated Travellers were combined with hostility towards settled Travellers. During the 1980s the main emphasis of halting site policy was to remove Travellers from the town. Two forms of exclusion were envisaged with the construction of a large halting outside the town at Drumcliffe. The first was to seek to compel Travellers living on the roadsides in Ennis to move of of town. It was considered that the provision of such a site would make prosecutions for illegal parking easier.[52] The second was to prevent such Travellers obtaining housing in the town.

The Drumcliffe halting site

In 1986 the Council opened a large halting site at Drumcliffe about two miles outside Ennis. The opening ceremony was marked by a photograph in the *Clare Champion*[53] with the caption that proclaimed 'a warm welcome to the new residents of Drumcliffe halting site'. The photograph showed a number of council officials and councillors, all named in the caption, a common feature of local newspapers, standing with some Traveller adults and children on the site. The newspaper contained 53 photos of over 200 named people.[54] However, none of the dozen or so Travellers in the Drumcliffe photograph were named. The development of the site had been marked not just by the usual objections by residents groups but by objections by Travellers and the voluntary sector that who argued that the site was unsuitable. The Travellers in the photograph were not members of the 'local' community as none of these had been willing to move onto the site. The site had remained unoccupied for many months after it was opened the previous year. The first occupants were people from outside the area who were offered places in an effort to justify the project.

In 1974 the County Council had located three caravans at Drumcliffe site which had been one of a number of sites identified in the early 1970s for small developments. The county manager reported at the time that Travellers were reluctant to use the site and it was agreed that it would be retained to provide emergency accommodation from time to time.[55] Such an emergency transpired almost two years later when a Traveller family lost all their belongings in a fire. They were offered one of the caravans but decided to emigrate instead.[56] Travellers in the Ennis area had a deep-rooted antipathy to the site because of its proximity to Drumcliffe cemetery where many of their dead were buried.[57] They also considered that the site was too far from the town. The Travellers who lived on the roadsides in and around Ennis by that time were the children and relatives of those living in houses in the town. Many had grown up in houses but became homeless when they married and had children of their own.

In 1983 the County Council agreed to develop accommodation for twenty-six families at Drumcliffe. Initially this was to consist of six houses and twenty caravan stands.[58] Plans for the six houses on the site were abandoned because of financial pressures rather than because of objections. Six additional caravan pitches were added in their place.[59] The County Council unanimously approved the revised scheme. The residents' objections mattered little in the face of the possibility of removing all unsettled Travellers from the town.[60] The development had been opposed from the outset by Travellers and by the settlement committee. A survey conducted by the committee in November 1984 of twenty-eight families living on the roadside and in Beechpark, an overcrowded site in Ennis, revealed that twenty-four families stated that they would not move to Drumcliffe under any circumstances.[61] Only one family was prepared to use the site but this was conditional on it being occupied by other local families. Officials were unwilling to meet with members of the committee to discuss the proposal in advance of it being approved by the Council.[62]

The Drumcliffe proposal precipitated Traveller activism. Ennis Travellers appointed spokespersons to represent their opposition to the development. Reports in the *Clare Champion* from early 1985 noted their objections to the development in considerable detail. They opposed the size and location of the scheme, the proposed mix of local and transient families, the distance of the site from the town and from amenities as well as its proximity to Drumcliffe cemetery.[63] The existence of these objections were denied by Council officials in the months that followed even when they were aired on the *Late Late Show*, the television programme with the highest ratings of the time.[64] Travellers refusing to move onto the site were threatened with prosecution for unauthorised parking.[65] At the same time motions were put before the local authorities that no housing applications from Travellers be accepted unless they were living on the Drumcliffe site.[66]

Harassment by the local authorities

One of the first to be prosecuted was a Traveller activist who had criticised the Drumcliffe site on the *Late Late Show* and had previously spoken out against anti-Traveller statements by councillors.[67] The vehemence with which officials pursued his prosecution reveals something of the extent of coercion at the time as well as the degree to which it was considered that the expressed views of Travellers could be discounted. Local authority officials were, at the very least, careless with the truth in the case they put forward. This was perhaps unsurprising within a culture where unfounded allegations about Travellers occurred on an ongoing basis, and where it was not expected that these would be contested by Travellers.

In this case, the Traveller was prosecuted under the Public Health Act (1878) for living without proper sanitary facilities on the outskirts of town. He contested the allegations about sanitation by arguing that his family had access to the public toilets at the nearby station. The council could not produce any evidence in support of their allegations about sanitation. The second strand of their case was that the Traveller refused an offer of suitable accommodation and had no grounds for halting on an unapproved site. Council officials gave evidence that the Traveller had refused a number of different offers of housing. One official told the court that the accused had been previously housed in Clarecastle but that he had subsequently vacated the property. He also stated that the Traveller had been offered accommodation in Traveller shared housing schemes and that he had 'refused' to apply for a standard local authority house. The Acting County Secretary informed the court that the defendant was one of the instigators of a campaign to stop Travellers moving to the Drumcliffe site which, he maintained, had been selected by the Council after several meetings had been held with Travellers representatives to find the best location.

The evidence given by officials in the court case was at the very least unreliable. Requests for meetings on the Drumcliffe proposal prior to completion by the Settlement Committee had been refused. The veracity of other evidence given by officials was also challenged. The Traveller had previously lived with his family in a house in Clarecastle. In 1981 he vacated this accommodation to emigrate to England along with many other Irish people. He stated that he had been offered a number of houses on Traveller schemes but he refused these because he wanted a house in the settled community for the sake of his children. He explained why he wanted to live in standard housing: 'I have a deaf and dumb child and there is nothing I would like better than to take her into her own home. I would love to give my children the luxury of being able to take a bath in their own house.'[68] He said that he was personally opposed to moving to Drumcliffe because his first child was buried there. He said that 'the Travellers had their own beliefs about settling in a place where their dead were buried and this was the problem with Drumcliffe'.

The judge ruled in favour of the local authority on the basis of an availability of suitable accommodation at Drumcliffe. The Traveller, and another whose case was heard in his absence, were evicted and fined. This cleared the way for the use of the courts to harass unaccommodated Travellers living in Ennis and contributed to a fear among remaining Travellers in the town that they would be forced onto the site.[69] By March 1985 fourteen families had left the Ennis area, which had been their home for many years.[70] The remaining four families still refused to move to Drumcliffe. Councillors at local authority meetings expressed anger at this and in August 1985 the chairman of the Urban District Council issued a statement 'which strongly condemned the action of the travellers for not occupying the site, opting instead to remain on the side of the town streets'.[71] The statement justified measures to exclude Travellers from the town by referring to fears in the town of Traveller violence. These claims had less bearing on reality than usual given that most of the unsettled Travellers had temporarily fled the town. It was also stated that Travellers who would not go to Drumcliffe would not be accepted onto housing waiting lists. Furthermore, it was contended that Traveller unwillingness to occupy the site would 'in the council's opinion, seriously call into question the desirability of providing any further accommodation for the travelling community.'

Early the following year the occupation of Drumcliffe by four transient families was heralded as a triumph by the County Council. Ennis Travellers continued to oppose being forced onto the site.[72] In 1987 a committee representing young Travellers argued that local families living in trailers wanted local authority houses and did not want to be herded off onto a site.[73] It stated that young people who had spent years in houses among the settled community had no wish to find themselves living on a site miles outside the town.

The failure of Drumcliffe

Warnings by Travellers and the voluntary sector about the consequences of accommodating a large number of incompatible families together were borne out in the years which followed. Some Ennis Travellers eventually moved onto the site to join the transient Travellers who lived there. Efforts to manage the site were minimalist.[74] In 1996 a violent incident involving about fifty Travellers occurred on the site.[75] This resulted in considerable damage to the site, a number of Traveller families being made immediately homeless and a High Court ruling that the site should be closed. The Drumcliffe site was closed in February 1997 and sixteen Traveller families were consigned to the roadsides around Ennis.[76] The High Court decision had ordered the provision of an alternative site.[77] Subsequent plans by the local authorities to develop a number of replacement halting sites some miles outside Ennis, against the long expressed wishes of the Ennis Travellers, met with considerable opposition from residents groups.[78] These plans were by and large unsuccessful in the face of High Court actions by residents groups.[79] A lack of alternative accommodation combined with overcrowding and poor conditions on existing approved sites in the county.[80] For example one site, at Beechpark in Ennis, had opened in 1973 as a temporary site for eight families. In 1981 Travellers living on the site complained that council workers had refused to collect refuse from the site for over two years and that all the families on the site had to share one tap and one broken flush toilet.[81] By 1998 it was occupied by eleven families. The local authorities had agreed that the number of families living on the site should be reduced to six but in the absence of alternatives the site remained overcrowded and improvements had been deferred for many years.[82]

Discrimination in housing allocation

Traveller demand for housing

There has been a tendency to regard claims that Travellers wanted housing as an expression of assimilationist ideology. However in Clare many Travellers expressed a preference for standard housing or group housing schemes rather than halting sites. The main aspirations of the Commission on Itinerancy (1963) to settle Travellers had been realised to some extent. By 1976 it was estimated that half the Traveller population in the country had been 'settled' even if a considerable number still wanted to travel.[83] Ironically, claims that Travellers did not want housing were used to justify discrimination by local authorities seeking to exclude Travellers from the town. Some Ennis Urban District councillors argued that the local authorities had fulfilled their obligations to Travellers. They put forward a motion in 1982 that no more Travellers be housed other than those already on housing waiting lists.[84] During the 1980s Ennis

Travellers contested what they described as discrimination in the allocation of Council housing on a number of occasions. Many of these were of a generation that had grown up in such housing in the town. As put by a spokesman of the Ennis Committee for Travelling People in 1987:

> Since the late 1960s, up to thirty families had been provided for in either standard or group housing schemes. No provision has been made for the children of Travellers who had been housed. These young people... had been born in or near Ennis, had attended school and the travellers training centre and had lived happily with their settled neighbours.
>
> Inevitably, they have grown up and married, thereby creating new families. Of necessity, they are then forced to go back on the roadside... From then on they were subjected to harassment forced to pay fines and legal fees for illegal parking and were constantly living with the threat of being moved. Unfortunately they had no choice other than moving onto another illegal parking place.[85]

In 1987 the local authorities came under considerable criticism for discriminating against Travellers. Statements by the local authorities that there was no demand for housing among Travellers were disputed. It was argued that eight out of the fifteen local families on the side of the road at the time wanted houses.[86] The Ennis Committee for Travelling People accused the Council of, in effect, maintaining separate housing waiting lists for Travellers and settled people. The local authorities argued that there were no plans to construct houses at the time because of an overall lack of demand. They discounted claims that Travellers wanted standard housing and argued that there was a significant demand for halting site accommodation.[87] These arguments masked an unwillingness to house Travellers in the Town. As reported in the *Clare Champion* at the time:

> The Assistant County Secretary acknowledged that there was a problem in the high marriage rate amongst young Travellers but he said that if they were prepared to consider locating to other areas of the county the Council would be able to help them. However, he said they had refused to do that.[88]

The argument that Travellers did not want housing and as such that there was no demand for such housing replaced more blatant statements at the time the Drumcliffe proposal was being considered, that Travellers would not be allowed onto waiting lists unless they moved onto the Drumcliffe site. Both were expressions of a desire to exclude Travellers from the town. These statements drew considerable criticism from the National Council for Travelling People that put forward the following analysis of what was happening:

The Assistant County Manager states that Clare County council cannot accommodate the fifteen local travellers presently on the roadside or the average eleven new marriages each year. At the same time he states that the Council have cut back on their housing programme because of a reduction in demand from settled people. In other words, if settled people need houses they can be built, if Travellers need them, forget it. Where citizenship is concerned some are more equal than others are.

During the course of a meeting with our committee, Mr O'Ceallaigh, the Assistant County Manager, made an even more astonishing statement that no Traveller family would be considered in the imminent allocation of vacant houses. Five local traveller families have applied for those houses, filled in the forms and have been visited by the health inspector who recorded the number of their children, their living conditions and how long they had been applying for a house. All five are married couples with from three to six children. All want a local authority house, not group housing or a site. All are local to the Ennis area. Some have lived in houses here as children and teenagers for up to fourteen years. They are very together couples with no problems their neighbours might object to. None has ever been in trouble with the law. Yet the council can deprive them of their constitutional rights to be considered for a home.[89]

The National Council of Travelling people complained about a lack of transparency in the allocation of houses. They stated that Clare County Council did not operate a points system in allocating houses that would enable houses to be allocated on the basis of need. Travellers were offered houses where vacancies arose in Traveller-only group housing schemes but were not considered for standard housing.

Discrimination

Officials spoke of the unwillingness to allocate houses to Travellers in veiled terms in comparison to councillors who remained adamant that Travellers should be excluded from waiting lists if they halted illegally or unless they agreed first to move to Drumcliffe.[90] The Ennis Committee for Travelling People issued a statement that they would support Travellers in taking legal action against the local authorities in response to various statements justifying discrimination.[91]

Complaints by local authority tenants about the allocation of two houses to Traveller families in 1987 resulted in demands from Ennis councillors to be consulted on all future letting decisions.[92] Two of these councillors were on record as opposing the allocation of any houses to Travellers.[93] Another two had argued that no more Travellers should be allowed to live on some estates.[94] The county manager acceded to this request in part. It was agreed that the councillors would be informed of any proposed letting decision in advance. Pressure to discriminate against Travellers persisted during the years, which followed. In 1991 a deputation of 150 residents from Clancy Park complained about conditions on the estate and that the estate already had 'more than its fair share of housed Travellers'. They protested against the proposed allocation of a house to a family. The objections of a spokesperson for the residents were summarised in the *Clare Champion*:

> Five traveller families are currently living in Clancy Park but he said that with the prospect of a sixth family moving onto the estate, residents were wondering where it was all going to stop and was it, in fact, going to become an 'estate of Travellers'.[95]

The notion that the allocation of six houses to Travellers, out of a total of 120 on the estate, constituted a crisis was highlighted by the insistence of the deputation that the Traveller issue took priority over their other grievances. These included problems resulting from the lack of maintenance of the estate in the eighteen years since it had been built. In 1994 a deputation of residents from Clarecastle, a village adjoining Ennis, protested against what they understood as the abandonment of a promise not to house any more Traveller families in the area:

> In the past and following representations on several occasions to the Co. Council, assurances were given that no further housing/re-housing of Travellers would take place in Clarecastle... since the last undertaking given by the Council that no further housing of travellers would take place in Clarecastle, one family has been housed in St Joseph's and one in Church Drive, one in Clarehill and one in six recently constructed houses on the road to the cemetery at Clarehill.[96]

These complaints might be understood, to some extent, as a response to the curtailment of earlier discriminatory letting policies. Opponents of the rights of Travellers to public housing now spoke of a sense of injustice among settled people that Travellers could be deemed to have a greater housing need because they tended to have more children than settled families. In other words, it was argued that the settled community was experiencing discrimination because of Travellers. One councillor argued, at the time when objections to Travellers in Clarecastle were being considered, that it was unfair that Travellers should move from the side of the road into a council house at the expense of a family who have been had been on a housing waiting list for years. Her suggestion that Travellers should be obliged to spend at least two years at a recognised halting site before being considered for a house was widely supported by other councillors.[97] In 1994 opposition of a number of residents groups to the construction of Council houses on the Watery road was based upon fears that some of these houses would be allocated to Traveller families.[98]

The persistence of Traveller exclusion

A number of Travellers, who had been evicted from Drumcliffe in 1997, were subsequently evicted from land adjacent to Ennis industrial estate following a High Court action by tenants of the estate.[99] They subsequently moved to open spaces around the town and to areas adjacent to existing Traveller sites.[100] This met with opposition from resident groups. For example, the arrival of five families on land adjacent to Traveller houses on the Watery road prompted local residents associations to raise funds for a possible High Court action against the local authorities.[101] As put by one Traveller representative: 'We have been treated like dogs since the Drumcliffe site was closed in December, being run from place to place around Ennis'.[102]

Councillors, facing pressure from residents, sought to exonerate the local authorities from the problem of Traveller homelessness. It was represented as the fault of Travellers. The Ennis Town manager, in the words of an article in the *Clare Champion* 'vowed to go to every court in the land' to have Travellers removed from the vicinity of one Ennis site, following claims that they were causing problems for local residents.[103] As put by the chairman of Ennis Urban District Council at the time: 'The Travellers cannot be allowed to rule the roost'.[104] Some of the displaced Travellers sought to counter this dominant perspective. As explained by one Traveller woman:

> We don't want to be illegally parked but have no option because the council hasn't provided any temporary halting site. We want to stay in Ennis because we are from the town and our children are going to school here. We understand that the car parks are not suitable but we have nowhere to go. Some Travellers looking for houses have been on the housing list for ten years and if they obtained houses this would help the situation considerably.[105]

In 1997 the Catholic Bishop, Dr Walsh, who was also chairperson of the Travellers Accommodation Advisory Committee, permitted four local Traveller families to halt on his lawn in a gesture 'aimed at encouraging a more positive response by the local authorities'.[106] However, this evoked considerable hostility from councillors who opposed the presence of Travellers in the town. One demanded that Dr Walsh should be prosecuted for being in breach of planning regulations.[107]

A Traveller Accommodation Advisory Committee had been established in 1997 to prepare to meet the statutory requirements of the Housing (Traveller) Accommodation Act (1998) to produce a Traveller accommodation plan for the county. It was agreed that the advisory committee would be made up of councillors, council officials and a representative of the Travelling community. A request for more than one Traveller representative on the committee resulted in a threat by the councillor who was to chair the committee that he would resign.[108] A decision to allow a second Traveller member to represent Travellers at Shannon resulted in his resignation.[109] Prior to the establishment of the advisory committee by the County Council in 1997 Travellers in Clare had never been formally consulted about accommodation proposals. The advisory committee quickly produced a report which set out the accommodation requirements of Travellers living in the county. It proposed seven group housing schemes, five single rural houses, seven serviced sites, twelve units local authority housing all to be located near the main towns in the county; Ennis Shannon and Ennistymon with, in the case of group housing or sites, fewer than six families in any one scheme. The report also stated the need to provide a number of transient sites in the county, to accommodate newly formed families awaiting permanent accommodation and to make provision for visiting Traveller families with a limit of eight families and twelve mobile homes or caravans on any one site. The report, as such, stated that most Travellers wanted housing and a minority wanted to be accommodated on halting sites and that such sites should accommodate small numbers.

The County Council received the report in October 1997. It was opposed by a number of councillors but was formally accepted, on the advice of officials that not to do so would potentially result in the matter being taken out of their hands by the minister of the environment.[110] The plan had little impact upon the proposals that emerged to provide accommodation for Travellers in the late 1990s. The Council constructed a halting site near Shannon. This contrary to the expressed wishes of the Travelling community and the report of the advisory committee consisted of a number of caravan pitches adjacent to small tigins. The County Council pursued plans to develop halting sites at a number of areas some miles from Ennis although the Travellers stated a desire to live in Ennis and the other towns in the county.

Officials had stated that an accommodation blueprint would be published in early 1999 but this was deferred in the face of potential public hostility pending the 1999 local government elections.[111] A report in the *Clare Champion* in September 1999 stated that councillors had 'trenchantly refused to allow a draft plan to confront the problem of accommodating Travellers to go on public display'.[112] This resistance brought yet another warning from the County manager that unless they 'got their house in order' they faced the prospect of having the final say on the make-up of the Travellers accommodation plan being taken away from them by the minister of the environment and local government.[113] In the absence of measures to address the accommodation needs of Travellers, the local authorities persisted in seeking through the courts to move Travellers on from unauthorised sites. However, the courts were increasingly reluctant to find in favour of the local authorities, given that they had failed in their obligations to provide accommodation.[114]

A census of Travellers undertaken in Clare by the local authorities in November 1998 noted that fifty Traveller families were accommodated in standard housing and Traveller-only group housing schemes.[115] Twenty families were living on serviced halting sites. Thirty-seven families were living on unauthorised sites. A further three families were living on private accommodation. Although councillors and officials often gave the impression that many of the unaccommodated families were transient outsiders, the Traveller Accommodation Sub-Committee had identified the need for an accommodation programme to cater for fifty-three 'indigenous' families in immediate need of permanent accommodation as well as eight transient families. The committee emphasised the need to take account of projected population increase and new household formations (an estimated five families) by 2004. However, as expressed by a spokesperson for a residents' association in October 1999:

> By my reading of the plan, it will not be until 2002 to 2005 before halting sites are provided. It is not easy on the community but there is sympathy for the travellers who are living in those conditions without running water, sanitation or refuse collection. There is a fire and health hazard in an area where there are between 12 and 15 caravans on a site just big enough to accommodate a bungalow... People living in Kosovo would not put up with the living conditions that the travellers are enduring.

A judge during the proceedings of an illegal parking case had expressed an even more pessimistic analysis two years previously. In reply to a statement by a Traveller woman that her 66-year-old father would be 70 by the time the council provided a halting site for her family the judge replied; 'You'll be 70 yourself by the time they provide a site'.[116]

Violence and social order

Speaking of violence

Opposition to Traveller accommodation was justified on an ongoing basis by allegations of violence by Travellers against settled people. Emotionally charged, hyperbolic or even apocalyptic language was a feature of most discussions on Travellers at local authority meetings. Newspaper accounts of discussions about Travellers frequently described residents and councillors as angry. Residents were often described by councillors and spokespersons as living in fear of Travellers, of being 'terrorised' by Travellers or of being 'harassed, abused and assaulted by Travellers'.[117] Allegations often focused on how elderly settled people or women at home during the day lived in 'a constant state of fear' of Travellers.[118] These often combined with allegations that Travellers posed a risk to the health of settled people. Similarly allegations that Travellers deposited excrement on the doorsteps of vulnerable 'old people' were made from time to time. However, allegations of these kinds were always vague. No specific instances of violence or harassment by a Traveller against any member of the settled community were identified by councillors, local authority officials or residents groups from 1963 to 1999 in Clare to support the various allegations which were made.[119]

In the 1990s some efforts emerged to curtail unfounded accusations of Traveller violence. On one occasion in 1996 the County manager 'pleaded' with those present to refrain from using what he called 'widely defamatory and unhelpful language'.[120] In 1996 Dr Walsh issued a statement which called upon settled people to desist from making inflammatory accusations of violence by Travellers against settled people:

> I have in mind particularly some suggestions in recent times which attempt to link travellers with the violence committed against people living in rural areas. Such suggestions are grossly unjust and unchristian.[121]

Travellers in Clare lived under a microscope where any real or imaginary transgressions were subject to intense scrutiny. However, the lack of evidence of Traveller violence did not prevent such allegations acquiring the status of 'truth'. In this context old unfounded accusations could be restated. For example, in 1985 the chairman of the Urban District Council alleged that old people in Ennis were 'living in fear of Travellers'. At that time there were only four Traveller families living on the roadside in and around the town. The wording of the accusation drew heavily upon accusations that first emerged in 1982. Such accusations might be understood as a racialised account of conflicts between settled and Traveller people. If threats of violence by Travellers were unfounded, antagonisms between settled people and Travellers were real enough. The anxieties of the settled community found expression within a racialised discourse of exaggeration that provided a justification for anti-Traveller feeling that could not be expressed through objections grounded in fact. Other accounts related to instances where residents stated that they were 'nearly attacked', or where it was claimed that a child had 'almost been kicked by a horse'.[122] Within such accounts Travellers constituted a 'nuisance' to be explained in terms of potential physical threat and danger rather than in terms of inconvenience. As such, vague allegations that Travellers attacked vulnerable members of the settled community with excrement were stated and restated instead of discussion of problems arising from the lack of sanitary services provided to Travellers in the town.

Anti-Traveller violence

Opposition by residents to Travellers who halted took a number of forms. It usually emerged through residents groups that lobbied councillors or took legal proceedings. Most such activism was bound up with efforts to exclude Travellers from a locality. Sometimes the actions of such groups took the form of boycotting or harassment. For example, in 1982 many of the residents on one road on the outskirts of Ennis agreed to refuse Travellers water in addition to pressing the local authorities to take legal action against them.[123] Some councillors considered that Travellers on unofficial sites should be deprived of all basic amenities, including water.[124] In other cases Travellers were physically prevented from halting. For example, in 1982 three councillors confronted Travellers attempting to halt at Drumbiggle in Ennis and 'informed them that further parking in the area would simply not be tolerated'.[125] The Travellers moved on. In 1992 residents who lived near an unofficial halting site outside Shannon hired a mechanical digger to make the site uninhabitable while many of its occupants were on a pilgrimage to Croagh Patrick. They physically prevented the Travellers from accessing the site on their return.[126] A Garda report at the time identified a problem of friction between the two communities.[127] The response to this problem, as outlined at a meeting of Clare County Council, had been the prosecution of eighteen Travellers on various unspecified offences. There was no discussion of prosecutions in relation to the anti-Traveller actions of residents.

Councillors predicted violence and threats to the social order in a number of local authority debates if Travellers were not excluded in some way. For example, in 1982 one councillor discussed the situation resulting from past decisions to develop provision for Travellers as an 'explosive' situation; 'We have started something in Ennis which could explode and

I am convinced that the fuse has been lit'.[128] Another frequently warned of the dangers of a 'mini-revolution' by residents if plans for Traveller accommodation were progressed.[129] People, he stated, could expect 'turbulent times' because a perception had gone out that 'Clare was a safe haven for Travellers'. In effect, the threat under discussion was one of potential violence against Travellers that might transpire if Travellers were not excluded. In other words, Travellers were a threat to social order because of the violence and hostility that they inspired in the dominant community. Such violence emerged on a number of occasions.

On St Patrick's Day 1985 a group of Travellers who had been drinking at a public house in the village of Sixmilebridge were surrounded by 'a crowd of about 100 drunk and aggressive locals chanting for blood'.[130] Six Travellers sought to escape in a van which was then attacked by some of the crowd who attempted to burn it and push it into a river until they were stopped by the Gardaí. The Gardaí had to use force to prevent the locals from assaulting the Travellers. Three Travellers were chased through the fields by some of the crowd. A witness described how one woman, fleeing in terror from a group of twelve or thirteen people armed with sticks, planks and hurleys, collided with her front door and fell through the glass window. The injured woman extracted herself from the glass and continued to run from the mob that had been chasing her. The witness was subsequently asked by the Gardaí to identify the Travellers but was not asked to identify any of the local people who were after them. Twelve Travellers were taken into custody and some of these were taken to Ennis hospital. None of the settled attackers were arrested.[131] Five of the Travellers were charged by the Gardaí with being drunk and disorderly but these charges were dismissed in court when their solicitor presented evidence of the attacks against them.

In 1986 a somewhat similar incident occurred on a council housing estate in Ennis when a large crowd of about one hundred gathered outside the home of a Traveller family chanting 'burn them out'.[132] The incident was a response to noise being made by 'drunken Travellers' in the house but the crowd that gathered included people from areas not affected by the disturbances. The Ennis Gardaí brought the situation under control with the assistance of reinforcements from around the county. Three settled people were charged with conduct calculated to lead to a breach of the peace. They included one man who, according to a Garda, attacked a Traveller with a hurley while leading the call to the house, and another man who was charged with assaulting one of the Gardaí. Their cases were adjourned for twelve months. However a number of Travellers were fined and bound over to the peace.

The different responses by the Gardaí to Travellers and to settled people on this occasion might be in part explained by evidence presented by a Garda that such arrests would not have been prudent. He said that the locals would not disperse unless the Gardaí took the Travellers into custody. He stated that the locals had weapons but the Travellers had none. It might also be explained by discrimination. Arguably the Gardaí were unwilling to criminalise residents. Some of the charges against the Travellers related to events which took place after they were taken into custody. They had become angry about their treatment by the Gardaí. It was alleged that a Garda was assaulted by one of the Travellers. The response of the Gardaí in this case and in the case of the attack at Sixmilebridge was to arrest Travellers so as to placate mobs of settled people. Travellers were arrested in both cases but not their attackers. The Gardaí tended to discuss the 'friction' between settled communities and Travellers as a problem to be addressed through the prosecution and criminalisation of Travellers.[133]

The Urban District Council responded similarly to the riot with criticism of the Travellers rather than their attackers. Officials stated that any tenants who, in future, caused annoyance or disturbance to their neighbours would have their tenancy terminated without further warning. However, it was clear that such warnings were principally directed at Travellers. Some councillors used the incident to argue that no local authority housing should be allocated to Travellers in future.[134]

The politics of Traveller exclusion

Racism and politics

Local political responses to Travellers from 1963 were characterised by the racialisation of Travellers as a threat and as a deviant and violent underclass. Anti-Traveller statements at local authority meetings were rarely challenged. Instead, they were prominently reported in the local media. The role of councillors on Traveller issues was one of opposition rather than leadership. Councillors played a central role in articulating anti-Traveller feeling and in opposing efforts to provide accommodation for Travellers even though they were the elected members of the local authorities with responsibility for providing such accommodation.

Since the 1960s local authorities could avail of central government funding to provide accommodation for Travellers but they were not required by law to do so prior to the Housing (Traveller Accommodation) Act (1998). In this context councillors could disassociate themselves from plans to provide accommodation and engage themselves in populist anti-Traveller protest. However, at the same time councillors were expected to deal with the problem of Travellers. Travellers lived on the roadsides because local authorities were unwilling to provide accommodation for them. Such unwillingness was in turn caused by opposition to sites for Travellers. The response of some councillors to this seemingly insoluble problem was to press for the exclusion of Travellers. A shifting and evolving racialised anti-Traveller discourse emerged to justify the politics of Traveller exclusion.

Travellers as an underclass

The representation of Travellers as a deviant and dangerous underclass was central to this discourse of exclusion. For example, in 1991 a councillor at a meeting of the Urban District Council (UDC) pronounced that 'itinerants were an absolute malaise and black spot'.[135] In 1996, in the aftermath of disturbances at Drumcliffe, another councillor described the Travellers as a well-organised criminal element that needed to be quelled by the army.[136] Depictions of Travellers as an underclass could be used to argue that they were undeserving of the same rights and entitlements as others in society as well as to argue for their physical exclusion. For example, in 1972 a councillor advocated removing the rights of Travellers to cash benefits.[137] He argued they should just receive vouchers for essentials. On another occasion councillors argued that Travellers should have their dole money stopped until they repaired damages at halting sites.[138] No such proposals were ever made in respect of other groups. Arguments that Travellers were welfare scroungers were used from time to time to justify their exclusion. There was a considerable preoccupation with stamping out begging through punitive measures. This was bound up with efforts to hide Travellers from public view. In 1964 one councillor opposed the development of campsites because they might be photographed by tourists and would show the Irish people in a poor light.[139] The 'tourism case' against Travellers continued to be made from time to time in the decades that followed.[140]

'Too much has been done for Travellers'

From the early 1970s there were criticisms that councillors and officials were failing in their duty to provide for the needs of Travellers. Such contestation emerged through a discourse that represented the local authorities as generous to a fault. This discourse became possible by appropriating the credit for the ongoing efforts of the voluntary sector to address the needs of Travellers. It was used to advance the argument that the people of Ennis had been 'too good to Travellers', that Travellers had exploited this generosity, and that the authorities were justified in doing no more.

By the early 1970s efforts to provide accommodation for Travellers had run out of steam. Local authorities and councillors became the focus of criticism from the voluntary sector for failing to provide accommodation and from residents for not having prevented Travellers from halting in their localities. During the 1980s many councillors advocated excluding Travellers from the town. Statements by councillors and officials often emphasised past generosity towards the Travellers. Ennis and Clare were depicted as having down more than any other town or county for Travellers in a number of statements during the 1980s and 1990s.[141] Thus, Ennis Urban District Council was described as having 'one of the most enviable records of housing Travellers'. Such statements emerged as a defence to accusations of neglect and discrimination by the local authorities against Travellers by voluntary organisations or local clergy.[142] Travellers were depicted as ungrateful when they made complaints or whenever complaints were made on their behalf. The persistence of a Traveller problem was represented as one that was caused by past and present generosity. As put by one councillor in 1995, who over the previous fifteen years or so had opposed all moves to develop provision for Travellers:

> Clare had done more than its fair share for Travellers in the past. And what have they done in return? They have wrecked group-housing schemes and they have wrecked the halting sites we have given them. This council is being kicked in the teeth even though it has done the most for Travellers.[143]

The argument that the local authorities could be expected to do no more was first articulated in the 1970s.[144] It continued to be made in various ways during the following decade. In 1982, for example, a councillor stated that the local authorities were 'too good to itinerants in Ennis'.[145] As put earlier by another councillor in 1974, the good people in Ennis had borne the brunt 'as regards accepting itinerants'.[146] The County Council should now 'look for some other towns in the county to take their share of itinerants in the Ennis area'. On another occasion another councillor claimed that because Ennis was a progressive town in its treatment of Travellers they were moving in from all over Ireland. 'They are playing on Ennis', he said.

Travellers as outsiders

Councillors frequently represented all unaccommodated Travellers on the roadsides in and around Ennis as outsiders. Arguments that Travellers living on the roadsides were outsiders were used from the 1970s to justify efforts to exclude them from the town. However, opposition to Traveller exclusion from the 1970s increasingly focused upon arguments that many of these Travellers had been born in and had grown up in Ennis. It was argued on many occasions that many of those living on the roadsides around the town were Ennis people being deprived of a home in their own town. Such arguments were used to contest discrimination in housing allocation from the mid-1980s. The contestation of such discrimination and of Traveller exclusion from the town resulted in some general acceptance that some of the Travellers were indeed local. For example, local media accounts of the objections of Travellers to the Drumcliffe site from the mid-1980s repeated arguments that many of the Travellers were Ennis people.

These claims were denied by some councillors who continued to falsely depict all Travellers on the roadsides as outsiders.[147] The term 'transient' came to be used in discussions of non-indigenous Travellers. Arguments that the local authorities had no responsibility to provide housing for transients persisted in discussions during the 1990s of the statutory requirement to prepare a Traveller accommodation plan. Transients were frequently described as an influx or as having flooded into Ennis and Clare within a discourse, which was quite, similar to that used to describe asylum seekers as 'illegal immigrants' from the late 1990s. It was increasingly argued that Travellers on the roadsides had come from England. This was certainly the case to some extent as many local Travellers had immigrated to Britain, as did many local settled people during the decade of high emigration that preceded the late 1990s. In the case of the Travellers some of these had been temporarily displaced by anti-Traveller hostility in the town during the mid-1980s. An argument emerged that any measures to provide for local Travellers would result in transients coming from abroad to take advantage of the generosity of the town. This was a variation of earlier claims that any provision to meet the needs of Travellers in Clare would result in the county being exploited by outsiders.

For example in 1972 a local senator argued that 'the rejects from other counties as far away as Kilkenny were coming to Clare'.[148] In June 1982 a councillor, who persistently opposed provision for Travellers in Clare, explained the presence of Travellers on the roadsides by stating that there were 'good pickings' in Ennis.[149] He used the outsider argument to claim that there were 'very few native Travellers left unhoused in Clare' and, as such, it was the responsibility of other local authorities to provide accommodation for them. Another councillor, at the same meeting, accused the Itinerant Settlement Committee of 'inviting strange Travellers into the area'.[150] Discussion of a proposed 'crackdown' on Travellers living on the roadside around this time (it was proposed to prosecute families living in Ennis) was accompanied by claims from the Assistant County manager that 'no town in Ireland had done better than Ennis in helping itinerants and no county better than Clare'.[151] In 1991 a councillor argued that Ennis would become a 'tinkers' town' if it made the maximum use of the money available for the provision of halting sites to Travellers.[152] He claimed that there had been an influx of non-indigenous Travellers to the town each time a new housing scheme was under construction.

These arguments were internalised to some extent by Travellers themselves. They were invoked by Ennis Travellers to claim rights as local citizens to local authority services. Local Travellers and the voluntary sector, on occasion, argued that only families native to the area should be accommodated.[153] These arguments were also bound up with an ongoing county-level chauvinism characterised by arguments that planning regulations should favour local people and by resistance to efforts by Limerick Corporation to extend the city boundary into Clare.[154] In 1997 the County manager was reported in the *Clare Champion* as promising that Clare would not become 'a haven for transient Travellers'. He said the mooted accommodation plan for Travellers would only include those who had already settled in the county prior to the 1996 census.[155] The chairman of Ennis Urban District Council opposed the accommodation plan because, he claimed, it would attract an influx of non-indigenous Travellers to Ennis. As he put it; 'There is a perception in the north and in England that "in Clare we care". Maybe it is time for us to be a little less caring.'[156]

Claims that Travellers were outsiders were arguably fostered by the segregation which existed between Travellers and settled people in the Ennis area. By contrast, some communal bonds between Travellers and settled people could be noted in some of the smaller towns in the county. For example, there were no campaigns against Travellers in Ennistymon between 1963 and the end of 1999. A Kilrush UDC debate on Travellers in 1982 demonstrated little of the hostility that generally characterised debates in Ennis. Claims were made by some councillors that Travellers camping in the area were not from the town. These argued that, as such, no official site should be provided for them. These claims were refuted on the basis that the UDC recognised that some Travellers were indeed related to people living in the town.[157] In contrast to county council or Ennis UDC debates discussion in Kilrush was characterised by a general mood of open-mindedness. As stated by one councillor:

> They are entitled to live too. They spend money in the area. They are on all the bends in Tralee. They are not objected to there as the people know they only come along for a few weeks anyway ... what's wrong with the

docks area for them. Circuses come and are welcome ... these people are human beings and should not be treated as outcasts.[158]

These discussions by Kilrush UDC ranked among the few ever positive local authority discussions of Travellers recorded in the *Clare Champion* from 1963 to 1999. In large towns such as Ennis and Shannon racialised claims that Travellers were, by definition, outsiders retained the status of 'truth'.

The construction of Traveller dependency

The responses to Travellers that emerged from the 1960s onwards were characterised by paternalism. In time the voluntary sector became more responsive to the views of Travellers themselves but local authority debates on Travellers from 1963 to 1999 never considered that Travellers might have views. The need to formally consult Travellers was not discussed until the late 1990s and even then there was considerable resistance to such consultation taking place. Nevertheless Travellers sought to articulate their own views on accommodation and other issues. Such articulations were often ignored or met with expressions of anger from councillors and officials.

The views of Travellers were not sought in the development of assimilationist responses to their 'needs'. Initial voluntary efforts to provide accommodation for Travellers were paternalistic. An explicitly moral discourse emphasised the need to focus on 'deserving cases'.[159] Over time, however, the voluntary sector became increasingly critical of the injustices faced by Travellers and acquired an advocacy role on behalf of Travellers and by degree it abandoned assimilationist aspirations. As the voluntary sector became more and more critical of the local authorities, the local authorities retorted that such groups lacked legitimacy because they were not representative of the community. This, unsurprisingly, was a notion of community that did not include Travellers.

By the 1980s, independent Traveller voices began to emerge. However, these tended to be ignored by councillors and officials. For example, in 1985 officials stated again and again (even under oath in court) that they were unaware of criticisms by Travellers of the Drumcliffe scheme, despite statements by Travellers on many occasions. Councillors and officials denied the authenticity of Traveller voices by arguing that they had been put to whatever objections they were making by the voluntary sector. Travellers were, in effect, denied agency within the anti-Traveller politics of exclusion. This led to frequent and ill-conceived attempts to press the voluntary sector to regulate Traveller behaviour and to take a form of parental responsibility for them. Such efforts were understandable given

the emphasis upon social control that existed within the Traveller settlement movement from the outset. In this context Traveller activism, such
as the opposition which emerged among Travellers to the Drumcliffe site,
was blamed on the voluntary sector. In 1987 a senior local authority official
castigated the local voluntary sector for fermenting discontent among
Travellers. As reported in the *Clare Champion*: 'It was clear his remarks
were aimed at what he called do-gooders allegedly concerned with the
issue and he told them in no uncertain terms that if they followed the
Christian example set by the local authority – instead of trying to undermine public confidence in the council – the issue would be nigh solved at
this stage'.[160] On another occasion, at a local government conference, these
'unChristian do-gooders' were identified by a councillor as the clergy,
nuns and social services working with Travellers in Ennis.[161]

The oppression of Travellers' voices

If it was difficult for voluntary groups to contest the oppression of Travellers, it was even more difficult for Travellers to do so themselves. In 1981
Travellers who complained about refuse collection at a local authority
meeting were praised by councillors and officials who noted that this
was the first time that Travellers had participated in a local authority
discussion of Traveller issues.[162] Such participation was very infrequent
for a number of reasons. One of these was that local authority meetings
were characterised by overt expressions of hostility towards Travellers on
an ongoing basis. Most accounts of anti-Traveller hostility from 1963 to
1999 recorded in the *Clare Champion* were drawn from the proceedings of
such meetings. Travellers, as a small minority, lacked political power.[163]
However, they had increasingly become involved in community development work, organising training projects, and arts projects and youth
clubs.[164] They organised events aimed at highlighting Traveller homelessness. For example, in 1987 Ennis Young Travellers undertook a survey
of homelessness in their own area and submitted the results, along with
those from other parts of the country to the minister of the environment.

From the mid-1980s Travellers contested housing discrimination in a
number of ways. In 1984 the Ennis Travellers Training Centre published
accounts by young Travellers of prejudice and discrimination in the
Ennis area. One account discussed how Travellers were not welcome in
most pubs and could never be sure of admittance to local dances. Others
argued that assimilation was unrealistic and that there was the need to
consult Travellers. As put by one Traveller writer: 'Travellers have a right
to be seated around every table where decisions affecting their lives are
being taken'.[165]

These arguments were reported positively in a number of articles in the *Clare Champion*.[166] One of these in 1985 noted that a musical group of young Travellers from Ennis would be 'making their mark' in an appearance on the aforementioned *Late Late Show*.[167] This television programme offered a rare media platform which was used by Ennis Travellers in the audience to criticise the proposal to accommodate Travellers at Drumcliffe and the actions of the official in charge of Traveller accommodation. Councillors and officials in Clare were angered by the criticisms of Travellers and they subsequently passed a resolution that officials write to the *Late Late Show* to demand that the allegations of the Travellers be retracted. The compère of the programme, Gay Byrne, advised them against overreaction. He wrote in his reply of a 'danger that the council members may over-react and in demanding official corrections may be seen to be anti-itinerant or generally hostile or may indeed be using an elephant gun to shoot gnats'.[168]

The Travellers who appeared on the programme were accused by councillors of mounting a conspiracy against the use of the 'magnificent halting site in Drumcliffe'.[169] One councillor alleged that the Travellers were being 'primed by people who were supposed to be concerned with the settlement of itinerants.' Individual Travellers on occasion contested prejudicial statements by councillors.[170] For example, in 1991 the *Clare Champion* reported the responses of a Traveller 'whose address is a caravan somewhere in Ennis' to allegations that there was an influx of non-indigenous Travellers into the town. He stated that indigenous families who were forced to move by Ennis UDC and Clare County Council to other towns and cities and to England had returned with the hope that the house or site for which they had waited many years would at last be available. He told the *Clare Champion* 'that he and his wife lived in houses with their parents prior to their marriage and he said they were currently in need of a home in the Ennis area'. As he put it:

> Why should my family and I have to go to an unsuitable site or to any other town or foreign country? All Ennis Urban Council have done so far for us is to take me to court for illegal parking, have me fined and then put me in prison when I could not pay. This carry on is very annoying to say the least. Our oldest child should be at school every day but it is not possible in our present circumstances.[171]

In 1997 another Traveller, a man who had lived in Ennis for twenty-two years, successfully sued a publican who had refused to serve him. When he asked why he was refused the publican had replied 'the citizens', which he took to mean he was being refused because the other customers would object. The court revoked the publican's licence which was then restored when the publican apologised to him.[172] The judge also delivered a strong criticism of the local bar. Local solicitors had refused to represent the Traveller in the case and the Traveller had to go to Gort to obtain a solicitor.[173] The solicitor who took the case was congratulated for 'his brave public spirit'.

Conclusion

In 1963 a District Court judge in Ennis, the largest town in the county, likened the nature and extent of exclusion faced by Travellers in Irish society to that of apartheid.[174] More recently the term 'ethnic cleansing' has been used to describe the nature of exclusion faced by Travellers.[175] Such terms, and the term 'pogrom', each capture some essence of the processes of exclusion faced by Travellers in Clare. As put by the judge, they 'were booted from town to town and place to place and got little chance to live from the people'. In the late 1960s efforts emerged to provide accommodation for Travellers. These were undermined by a persistent hostility among settled people to the presence of Travellers in their communities. In essence, such communities vehemently rejected efforts to assimilate Travellers as much if not more so than the Travellers themselves did. Accommodation schemes were shaped by political expediency and ameliorated by the demands of opponents. They were ill-suited to the needs of Travellers.

Political hostility against Travellers was justified in a number of ways within a racialised discourse that depicted them as a deviant and violent underclass. Travellers were constructed as a threat to the dominant community by local politicians on an ongoing basis within a racist discourse that had some similarities with the 'new racism' associated with Enoch Powell in Britain. If there was no reference to 'rivers of blood', there were plenty of apocalyptic references to 'explosive situations' and 'fuses that have been lit' by decisions to permit Travellers to live in Ennis. Councillors and officials played a pivotal role in articulating such racism. Few local authority debates on Traveller issues were reported between 1963 and 1999 without central prominence been given to vehement anti-Traveller statements.

The term 'new racism' emerged in an attempt to explain a racist discourse against black and minority ethnic groups in Britain which was not grounded in claims that such groups were biologically inferior. It was a sophisticated discourse with many levels. At the apex, politicians opposed to the presence of such minorities could deny racism (of course we don't believe that black people are inferior) but at the same time pursue racist goals of exclusion within an anecdotal discourse which represented the imagined grievances of the (white) community against black people.[176] This might be understood as a response to a prohibition of 'race' talk in public space.[177] Anti-Traveller racism in Clare local politics might be understood as unfettered by comparison. Open hostility by councillors and officials from the 1960s onwards was virtually uncontested until the 1990s when occasional requests for moderate language were made. There were few objections to anti-Traveller tirades at local authority meetings until the late 1990s. Instead, racialised accusations which emerged at these meetings were reproduced as truths the local media and subsequently repeated by councillors, by officials, by residents groups and in public discourse to provide justifications for the exclusion of Travellers. Expressions of anti-Traveller racism in Clare were never concealed, as they were arguably within the 'new racism' in Britain, behind the political expediency of having to deny holding blatantly racist views.

The claims, which were mobilised to justify anti-Traveller discrimination in Clare, were often shrill fictions that could only be sustained through acceptance of hegemonic racialised 'understandings' of Travellers. It cannot be denied that grounds for conflict existed between residents and Travellers. The presence of Travellers in a nearby camp or roadside might be understood as a negative externality; a burden in land use planning terms similar to the loss of some local amenity or overdevelopment.[178] Residents often complained that the presence of Travellers would, in effect, constitute a planning blight, by claiming that the price of houses would fall if Travellers moved into an area. These claims were bound up with some understanding of a societal consensus that the presence of Travellers was a bad thing. However, such 'rational' grounds for opposing the presence of Travellers were compounded by anti-Traveller hostility that could be understood as a hatred of them rather than frustration about the nuisance caused by their presence. Racialised accounts of the threat of Traveller violence offered a means of articulating anti-Traveller hostility even if such accounts were patently untrue. The allegations of violence by Travellers against settled people put forward by residents were never specific. Only a few distinct allegations were documented in the *Clare Champion* over almost four decades. Exaggerated claims of violence by Travellers against settled people were mobilised as an essential truth so as to justify the exclusion of Travellers from Ennis.

It is argued that the spatial exclusion of Travellers and discrimination in the allocation of local authority housing was often justified by racialised accounts of Traveller deviancy and violence. These drew upon claims about past transgressions by Travellers rather than specific events. This history was invoked to suggest that the settled community and the local authorities were the victims of Travellers. It contrasted with an actual history of unremitting spatial exclusion and anti-Traveller hostility. This goal of exclusion persisted in so far as efforts to provide accommodation for Travellers remained politically unfeasible despite, statutory obligations to provide such accommodation. By the end of the century a top-down national project of integration, exemplified by the *Report of the Task Force on the Travelling People* (1995) remained unreconciled with the persistence of a politics of exclusion among the local authorities to whom 'the Traveller problem' had been devolved. The role of the state in the persistence of anti-Traveller racism is examined in the next chapter.

Notes

1 J. Barry, B. Herity and S. Solan, *The Travellers Health Status Study* (Dublin: Health Research Board, 1989).

2 N. Crowley, 'Travellers and Social Policy', in S. Quin, P. Kennedy, A. O'Donnell and G. Keily (eds), *Contemporary Irish Social Policy* (Dublin: University College Dublin Press, 1999), pp. 243–65.

3 The accounts of the views or statements of councillors, officials, residents and Travellers in this chapter are referenced by the date of the issue of the *Clare Champion* in which these appeared. As such, these generally occurred in the preceding week. Hereafter, these are referred to by date.

4 14 June 1991; 10 October 1997; 19 October 1998.

5 6 December 1964.

6 It was agreed that Clare County Council, in conjunction with Limerick County Council, Limerick City Corporation and Tipperary North Riding Council would request the minister of defence to make the site available and it was agreed that costs should be shared between the four local authorities (18 June 1966).

7 6 June 1964.

8 18 June 1966.

9 Senator D. P. Honan.

10 As late as 1987 an anticipated motion before Limerick Corporation for the use of Knockalisheen as a halting site was opposed by a number of politicians in Clare. As put by one of these: 'rounding up all Limerick's Itinerant families and putting them into 30 acres of Clare land is inhuman and stupid'. However, the main objection was to accommodating Limerick Travellers in Clare.

11 9 December 1967.

12 The following definition of rehabilitation was offered at the 1973 AGM of the Ennis Itinerant Settlement Committee: 'The word rehabilitation, or correctly habitation, is used very broadly and in the case of the travellers it means helping and supporting them while they grow accustomed to their new way of

life. This is a very gradual process and we must be very patient' (7 December 1973).

13 4 January 1969.
14 9 December 1967.
15 22 February 1969.
16 Tigins, from the Irish for 'little houses', were envisaged as the principal form of accommodation to be used in the initial settlement of Travellers. The tigin featured in the logo of the settlement movement.
17 *Clare Champion* (1963–99).
18 9 January 1971.
19 18 January 1969.
20 15 February 1969.
21 22 February 1969.
22 22 February 1969.
23 3 May 1969.
24 11 October 1969.
25 17 June 1972.
26 7 November 1970.
27 The committee ran a campaign in 1972 which began with a newspaper advertisement which ran for a three months: 'Wanted urgently; shelter for fifty children born in Ennis, living in sub-human conditions on the road-side. Do you care enough to help?'.
28 17 October 1970.
29 17 June 1972.
30 5 December 1970.
31 22 February 1969; 17 November 1970.
32 4 June 1972.
33 17 July 1972.
34 17 July 1972.
35 17 July 1972.
36 17 July 1972.
37 26 June 1971.
38 26 June 1972; 14 July 1972.
39 26 June 1971.
40 29 March 1974; 11 June 1976; 9 December 1977; 7 August 1982; 9 March 1984.
41 13 February 1971.
42 15 February 1974.
43 For example, in 1972 three Travellers were fined a total of IR£40 for allowing their horses to wander on the roads for a number of nights. At the time a return train journey from Ennis to Dublin cost IR£3.00 (15 January 1972).
44 20 January 1984.
45 In 1984 an official reported that the local authorities were responsible for twenty unaccommodated indigenous families in the area (7 December 1984).
46 13 May 1988.
47 11 June 1976.
48 31 October 1970.
49 21 October 1977.
50 7 August 1982.
51 29 March 1974.

52 17 January 1974.

53 10 January 1986.

54 The only exceptions were four babies in one photograph of an Irish Child-birth Trust event and the individual members, all children, of a group of carol singers in another group photograph (10 January 1986).

55 22 February 1974.

56 5 March 1976.

57 Travellers have been noted to avoid places where deaths of family members occurred. In common with many Gypsy and Traveller cultures, 'the standard way of coming to terms with a bereavement is to move away' (see A. Binchy, 'Travellers' Language: A Sociolinguistic Perspective', in M. McCann, S. O'Siochain and S. Ruane (eds), *Irish Travellers: Culture and Identity* (Belfast: Institute of Irish Studies, 1996), pp. 134–54).

58 24 June 1983.

59 16 March 1984.

60 A group of about eighty residents asked for some compromise on the proposals but no concessions were offered (9 March 1984).

61 17 May 1985.

62 24 May 1984.

63 13 March 1985.

64 The assistant county secretary stated that, 'he was not aware of any large-scale objections to the site. He understood that one or two families had expressed reservations' (13 May 1985).

65 13 May 1985.

66 13 May 1985.

67 16 May 1984.

68 13 May 1985.

69 As put in a statement by the Ennis Travellers Committee: 'faced with court fines and heavy legal costs and fearful of being moved forcibly to Drumcliffe, the Travellers began to move out' (17 May 1985).

70 *Ibid.*

71 9 August 1985.

72 10 January 1986.

73 7 February 1987.

74 The lack of a site management agreement was cited by the County manager as the reason why various disruptions and vandalism had occurred (20 May 1994).

75 This was explained as the result of a feud between Traveller families, dating back more than thirty years (13 December 1996).

76 21 January 1997.

77 4 January 1997.

78 This included picketing of county council offices and alleged intimidation of council staff seeking to inspect a proposed site (23 March 1996).

79 1 March 1996; 22 March 1996; 16 May 1997.

80 27 February 1987.

81 25 September 1981.

82 2 January 1998.

83 Report by the chairman of the National Council of Settlement Committees (3 March 1976).

84 12 November 1982.
85 15 November 1985.
86 Statement by Ennis Committee for Travelling People (20 February 1987).
87 20 February 1987.
88 20 February 1987.
89 Letter quoted in the *Clare Champion* (27 February 1987).
90 3 April 1987; 27 October 1987.
91 27 May 1988.
92 8 July 1988.
93 13 May 1988.
94 For example, both councillors stated that they opposed allowing further families to be housed on Cloughleigh in Ennis (13 May 1988).
95 4 October 1991.
96 18 March 1994.
97 25 March 1994.
98 4 October 1994.
99 25 April 1997.
100 4 April 1997.
101 27 June 1997.
102 27 June 1997.
103 9 January 1998.
104 2 May 1997.
105 20 June 1997.
106 4 July 1997.
107 1 August 1997.
108 4 July 1997.
109 16 May 1997.
110 4 July 1997; 10 October 1997.
111 A prediction that the plan would be deferred pending the 1999 local government elections was made by a councillor who was a member of the Traveller Accommodation Advisory Committee following newspaper coverage of the threat of hostility by residents to such a plan. The view that it should be deferred was shared by a number of councillors (19 September 1998).
112 17 September 1999.
113 17 September 1999.
114 29 October 1999.
115 8 January 1999.
116 21 September 1997.
117 13 May 1988.
118 17 July 1972; 12 December 1982.
119 Only a few specific allegations of violence by Travellers against settled people in Clare were recorded in the *Clare Champion* (1963–99). These, with one exception, related to evidence given by the Gardaí that Travellers had resisted arrest. The exception was an account of a court case against a Traveller who had detained a settled woman in a field without touching her. It was described in the article as a 'case of rape'. The Traveller was sentenced to three years in prison (7 December 1963).
120 12 April 1996.
121 12 April 1996.

122 21 October 1977; 25 June 1982.

123 Interview with a former resident.

124 4 June 1996.

125 2 July 1982.

126 13 November 1992.

127 13 November 1992.

128 12 November 1982.

129 12 December 1997.

130 2 August 1985.

131 The Gardaí told the court that the witness found it hard to identify any local people who were involved (2 August 1985).

132 9 January 1987.

133 13 November 1992.

134 6 February 1987.

135 9 May 1991.

136 He stated, 'we all know about the problems at Drumcliffe and I have a sneaking suspicion that you have the worst of the travelling community in Ireland there' (20 December 1996).

137 14 July 1972.

138 20 December 1996.

139 26 December 1964.

140 For example, arguments that parking of caravans was very unsightly on tourist routes (22 October 1982).

141 9 May 1991.

142 In February 1989 the Catholic Bishop, Dr Harty, gave a sermon which urged greater acceptance of minority groupings like Travellers. A number of councillors interpreted this as a criticism of the UDC. One councillor said at a UDC meeting that she had squirmed in her seat during the sermon. Another councillor stated that he found the bishop's remarks personally insulting and ill-informed (3 February 1989).

143 3 November 1995.

144 22 April 1974.

145 30 April 1982.

146 22 April 1974.

147 In 1984 an official reported that the local authorities were responsible for twenty unaccommodated indigenous families in the area (7 December 1984).

148 26 February 1972.

149 30 April 1982.

150 25 June 1982.

151 30 April 1982.

152 9 May 1991.

153 21 January 1997.

154 This has been an ongoing saga for decades. Efforts by Limerick Corporation in 1987 to accommodate Limerick Travellers over the county line in the Knockalisheen army camp were resisted in this spirit. A Clare TD who opposed the proposal expressed the underlying county-level chauvinism in the following terms: 'We in Clare have a great reputation for solving our own problems'.

155 10 October 1997.

156 12 December 1997.

157 22 October 1982.

158 17 September 1982.

159 23 December 1967.

160 3 April 1987.

161 B. Fanning (2000) 'Asylum Seekers, Travellers and Racism', *Doctrine and Life*, 50(6) (2000), pp. 358–66.

162 25 September 1981.

163 An article prior to the 1991 local elections noted that approximately one hundred Travellers were registered voters in Ennis. The article commented that Travellers were unlikely to vote for two candidates. Both of these 'had taken hard line attitudes on the Traveller Question'. One topped the polls on a number of occasions. Both have served as chairperson of Ennis UDC (14 June 1991).

164 20 July 1984; 12 June 1987.

165 20 July 1984.

166 These invariably appeared on the Ennis news page and contrasted vividly with lengthy, more prominent and usually front-page articles reporting the anti-Traveller statements of councillors, officials and residents.

167 29 March 1985.

168 24 May 1985.

169 26 April 1985.

170 16 March 1984; 10 May 1991.

171 11 May 1991.

172 26 September 1998.

173 20 October 1998.

174 7 December 1963.

175 M. Mac an Ghaill, *Contemporary Racisms and Ethnicities* (Buckingham: Open University Press, 1999), p. 71

176 For example, A. Brown, '"The Other Day I Met a Constituent of Mine": A Theory of Anecdotal Racism', *Ethnic and Racial Studies*, 22(1) (1999), pp. 23–55.

177 *Ibid.*, p. 23.

178 K. Cox defines externalities as uncompensated welfare impacts or costs which will be borne by those within the immediate area of development. It is this lack of compensation and a resulting sense of injustice which is seen to result in controversy (*Urbanisation and Conflict in Market Societies* (London: Maarouf Press, 1978), p. 110).

7

Legacies of anti-Traveller racism

This chapter examines changes in responses by the state to Travellers from the establishment of a Commission on Itinerancy in 1960. If assimilation was the ideal, the reality, exemplified by the kinds of local politics described in the previous chapter, was the ongoing segregation of Travellers from the wider community. This chapter documents the intergenerational persistence of Traveller segregation, poverty and experiences of discrimination against the backdrop of shifts in government policy. It also describes campaigns to have Travellers recognised as a distinct ethnic group. The case for Traveller ethnicity emphasised the distinctiveness of Traveller ways of life, even as these changed from generation to generation. It was made as a means of securing recognition of the racism experienced by Travellers. Travellers became so recognised in Northern Ireland and the United Kingdom and organisations such as the Equality Authority and the National Consultative Committee on Racism and Interculturalism (NCCRI); key figures in both of these had previously worked for Traveller organisations. However, the mainstream of the Irish state has long resisted according ethnic status to Travellers, or 'travellers' as these have been generally referred to in lower-case. Traveller-led and human rights organisations in Ireland and international anti-racism and human rights bodies have variously argued that the denial of Traveller ethnicity has fostered a denial of anti-Traveller racism by the Irish state.

On Monday 28 June 2010 the RTE current affairs programme *Frontline* broadcast a 'special programme on travellers'; RTE online materials about the programme declined to use upper-case.[1] The picked audience consisted of Travellers and people hostile to Travellers including councillors and journalists. The panel of speakers on the programme included the sociologist Niamh Hourigan who described the set-up in the following terms: 'Beforehand all the Travellers were kept in one hospitality room, all the anti-Traveller types in another and I was in a room on my own watching the World Cup! The set-up seemed to be designed to create a Jerry Springer type atmosphere.'[2] In debating the barriers faced by Travellers in twenty-first century Ireland a Jerry Springer atmosphere is hard to avoid, even in the staid environment of the university. Otherwise reasonable settled people feel entitled to openly express anger and hostility towards Travellers in everyday discourse and on the airwaves. My attempt to explain policies of recruiting ethnic minority police in American cities to social work students back in 2001, by asking them to imagine those being recruited were Travellers, resulted in the class bursting into incredulous laughter. More recently, in 2010 a class I taught on Travellers and social policy was interrupted a number of times by shouts of 'knacker' and other pejorative terms for Travellers, from students outside the door of the lecture theatre. Anti-Traveller racism in Irish society is difficult to deal with but easy to exploit whether for political gain or as media entertainment.

During the *Frontline* debate various settled people insisted that Travellers did not constitute an ethnic minority and disparaged claims that Travellers had a distinct culture. How this has become the position of the Irish state is addressed later in the chapter. Among the most vehement deniers of Traveller ethnicity on *Frontline* was an Enniscorthy councillor who claimed that the presence of Traveller tenants on local authority estates was leading to 'ethnic cleansing' of the local population. Yet, the programme highlighted some positive stories of young Travellers who had managed to embark on careers or third-level education despite extensive obstacles. But there was also considerable discussion of violence and feuds among Travellers. For all that the programme rehearsed the contours of past debates on the issue – Travellers' claiming cultural distinctiveness and describing experiences of discrimination, settled commentators denying Traveller ethnic distinctiveness and highlighting crime and anti-social behaviour among Travellers – it nevertheless emphasised many of the legacies of Traveller exclusion discussed in this chapter.

Shifting responses to Travellers

The economic 'take-off' that began in the late 1950s changed Ireland from a predominantly rural to a predominantly urban society.[3] It also resulted in the displacement of the Travelling People, Ireland's largest ethnic minority, from their precarious niche in rural society. Prior to the 1960s, the position of the Travelling community in relation to the dominant settled community was characterised by gradual economic and social closure. By the 1960s, the economic and social displacement of Travellers had occurred to an extent sufficient to precipitate overt policies of assimilation by the state. The terms of reference of the Commission on

Itinerancy established in 1960, for example, envisaged the solution to 'the problem arising from the presence in the country of itinerants in considerable numbers' in the following terms:

(a) to promote their absorption into the general community (b) pending such absorption, to reduce to a minimum the disadvantages to themselves and to the community resulting from their itinerant habits.

Travellers were depicted as a problem for Irish society. Their cultural distinctiveness became depicted, within a highly racialised discourse of Traveller deviance and inferiority, as justification for spatial exclusion and discrimination. Within the dominant discourses of the time Travellers were not to have equal rights to welfare unless they first ceased to be Travellers. The price of social citizenship, within the assimilationist logic of the social policies which emerged to address the 'problem of itinerancy' included the surrendering of identity and difference.[4] The reports of the *Commission on Itinerancy* (1963), *The Report of the Travelling People Review Body* (1983) and *The Report of the Task Force on the Travelling People* (1995) reveal shifting official responses to Travellers. One account of these shifts might be summarised as follows:

- a shift from depicting Travellers themselves as a problem experienced by 'normal' people (i.e. the settled community) to depicting the problem in terms of the relationship between Traveller and settled communities with, by 1995, some emphasis on discrimination against Travellers by the settled community;
- a growing acceptance that Travellers have a distinct culture and, by 1995, acknowledgement that this culture is not inferior to that of the dominant community. In 1963 the implication that Travellers' 'lifestyle' was inferior made assimilation a legitimate policy goal. By 1983 they were recognised as an identifiable group within Irish society but their distinctiveness was regarded as an expression of individual choice within a narrow interpretation of the meaning of culture. The 1995 report recommended that Traveller cultural distinctiveness should be supported by public policy.

The *Report of the Review Body* (1983) acknowledged the failure of earlier assimilationist responses to Travellers yet persisted in advocating assimilation as the solution. This was fostered by a narrow interpretation of the cultural distinctiveness of Travellers.[5] The report depicted cultural difference as an expression of individual choice rather than in terms of collective rights. It was argued that the extent to which Travellers would integrate with the settled community would depend on individual decisions by them and not on decisions by Travellers as a whole or of any group of them. This, in effect, denied the structural inequalities which precipitated and maintained the exclusion of Travellers in Irish society. The report emphasised a form of integration designed to support Travellers adapting to the settled 'norm'. The nomadic way of life, identified by Travellers as an important part of their cultural identity, was not seen as warranting support.[6]

The *Report of the Task Force* (1995) placed a strong emphasis on addressing inequalities encountered by Travellers. It contained more that 400 recommendations, most of which dealt in some way with the mechanics of exclusion experienced by Travellers in areas such as education, accommodation and health care. It was unequivocal about the existence of widespread prejudice and discrimination against Travellers within Irish society:

> The 'Settled' community will also have to accept that their rejection of Travellers is counter-productive and that incidents of social exclusion and discrimination against the Traveller community, such as the refusal of service in hotels, public houses and other establishments and the segregation of Travellers in the provision of facilities, must end.[7]

The *Report of the Task Force* (1995) interpreted the meaning of culture, and hence the cultural distinctiveness of Travellers, more broadly than the 1983 report but stopped short of recognising claims by Travellers that they constituted an ethnic minority. Consequently, it placed little emphasis on examining the discriminations and exclusions encountered by Travellers as manifestations of racism. Nevertheless, the report contained a few references to racism.[8] One of these acknowledged the role of anti-racism skills in work taking place to improve relationships between Travellers and the settled community. The Task Force recommended that 'modules on Traveller issues and anti-racism' be developed for public servants. Another recommendation referred to guidelines on 'race reporting' for journalists. Yet, there was no explicit acknowledgement that Travellers experienced racism.

The absence of an emphasis upon racism, or related conceptual approaches to prejudice related discrimination, left the Task Force with few tools for addressing discrimination. In this context it was difficult for the Task Force to move beyond interpretations of Traveller marginalisation set out in earlier reports. The Task Force represented prejudice and discrimination as counter-productive and unreasonable. The use of such language, in the absence of a critique of anti-Traveller racism in Irish society, suggested an appeal to the dominant community for mercy or charity. This was framed in such a manner as to indicate that this was a matter that was in their best interests to address but one where they had the final choice whether to do so or not.

Table 7.1 Shifting perspectives in official reports on Travellers

	Report of the Commission on Itinerancy (1963)	Report of the Review Body (1983)	Report of the Task Force (1995)
Membership	A judge Farmers' representative Garda representative A county manager Doctors Civil servants No representation or inclusion of Travellers	Doctors County managers Civil servants were on the Review Body Representatives of Tenants Associations replaced farmers (reflecting urbanisation) Bodies involved in the settlement and education of Travellers The National Council for Travelling People (not run by Travellers)	Representatives of organisations consisting of and run by Travellers (Pavee Point and the Irish Travellers Movement) Less representation from the voluntary sector than before No tenants and farmers Civil servants and representatives of the political parties
Sample terms of reference	To promote their absorption into the general community Pending such absorption, to reduce to a minimum the disadvantages to themselves and to the community resulting from their itinerant habits	'To review current policies and services for the Travelling people and to make recommendations to improve the existing situation'	To advise on the needs of Travellers and on government policy generally in relation to Travellers To explore the possibilities for developing mechanisms to enable Travellers to participate in decisions affecting their lifestyle and environment
Explanation of inequalities experienced by Travellers	Resulting from deviance and cultural inferiority	Poverty resulting from nomadism and lack of adaptation to settled ways of life	Discrimination resulting from hostility against Travellers by the 'settled' majority Hostility, in part explained by actions of some Travellers (1995: 61)
Response	Rehabilitation and assimilation: 'It is not considered that there is any alternative to a positive drive for housing itinerants if a permanent solution to the problem of itinerancy, based on absorption and integration, is to be achieved' (1963: 62)	Mediation and assimilation: emphasis on 'the way in which barriers of mistrust between the settled and travelling communities can be broken down and mutual respect for each others' way of life increased' (1983: 3)	Mediation and integration: some emphasis upon contesting anti-Traveller prejudice A reluctance to acknowledge this prejudice as racism related to a reluctance to regard Travellers as an ethnic minority

Minority report

All three reports represented accommodations between interest groups represented on the bodies that prepared them (Table 7.1). The *Report of the Task Force* (1995), unlike the earlier reports, included representatives from Traveller organisations. Their influence was acknowledged in an account of how perspectives on Travellers set out in the report differed from those contained in previous reports. This account also pointed to conflicts between the perspectives of Traveller organisations and others represented on the Task Force:

> A shift in focus has taken place, from a welfare approach inspired by charity to a more rights based approach inspired by a partnership process, in seeking to improve the living circumstances and general welfare of Travellers.
>
> There is an increase, that is both quantitative and qualitative, in Traveller participation in Traveller organisations. This increase is related to the more developmental approaches and work methods that have evolved within Traveller organisations.
>
> The recognition of the importance of concepts of culture, ethnicity, racism and discrimination has entered the debate about the situation of Travellers. This has resulted in a redefinition of the Traveller situation in terms of cultural rights as opposed to simply being a poverty issue.
>
> The emergence of a range of more conflictual relationships with statutory bodies is evident. These relationships were preceded by an earlier consensus around a welfare agenda. The present thrust is now towards a new partnership based on a common understanding of the cultural rights of Travellers and of the urgent need to response to the situation of Travellers.[9]

Traveller perspectives were particularly in conflict with those of Task Force members who were local government councillors and officials. A minority report, signed by four of its eighteen members, was set out as an appendix to the main report. It reiterated many of the assimilationist perspectives of the 1963 and 1983 reports. It is worth noting that three of the authors of the minority report were councillors and one was a local government official. They arguably reflected a constituency within which, as explored in the previous chapter, support for the provision of accommodation and other amenities for Travellers was often politically unfeasible. The minority report rejected the broader definition of culture employed by the Task Force. It identified the lifestyle of Travellers the cause of the disadvantage they experienced. The account of Travellers set out in the minority report depicted them as a deviant and transgressive underclass. It spoke of the 'failure of travellers and travellers organisations to recognise that today's society finds it difficult to accept a lower standard of conduct from a section of the community who consciously pursue a way of life which sets its members apart from ordinary citizens'.[10]

From this perspective it was argued that the hostility of the settled community to Travellers was justifiable. The minority report claimed that the 'vast majority of the settled community are appalled at the prospect of a traveller halting site next to them and the arrival of a group of travellers in an area usually provokes panic and fear among the settled community.'[11] In common with the 1963 report, it identified assimilation as the price of social membership and social inclusion. The minority report stated that 'it must be recognised that the traveller community, in common with any marginalised minority, cannot make the transition to full citizenship unless the majority population, whose values society reflects, makes the space available for than transition to take place'.[12] It opposed any measures to address the marginalisation of Travellers that challenged the effective veto of settled communities. The views set out in the minority report explained, to an extent, the resistance of the Task Force to recognising Traveller ethnicity.

Traveller ethnicity and anti-Traveller racism

The discourses on culture and ethnicity within the *Report of the Task Force* (1995) represented ideological conflicts between a dominant monoculturalism and a nascent Irish multiculturalism which owed much to the influence of Traveller organisations. This conflict was marked, at a semantic level, by the use of upper-case references to 'Travellers' in the main report, and lower-case references to 'travellers' within the minority report. A number of reports by Travellers organisations, in the years prior to the publication of the *Report of the Task Force* (1995), argued that Travellers were an ethnic group. Such claims sought to contest dominant representations of Irish society as homogenous and to contest prevalent racialisations of Travellers as a deviant minority. They identified anti-Traveller prejudice as racism. However, Traveller claims of ethnicity met with strong resistance and rebuttal in the years preceding the publication of the Task Force report.[13] The ongoing opposition to Traveller ethnicity within this context was exemplified by an article about a survey conducted by Amnesty International of racism in Ireland by the *Irish Times* columnist John Waters in May 2001:

> To place Travellers in the 'racism equation' is a mistake to begin with as Travellers are not an ethnic group. According to the Amnesty survey, 40 percent of Irish people would be reluctant to welcome Travellers into

their area. Two things strike me about this: (1) it is a ludicrous under-estimate of the hostility towards Travellers; and (2) the question implies, against massive evidence, that objections to having Travellers as neigh-bours could result only from prejudice.[14]

In a reply article, Thomas McCann and Fintan Farrell, two workers with the Irish Traveller Movement, cited a UNESCO definition of racism as 'any theory involving the claim that racial or ethnic groups are inher-ently inferior'. They argued that the belief that the Traveller way of life is inferior to the 'sedentary' way of life has been central to responses to the needs of Travellers for decades. They contested an argument by Waters that anti-Traveller hostility was justified by also referring to the Amnesty International research. This found that although 42 per cent of Irish people were unfavourably disposed towards Travellers some three-quarters of Irish people did not know any Travellers. This notion of anti-Traveller prejudice without personal contact or relations with Travellers pointed to a racialisation of Travellers within Irish society which resembled forms of anti-Semitism in communities without Jews noted in Chapter 4.[15]

The *Report of Task Force* (1995) stated that Traveller nomadism, the Traveller language and the structure of the Traveller economy all provided visible or tangible markers of a distinct culture.[16] Traveller cultural distinc-tiveness was discussed at length in the report alongside case law from the United Kingdom which identified the Travellers as an ethnic minority. The Task Force had commissioned research on the use of legislation in the UK to protect the cultural rights of Travellers.[17] This found that the Travel-ling community could be regarded as an ethnic group under British law. The Task Force report argued that anti-discrimination law along British lines was capable of providing protection to the Travelling community especially if it was made explicit that ethnic groups were intended to benefit from protection afforded by the legislation.[18] It cited a UK court ruling from 1983 which offered a definition of ethnicity:

1 a long shared history, of which the groups is conscious as distin-guishing it from other groups, and the memory of which it keeps alive;

2 a cultural tradition of its own, including family and social customs and manners, often, but not necessarily associated with religious observance.

In addition to those two essential characteristics the following character-istics are, in my opinion relevant:

3 either common geographical origin or descent from a small number of common ancestors;

4 a common language, not necessarily peculiar to the group;
5 a common literature peculiar to the group;
6 a common religion different from that of neighbouring groups or from the general community surrounding it;
7 being a minority or being an oppressed or dominant group, for example a conquered people (say the inhabitants of England shortly after the Norman conquest) and their conquests might both be ethnic groups.[19]

The Task Force implicitly acknowledged Traveller ethnicity insofar as it considered that Travellers met the above criteria. However, this discussion was located within the chapter of the report that set out proposals to address discrimination rather than in the chapter on Traveller culture which assiduously avoided reference to ethnicity. The chapter on discrimination proposed the development of equality legislation modelled, to an extent, on the remedies arrived at by the British courts whereby a number of grounds on which discrimination would not be permissible would be set out. These would include membership of the Traveller community and race but not, as in Britain, ethnicity. Within the *Report of the Task Force* (1995), and within subsequent legislation, the rights of Travellers were set out on an exceptional basis that acknowledged them as a distinct community but not as an ethnic group. The Equal Status Act (2000) contained an explicit definition of the Traveller community:

'Traveller Community' means the community of people who are commonly called Travellers and who are identified (both by themselves and others) as people with a shared history, culture and traditions including, historically a nomadic way of life on the island of Ireland.

The recognition of Travellers as a special case rather than an ethnicity minority per se mirrored their categorisation within the census. Prior to 1996, census records of the Travelling community were based on determinations by enumerators as to whether those surveyed were or were not Travellers. This resulted in only those in halting sites and on the roadside being classified as Travellers and the underestimation of the Traveller population by approximately 100 per cent. The forthcoming census includes a question which will ask whether or not the person being surveyed is a Traveller. The rejection of proposals by Traveller groups for a question which asks respondents to identify their own ethnicity could be seen as part of the unresolved struggle for ethnic status. The rejection of a question on ethnicity also pointed to the persistence of ideological monoculturalism within state practices.

The persistence of discrimination

The *First Progress Report of the Committee to Monitor the Implementation of the Recommendations of the Task Force on the Travelling Community* (2000) was published five years after the launch of the *Report of the Task Force* (1995). It noted a 'lack of real improvement on the ground'. It reiterated and quoted the criticisms of responses to Travellers set out in a report published by the Economic and Social Research Institute (ERSI) in 1986 as still pertinent in the year 2000. The ERSI report states that the 'circumstances of the Irish Travelling people are intolerable. No decent or humane society, once made aware of such circumstances, could permit them to persist.'[20] The *Report of the Monitoring Committee* (2000) stated that the daily reality of discrimination made it very difficult for a large section of the Traveller community to have faith in the promises contained within the recommendations of the *Report of the Task Force* (1995).[21] The experiences of Travellers in the areas of health, education and accommodation, illustrate the failures of social policy in Ireland in addressing such circumstances.

Health inequalities and institutional racism

According to the *Traveller Health Status Study* (1989) Travellers lived on average 12 years fewer than their settled peers. Travellers were found to have significantly higher death rates for all causes. Traveller infant mortality rates for live births were found to be 18.1 per 1,000 in comparison with 7.4 per 1,000 for the population as a whole.[22] The study likened the life expectancies of Travellers to those of settled Irish people during the 1940s. There are no indications that disparities between the health of Travellers and the population as a whole have diminished in recent years.[23] The Primary Health Care for Travellers Project has identified poverty, poor accommodation and cultural stress resulting from discrimination and exclusion as causes of health inequalities experienced by Travellers.[24] These inequalities were described by Niall Crowley, the inaugural Director of the Equality Authority, as graphic evidence of institutional racism.[25] Even with the best of intentions policies and practices designed to serve some dominant notion of community produce inferior outcomes for those outside the dominant group. Travellers experienced a number of institutional barriers. For example, existing patterns of health provision assumed literacy and a sedentary lifestyle. Notifications of appointments often took place by post. Travellers living on unofficial sites often did not receive their post or it was often the case that Travellers living on such sites receive post at infrequent intervals. The medical card system provided eligibility to services on the basis of locality. This discriminated against those who do not live sedentary lives.[26] The persistence of access barriers to medical cards was compounded by a widespread refusal of GPs to accept Travellers as patients.

These access barriers were acknowledged by the Task Force (1995) which noted that 'GPs tend to be reluctant to accept Travellers as registered patients because of fear that to treat them will result in the loss of other patients and because of their high consultation rate'.[27] It called for the introduction of a scheme to ensure access to services when Travellers moved from one Health Board jurisdiction to another.[28] It recommended the introduction of measures to pay doctors with medical card patients without delay and so remove a perceived financial disincentive to the acceptance of Traveller patients. These recommendations were aimed at removing administrative barriers. They did not address the racism-related 'fear factor' which was identified as a cause of discrimination.

In any case, the *Report of the Monitoring Committee* (2000) noted ongoing resistance from the Department of Health and Children to the introduction of any special arrangements for Travellers.[29] It recommended that procedures regarding access to such services should be reviewed. It noted that existing contracts between general practitioners and the Department of Health and Children permitted doctors to refuse 'to accept a person as a registered patient solely on the basis that he or she is a Traveller'.[30] These contracts were seen as contrary to the Equal Status Act (2000) which prohibited discrimination in the provision of goods and services on nine grounds; including membership of the Travelling Community. The Monitoring Committee called on the General Medical Service (GMS) to seek an explanation in cases where GPs refuse service to Travellers. The adequacy of this proposal for non-statutory monitoring was questionable given the scale of discrimination. Research published in 2001 by the Travellers Health Unit relating to the Eastern Regional Health Authority, which contained most of Travellers living in Ireland, found that the majority of GPs still refused to take on Traveller patients. This study of the use of hospital services by Travellers showed that all patients in the region were admitted through casualty services only and that none were referred to hospital by a GP or by a consultant.[31] Such forms of discrimination have been described by Traveller women primary health care workers as expressions of racism.[32] The monitoring committee did not have a remit to examine racism. It could only note the non-implementation of the recommendations of the *Report of the Task Force* (1995). A lack of contestation by the state of institutional racism in the area of health has been mirrored in other sectors.

It was not until 2008 that follow-up research to the *Traveller Health Status Study* was undertaken. The *Our Geels: All Ireland Traveller Health Study* published in 2010 found that life expectancy at birth for male Travellers remained at the 1987 level of 61.7 years, which was 15.1 years fewer than for men in the general population, representing a widening of the gap by 5.2 years. The Standardised Mortality Ration (SMR) for Male Travellers in 2008 was 272 compared with 352 in 1987, while in the same period the SMR of males in the general population had reduced from 161 to 100. This meant that Traveller males experienced 3.7 times the mortality rate of males in the general population.

Life expectancy for female Travellers was found to be at 70.1 years, which was 11.5 years fewer than women in the wider population. The SMR for female Travellers in 2008 reduced to 309 from 472 in 1987. The SMR in the general population declined over the same period from 150 to 100. This meant that Traveller females experienced 3.1 times the mortality rate of the general population. According to the 2006 Census, older Travellers (i.e. those aged 65 and over) accounted for just 2.6 per cent of the total Traveller population compared with 11 per cent for the general population.

The *Our Geels* study estimated that Traveller infant mortality at 14.1 per 1,000 live births. This compared to an infant mortality rate of 3.9 per 1,000 live births or a rate 3.6 times higher than in the general population. The *Our Geels* study concluded Travellers in twenty-first century Ireland were experiencing 'the mortality experience of previous generations 50–70 years ago' and that the mortality gap between Travellers and the general population has widened in the past twenty years.[33]

Why was this the case? The suicide rate among male Travellers was found to be 6.6 times higher than in the general population.

In its findings, under the heading 'Racism, Discrimination and Disadvantage: Its Impact on Health and Wellbeing' *Our Geels* noted that Travellers reported high levels of discrimination from and low levels of trust in health service providers. The Report observed that even if this had been a collective misperception and had no basis in objective fact, such a perception would undermine the efficacy of health care and be damaging to health and wellbeing. Regrettably, *Our Geels* concluded, it was all too likely that there was a very real basis to this perceived discrimination.[34]

Education and institutional racism

The *Report of the Commission on Itinerancy* (1963) envisaged education primarily as a means of assimilation. It stated that the 'almost complete illiteracy of itinerants accentuates their isolation from the settled population and in itself makes all the more difficult any attempt to change over to the settled way of life'.[35] This must be understood as a very different educational goal to that which predominated within the mainstream education system. Segregation was justified by qualitative differences in the perceived educational needs of Traveller children to other children. It took the form of special classes and schools for Travellers. This was accompanied by segregation in school playgrounds. Travellers did not receive the same admission rights to education as other children until 1970.[36] Segregation within classes and apartheid within the playground have persisted to some extent. The *Report of the Task Force* (1995) noted that an estimated 4,200 Traveller children attended primary school out of a total of approximately 5,000 Traveller children of primary school age in the state.[37] Of these 1,800 were in mainstream classes while the remaining 2,400 were taught by special teachers for Travellers. There were also four special schools for Travellers with an aggregate enrolment of 260. Disparities between the educational attainment of Travellers and the population as a whole within primary education were a product of a number of factors. These included the inability of the education system to accommodate non-sedentary ways of life, stigma, lower attainment goals within segregated education and racism within schools. In 1988, 640 Traveller children between 12 and 15 years of age were still in primary education.[38]

Policies of including Traveller children in mainstream primary school classes were mooted in the *Report of the Task Force* (1995) and were subsequently introduced by the Department of Education and Science. In some cases, these have been opposed by parents of settled children. In 2001, for example, parents in Rathkeale, County Limerick, threatened to withdraw their children from two primary schools. They stated that they did not object to the presence of Traveller children but to their inclusion in classes appropriate to their ages which, the parents considered, would undermine the ability of the schools to meet the educational needs of their own children. In effect they opposed the inclusion of Traveller children in mainstream classes. The schools were not in a position to reintroduce segregation. However, they institutionalised different leaving times for Traveller and settled children at the end of the school day.[39] A few months later parents in Menlough, County Galway, withdrew their children from a small primary school following proposals to admit five Traveller children. Their action was referred to as a boycott in newspaper accounts.[40] This echoed a concurrent dispute at Holy Cross School in Belfast where a much condemned loyalist blockade sought to prevent Catholic children from attending the school. Widespread concern about Holy Cross, and acknowledgement of the trauma experienced by the children at that school, culminated in an invitation from the president to all children from the school to attend the lighting of the Christmas tree at Aras An Uachtaran.[41] No such symbolic support was offered to the Traveller children in Galway or elsewhere.[42]

The barriers encountered by Traveller children within primary education to some extent explain their low levels of completion of secondary education. The Review Body (1983) noted that only 10 per cent of those who finished primary went onto secondary school and that most of these dropped out within two years. Analysis of the reasons for this was limited. However, it was suggested that the monocultural nature of the school curriculum was a factor. The report of the Review Body stated that it 'has been recognised that curricula may need to be broadened to embrace subjects more attractive to Travellers in order to sustain their interest and attendance'.[43] This was interpreted as a need for segregationalist vocational provision for Travellers between 12 and 15 years. There was no emphasis upon addressing access barriers to the mainstream secondary education system. Subsequently, the *Task Force on the Travelling People* (1995) made 167 specific recommendations on Traveller education. Some of these emphasised flexibility in the provision of education which would take into account the differences between Traveller and sedentary ways of life. However, no evaluation of the efficacy of education provision for Travellers was mooted and no such evaluation has ever been undertaken by the Department of Education.

The glaring inadequacies of data about the Traveller participation levels in secondary education point to an ongoing lack of emphasis on the needs and rights of Traveller children on behalf of the Department of Education. As of 2000, no data were collected which would allow numbers of children at various stages of the secondary education system to be identified. Nor was any data on educational attainments gathered. The inadequacy of data was explained by a Department of Education statistician, in a comment that reflected the monocultural presumptions underpinning education policy, in the following terms: 'You see, we treat everyone the same'.[44]

Some surveys have sought to estimate Traveller participation in secondary education. One study carried out in 1991 estimated that about 20 per cent of Traveller children of appropriate ages attended mainstream secondary education.[45] However, a 1993 estimate (which looked at children between 12 and 15 years only) put the percentage at around 5 per cent.[46] Most of those Traveller children who attend mainstream secondary education were estimated to have dropped out after two years.[47] Traveller children continue to experience widespread institutional racism in education. This mirrors the experiences of Travellers in relation to health care.

According to the 2006 Census 53 per cent of Travellers over the age of 15 years had only a primary education and just under 3 per cent of Travellers over the age of 15 years had completed their education at secondary level. Just over 1 in 200 Travellers (0.57 per cent) over 15 years of age had completed third-level education. Qualitative research findings of the *Our Geels* health study published in 2010 identify many of the same experiences of the education system as experienced by earlier generations of Travellers. These include discrimination by teachers, bullying and name calling, peer pressure, feeling isolated, differences between the social and family lives of Traveller and 'settled' children, lack of positive emphasis on Traveller identity within schools and negative portrayals of Traveller identity in schools.

The Education Inspectorate published *Guidelines on Traveller Education in Primary Schools* in 2002. The stated aim was 'the meaningful participation and highest attainment of the Traveller child so that, in common with other children of the nation, he or she may live a full life as a child and realise his or her full potential as a unique individual, proud of and affirmed in his or her identity as a Traveller and a citizen of Ireland'.[48] However, these guidelines were not accompanied by concrete policies aimed at furthering such goals.[49]

In recent years there has been a considerable increase in the percentage of Traveller children who transfer from primary to secondary education. In 2008 just over 90 per cent of Traveller children did so. No data is collected on the academic achievement of Travellers at post-primary level. All that can be gleaned from official data are participation rates. The completion rate among Traveller children for the 2008 Junior Certificate was less than 20 per cent compared with a national average of 84 per cent. Furthermore the completion rate for Traveller boys was considerably lower than it was for Traveller girls. It is clear that most Traveller children fall out of and are failed by the secondary school system at an early stage. In effect, this might be understood as the institutional rejection of Traveller children. Girls are twice as likely to stay on than boys. The pressures that remove Traveller children are both a result of institutional indifference – the absence of policies and measures that might support adequately children and their families – but also a rejection of the education system by many Travellers.

The long history of Travellers being failed by the mainstream primary and secondary education systems has resulted in particular emphasis on adult education for Travellers. A system of thirty-three Traveller Training Centres was developed around the country from 1974 with the first centre established in Ennis County Clare. Their target group was mainly young

Travellers who had left school with either minimal or no qualifications. Most centres were segregated from the mainstream system of adult education run by county Vocational Educational Committees (VECs). The Traveller Training Centres have a poor track record of achieving what they set out to do, that is, progression to further education and employment. As in the school system the participation of Traveller females greatly outnumbers that of males. Women have outnumbered men six to one in Traveller Training Centres.[50]

Traveller Training Centres became refuges from the wider world of discrimination where Traveller culture and identity was respected and where some educational gains were achieved. The Centres also ran programmes aimed at improving literacy and boosting capabilities in dealing with the wider social and system, for example, how to engage with officials and teachers, and to cope in mainstream social settings. A 2010 evaluation of the Traveller Training Centres emphasised how segregation from mainstream society has been fostered by both discrimination and exclusion perpetrated by the 'settled' community but also by reluctance by Travellers to step outside their own culture and imposing pressures on one another that impede progression in education and employment.

Accommodation and anti-Traveller racism

The *Report of the Task Force* (1995) made many recommendations concerning good practice in the provision of accommodation for Travellers. It also emphasised the need for measures aimed at overcoming barriers to the development of such accommodation. In particular, it recommended the establishment of a statutory Traveller Accommodation Agency. As with a number of other proposals, such as those relating to access to health care, discriminations were acknowledged. It was envisaged that the agency would draw up, agree and monitor a national programme of Traveller accommodation but it was not recommended that the proposed statutory agency would supersede the powers of local authorities. One member of the Task Force recorded his disagreement with this recommendation. He opposed it on the grounds that it would undermine the autonomy of local authorities and that it would provide a further focus for opposition to halting sites.[51] He argued that none of the recommendations would, in any case, remove community opposition to such sites. These, he said, could only be addressed at local level. The recommendation to establish a Traveller Accommodation Agency could be interpreted as an implicit acknowledgement of the exclusionary practices of local authorities. However, as in other areas of the report, the absence of a critique of such practices resulted in measures which were inadequate to overcome the forms of accommodation exclusion explored in Chapter 6.

The agency was not established but a number of the recommendations of the *Report of the Task Force* (1995) were incorporated within the Housing (Traveller Accommodation) Act (1998). This placed, for the first time, a statutory duty upon local authorities to meet the current and projected accommodation needs of Travellers. As noted in Chapter 6, a duty to develop accommodation plans did not translate into a political willingness to do so. In Clare, as elsewhere, opposition to Traveller accommodation schemes persisted. For example, one Dublin TD considered that the loss of her seat in the Dáil during the 1997 general election, was, in part, due to her unwillingness to oppose Traveller accommodation plans in her constituency. She described how residents groups sought pre-election commitments from candidates for local and national elections to oppose such plans.[52] The politicisation of the Traveller issue arguably deepened in the run up to the 2002 general election. For example, Olivia Mitchell TD, the Fine Gael spokeswoman on local government, emerged as a high-profile populist opponent of expenditure on accommodation for Travellers. A consistent opponent of establishment of halting sites, she proposed the introduction of new legislation that would make it easier to evict Travellers from unauthorised sites and allow for the confiscation of Traveller caravans even where the local authorities had failed to meet their statutory responsibilities.[53] Anti-Traveller prejudice found new forms of expression in the Ireland of the Celtic Tiger. One example was reported in the property supplement of the Irish Times:

> The best story doing the rounds at the moment concerns one of south Dublin's most expensive new housing developments. One of these mansions was recently acquired by a solicitor in trust for a client. The developer and his agents were subsequently reduced to a state of near apoplexy when the mystery purchaser turned up two weeks later in a white Hi-Ace van. He turned out to be a member of the travelling community who had recently won the Lotto and was reversing most of his prize money into bricks and mortar. The developer was quick to offer not only to return his deposit but also to give him £180,000 to move his Hi-Ace and his family off site pronto.[54]

This article highlighted a casual and unquestioning acceptance within Irish society of the legitimacy of discrimination against Travellers. It took, as given, that it was reasonable for the developer to prevent Travellers from purchasing a house. This mirrored similarly uncontested perspectives within the *Report of the Task Force* (1995) and elsewhere that it was reasonable for residents to oppose Traveller accommodation because it would devalue their homes, or that it was reasonable for doctors to refuse to accept Travellers as patients because it would be bad for business. In this context, the introduction of the Equal Status Act (2000), which prohibited discrimination in the provision of goods and services, was of considerable importance.

The *Report of the Monitoring Committee* (2000) called for a review of the Housing (Traveller Accommodation) Act (1998) by 2002 and for an examination of the need for stronger land acquisition measures to expedite the accommodation programme. It stated, without exaggeration, that progress in the provision of new accommodation had been 'very slow'.[55] For example, between 1998 and 1999 the overall number of families in local authority accommodation rose by only 68 for the country as a whole. During the same period the numbers of families on the roadside or in other unauthorised sites rose from 1,148 to 1,207. Between 1996 and 1999 the number of families on the roadside had increased from 1,040 to 1,207. This resulted in extreme deprivation among a significant proportion of Travellers:

> The Monitoring Committee is aware that in reality one in every four Traveller families are currently living with no access to water, toilets and refuse collection. The accommodation provision has not kept pace with the increasing demand over the past five years and the Committee would like to emphasise in the strongest terms the importance of local Traveller accommodation programmes… Local authorities have a crucial role to play in this area.[56]

The harsh realities of ongoing exclusion have been highlighted by the Citizen Traveller campaign, funded by the Department of Justice, Equality and Law Reform (DJELR). One poignant radio advert, used during 2001, consisted of the voices of Travellers discussing various forms of discrimination. The advert ended with the announcement; 'Citizen Traveller, working to further the Traveller accommodation programme'. The campaign 'aimed at promoting an environment where Travellers can participate as equal citizens in Irish society'.[57] It was clear in the area of accommodation, as in other areas, that existing policies and programmes were insufficient to realise such goals.

The 1998 Act which imposed duties on local authorities to develop accommodation for Travellers became undermined by resistance at a local political level. For a few years courts found in favour of Travellers prosecuted for halting on land and sites own by local authorities who had failed in their statutory obligation to provide sites for Travellers. The very local politicians who opposed sites for Travellers now demanded new restrictions on Travellers. New legislation which criminalised halting on unofficial sites under any circumstances, the Housing (Miscellaneous

Provisions) Act (2002), was passed by an overwhelming cross-party majority. The 2002 Act allowed Travellers to be evicted and to have their caravans seized even where their statutory accommodation entitlements had not been met. Citizen Traveller ran a campaign describing the 2002 Act as racist. As a direct result, following an intervention by Michael McDowell, Minister of Justice, Equality and Law Reform, the group lost its state funding and was shut down.[58]

A study of Traveller accommodation by the Irish Traveller Movement identified 6,991 Traveller families in 2004, rising to 8,398 families in 2008. The numbers and overall percentage of these living in halting sites declined over this time from 1,321 families in 2004 to 1,035 families in 2008. By 2004 most Traveller families were accommodated with local authority assistance (5,106 families or 73 per cent). The number of families accommodated with local authority assistance rose to 5,500 by 2008 but this did not keep pace with new family formation. As a result just 65 per cent of families were so accommodated in 2008.

There is a steady and significant increase in the number of Travellers living in private rented housing, rising from 486 such families in 2004 to 1,516 such families in 2008. By 2008 nearly 20 per cent of all Traveller families had come to live in private rented accommodation. Yet, it is notable that there was no significant decline in the number of families living on unauthorised sites such as roadside encampments. In 2004 there were 601 such families. By 2008 there were 524 families.[59]

Hostility towards Travellers from resident groups, even when what is being proposed is the accommodation of single families in standard housing, has persisted. The challenges facing local authorities in implementing Traveller Accommodation programmes as required under the 1998 Housing Act, even when councillors do not seek to undermine these can be illustrated by opposition from a residents' group in Ballina in County Tipperary to the purchase of a house for a Traveller family.[60] From September 2008 a residents' group for six weeks blockaded a house which was purchased to accommodate a Traveller family that had been on the local authority housing waiting list for nine years. The local authority sought an order against the residents' blockade from the High Court. The residents in turn argued in the High Court that the letting of the house to Travellers did not comply with the local authority's Traveller Accommodation Programme. This programme, they maintained, stated that housing would be provided from the local authority's own standard housing stock, in group schemes, in rural areas or on a stand-alone basis or via housing loans but did not cover this particular house. The local authority in response emphasised the 'significant needs' of the family and argued that it had powers to address the significant needs of the public in general and that it would be 'absurd and unconstitutional to exclude this family because of their status as Travellers'.[61] The High Court found in favour of the local authority but the residents' protest continued. In addition to the blockade picket on the house the locks on the doors of the house had been glued so that it could not be accessed The unoccupied house was destroyed by fire on the night of 2 July 2009.[62]

Equality and ethnic status

The persistence of assimilationism

The *Report of the Task Force* (1995) emphasised the need to address inequalities and discrimination experienced by Travellers but was most reluctant to refer to prejudice against Travellers as racism. It set optimistic targets for addressing the exclusions experienced by Travellers yet contained an addendum that painted, in the starkest of terms, a picture of overwhelming resistance within Irish society their inclusion. This augured poorly for the responses to various recommendations. It pointed to a profound disjuncture between an official discourse of inclusion and a dominant racialised one which justified the exclusion of Travellers.

The reluctance by the state to recognise Traveller ethnicity can be understood as an expression of the ideological monoculturalism institutionalised within state practices. Almost fifty years after the *Report of the Commission on Itinerancy* (1963), the extent to which the ideology of assimilation set out in that report had ceased to be the dominant ideological response to Travellers was questionable. The setting up of the Task Force was, to some extent, a top-down initiative aimed at promoting inclusion in the face of antipathy to such goals at a local level. In a sense, the accompanying minority report, which dissented from the main report, was a majority report. This, in keeping with the *Report of the Commission on Itinerancy* (1963) and the *Report of the Review Body* (1983), located Travellers within a narrative of social modernisation and nation-building within which their way of life was outmoded and dysfunctional. A 'softly softly' approach to some aspects of anti-Traveller discrimination, notably within local government, was arguably politic in so far as the purpose of the Task Force was to shift national policy and its legitimacy was to be achieved through the articulation of a consensus. This could be seen in the lack of challenges to dominant presumptions that the majority settled community had a right to exclude Travellers. As a result, the measures the Task Force advocated in areas such as education, health and accommodation fell far short of being able to overcome the exclusions experienced by Travellers. This dominant consensus paradigm, to an extent, shaped subsequent equality legislation and the remit of state-supported multicultural practices.

Equalities legislation

Yet, the Task Force instigated progressive legislation such as the Housing (Traveller) Accommodation Act (1998) which imposed, for the first time, a statutory duty on local authorities to accommodate Travellers and the Equal Status Act (2000) which prohibited discrimination in the provision of goods and services. It recommended, in the case of the latter, strong measures to address indirect discrimination. It proposed that equal status legislation would define indirect discrimination in a manner that incorporated not only terms and conditions set for the provision of goods, services and facilities but also policies or practices relating to these. It sought the inclusion of a strong definition of indirect discrimination which required that any differential in excess of 20 per cent between communities, in their access to goods, services and facilities, would be investigated to ascertain whether or not indirect discrimination had occurred.[63] However, the case for such a recommendation was not explicitly made. The emphasis on indirect discrimination was not related to any specific conceptualisation of institutional racism. Nevertheless it emanated from an implicit critique of the institutional inequalities experienced by Travellers that shared much with the analysis set out in the McPherson Report (2000) a few years later in the UK of institutional racism.[64]

The recommendation was not incorporated in full within the subsequent Equal Status Act (2000). The Act stated that indirect discrimination occurs where access to goods, services or facilities is dependent upon compliance with some condition which has a disproportionately adverse effect on a particular group. The relevant factor identified in the Act, which determines whether indirect discrimination is occurring, is that 'substantially more people' outside the particular 'community' (the discriminated against or affected category) than within it, can comply with the particular condition being imposed by the service provider. The Monitoring Committee (2000) endorsed the original Task Force recommendation, concerning the identification of a 'twenty per cent differential between communities in their access', as means of shifting the focus of the Equal Status Act (2000) from individual cases to 'a more relevant group dynamic'.[65] It expressed concern that there was no automatic trigger for the investigation of indirect discrimination.

The Equality Authority was empowered to investigate discrimination in the provision of goods and services in some cases. Section 69 of the

Employment Equality Act (1998) provided for audits and examinations of factors relevant to the promotion of equality of opportunity. The Equality Authority also had the power to carry out equality reviews of businesses with more than fifty employees. The Equal Status Act (2000) empowered the Equality Authority to undertake equality reviews relating to the provision of goods and services and to prepare and implement equality action plans. The Equality Authority could also invite public service providers or those in other sectors to undertake such reviews. The ability of these mechanisms to contest the full scale of direct and indirect discrimination is open to question. One year after the introduction of the act, more than 500 cases of alleged discrimination against individuals were being pursued by the Equality Authority. These related to allegations of discrimination in the provision of services by pubs and clubs, landlords, insurance companies, transport organisations rather allegations of institutional discrimination by public services or local authorities. However, complaints were registered about discrimination by schools. In this context, the ability of the Act to challenge indirect discrimination was called into question by the Monitoring Committee.

During the late 1990s a new agenda of anti-racism emerged in response to immigration. In 1997 the Irish National Co-ordinating Committee for the European Year Against Racism, established by the Department of Equality and Law Reform, focused upon anti-Traveller racism.[66] The subsequent establishment by the DJELR of the National Consultative Committee on Racism and Interculturalism (NCCRI) in 1998 furthered official recognition of Traveller ethnicity and the existence of anti-Traveller racism. The European Year Against Racism coincided with rapid increases in the numbers of asylum seekers coming to Ireland and, as noted in earlier chapters, to the emergence of new expressions of racism within Irish society.

In the same vein the DJELR funded a three-year 'Citizen Traveller' campaign with a remit to promote the rights of Travellers. In 2001 it launched a 'Know Racism' campaign. Both of these initiatives embodied broader notions of ethnicity and racism than those acknowledged by the Task Force. At the same time they were located within the dominant equality paradigm. Campaigns with a limited remit educate the public about racism coexisted with a general lack of emphasis on racism within the practices of state institutions.

The denial of Traveller ethnicity

Irish Travellers came to be recognised as an ethnic group in the UK and in Northern Ireland but not in the Republic of Ireland. More precisely, bodies such as the Equality Authority and the NCCRI (under leaders who had previously worked with Traveller organisations) advocated recognition of the ethnic distinctiveness of Travellers. Such recognition has continued to be opposed by successive Irish governments in the face of some international pressure. In 1992, Ireland's first report under the International Covenant on Civil and Political Rights refused to define Travellers as an ethnic group:

> Allegations are sometimes made of discrimination against the travelling community. This is a community whose members, like the gypsies in other countries, used to travel from place to place in pursuit of various traditional callings. Many of these occupations in the modern economic climate are obsolete. Nowadays travellers tend to live in caravans close to the major cities. Some of the bodies representing travellers claim that members of the community constitute a distinct ethnic group. The basis of this claim is not clear.[67]

This position reflected the status quo prior to the publication of the *Report of the Task Force on the Travelling People* in 1995. In 1996 Ireland's Report under the Convention on the Rights of the Child noted 'the claim that Travellers were an ethnic group' but did not comment on it one way or the other. A similar approach was adopted in Ireland's 1996 Report under the International Covenant on Economic, Social and Cultural Rights.[68] Ireland's *First Report under the European Framework Convention on National Minorities* (2001) described Travellers as 'an indigenous minority who have been part of Irish society for centuries'. It stated:

> While Travellers are not a Gypsy or Roma people, their long shared history, cultural values, language (Cant), customs and traditions make them a self-defined group, and one which is recognisable and distinct. The Traveller community is one whose members, like the Gypsies in other countries, travelled from place to place in pursuit of various different traditional vocations. Despite their nomadic origins and tendencies, the majority of the Traveller community now live in towns and cities.
>   Their culture and way of life, of which nomadism is an important factor, distinguishes Travellers from the sedentary (settled) population. While Travellers do not constitute a distinct group from the population as a whole in terms of religion, language or race, they are, however, an indigenous minority who have been part of Irish society for centuries. The Government fully accepts the right of Travellers to their cultural identity, regardless of whether they may be described as an ethnic group or national minority.

Here it seemed a degree of implicit recognition of Traveller ethnicity was forthcoming. In what might have been an unintentional typographical slip the report referred on page 47 to 'Travellers and other minority ethnic groups'.[69]

Typically such submissions reflected pressure place upon the Irish state from two directions. First, having ratified international conventions against racism there was pressure to acknowledge international norms, such as definitions of racism and ethnicity. At the same time NGOs including Traveller organisations used such conventions as opportunities to press for recognition and reform. Documents went through many drafts and sometimes there was a slip of the pen such as the above-quoted page 47 acknowledgement that Travellers were like other ethnic groups.

In this context a number of state-funded organisations with equality (the Equality Authority) anti-racism (the NCCRI) and human rights (the Human Rights Commission) made strongly worded submissions aimed at supporting Traveller demands for ethnic status. A 2004 Human Rights Commission discussion paper on Ireland's obligations under the Convention on the Elimination of all forms of Racial Discrimination (CERD) directly challenged statements by Michael McDowell, Minister for Justice, Equality and Law Reform who was a strong political opponent of Traveller recognition and the equalities agenda he held ministerial responsibility for:

> On this issue the Minister is emphatic that the Government does not believe that Travellers are ethnically different from the majority of the Irish people. The Human Rights Commission disagrees and believes that the refusal to recognise Travellers as an ethnic minority for the purposes of CERD suggests a lack of understanding of the importance to Travellers of recognition of their culture and identity. It also, in the view of the Commission, raises concerns that sufficient weight may not be given in policy making to the need to respect and promote that culture, while the lack of recognition may place obstacles in the way of Travellers accessing all the protections of CERD and other international human rights conventions.[70]

CERD, the Human Rights Commission noted, had defined the term 'racial discrimination' to mean any distinction, exclusion, restriction or preference based on race, colour, descent, or national or ethnic origin which has the purpose or effect of nullifying or impairing the recognition, enjoyment or exercise, on an equal footing, of human rights and fundamental freedoms in the political, economic, social, cultural or any other field of public life.

The Human Rights Commission argued that the Irish legislation which addressed Ireland's obligations under the CERD Convention – the Employment Equality Act (1998) and the Equal Status Act (2000) – had

fudged the issue as to whether Travellers came within the CERD definition of racial discrimination. The 1998 Act prohibited discrimination on
the basis of 'race, colour, nationality, or ethnic or national origins' and then
separately prohibited discrimination on the basis of membership of 'the
traveller community'.[71] The 2000 Act contained a definition of 'Traveller
community' (in upper-case this time), virtually identical to one set out in
legislation from Northern Ireland where Travellers *were* acknowledged
as a 'racial group'.[72] The following definition was set out in section 2 the
Equal Status Act:

> 'Traveller community' means the community of people who are
> commonly called Travellers and who are identified (both by themselves
> and others) as people with a shared history, culture and traditions
> including, historically, a nomadic way of life on the island of Ireland.

The irony, highlighted by the Human rights Commission report was that
some Travellers lived on both sides of the border at various stages of their
lives or had close relatives on the other side from where they lived. The
same people were in effect differently classified in both jurisdictions.[73]
In effect, on one side of the border they were understood to experience
racism while on the other, Republic of Ireland, the very existence of racism
against Travellers could be denied.

In a 2006 report *Traveller Ethnicity* the Equality Authority noted that
international agreements and EU legislation did not name specific
ethnic groups from particular states within their provisions on ethnicity.
Traveller ethnicity needed to be recognised to ensure Travellers could
enjoy the protections and benefits that flow from such agreements and
legislation.[74] By denying Travellers ethnic status the Irish state was, in
effect, denying that various anti-racism conventions ratified by Ireland
applied to Travellers.

Ireland's First Report under the CERD Convention in 2006 represented
what the Equality Authority described as a 'surprising and somewhat
disturbing change in direction' and as a hardening of the Irish government position. For the first time the Irish state explicitly denied that
Travellers constituted a distinct group from the population as a whole.
In effect, the argument of the Irish state was that Travellers could not be
deemed to experience racism and that the CERD obligations to address
racist discrimination did not apply to Travellers. As put in paragraph 28
of the Irish government report:

> [I]t should be noted that some of the bodies representing Travellers
> claim that members of the community constitute a distinct ethnic group.
> The exact basis for this claim is unclear. However, the Government of

Ireland accepts the right of Travellers to their cultural identity, regard-less of whether it may be properly described as an ethnic group and is committed to applying all the protections afforded to ethnic minorities by the CERD equally to Travellers ... The Government's view is that Travellers do not constitute a distinct group from the population as a whole in terms of race, colour, descent or national or ethnic origin.

The Human Rights Commission summarised the implications of this refusal of ethnic recognition in the following terms. Ireland had declared itself bound by Article 14 of the CERD Convention, which allowed individuals to complain to the CERD Committee about violations of their rights under the Convention – rather like taking a case to the European Court of Human Rights or the UN Human Rights Committee. But if the government did not recognise that discrimination against Travellers constitutes racial discrimination for the purposes of the Convention, then they would presumably claim that any complaints made by Travellers to the CERD Committee are inadmissible. The Human Rights Commission was also concerned that refusal to recognise Travellers as a group with a distinct ethnic origin suggests that the government might claim that they are not covered by the EU Race Directive, which appeared to provide some protections additional to existing anti-discrimination law.[75]

The Irish government has continued to refuse such recognition despite pressure from the Council of Europe and the International Convention on the Elimination of all forms of Racial Discrimination (CERD). For example, the Council of Europe's Advisory committee on the Framework Conven-tion on National Minorities, in its Second Opinion on Ireland (2006) was critical of the Irish government's unwillingness to consider the issue.[76] The 2011 Irish government report to CERD relegated reference to Travellers to an appendix, and made no reference to the issue of ethnic recognition. In effect, the Irish government position was that its obligations under the UN Convention on the Elimination of All Forms of Racial Discrimination did not apply to Travellers. Pavee Point produced a shadow report for submission to CERD which argued otherwise.

Segregation and harsh realities

Such efforts to deny Traveller ethnicity cannot be understood without reference to the political salience of anti-Traveller prejudice in Ireland. From the early 1960s, when Travellers first became identified as a social policy problem by the mainstream population of an urbanising Ireland efforts to assimilate have been undermined by an impetus to exclude and to segregate. Only ideological assimilation, in the form of the denial of ethnic distinctiveness, has proved possible. Irish society has changed hugely since the 1960s and as it modernised and changed so too have the lives of Travellers. Segregation endorsed by the state whether through neglect in the areas of education, health care and accommodation, and experiences by Travellers of discrimination and racism coexist with an unwillingness of many Travellers to participate in the mainstream society that has rejected them.

Many Travellers are clearly not integrated into wider Irish society. Explanations of Traveller culture by advocates of Traveller rights typically focus on traditions of nomadism and keeping horses. Yet it is apparent that the lives of many Travellers have changed during the last several decades. Pejorative accounts of Traveller culture, which focus on deviance, crime and disorder have also shifted over this time. Studies by Traveller advocates have become more frank about difficulties within Traveller society. For example, Hourigan and Campbell in their study of Traveller education describe how violent feuds have prevented children from attending school.[77] They also describe how various communal pressures within Traveller communities including fears of peer rejection have been found to undermine Traveller participation in education. As put by one girl cited in their 2010 report: 'you just feel that the cost is too great, you might become just like the settled girls and then your own won't want you'.[78]

A 2006 book *The Outsiders* by *Sunday World* journalist Eamon Dillon, draws attention to many features of twenty-first century Traveller life not addressed by advocates of Traveller rights. While his account is presented as an expose of Traveller crime it also in many respects a frank ethnography, which draws on dozens of interviews. Travellers tend to be blandly portrayed in reports by advocates of their rights. In Dillon's *The Outsiders* individuals are vividly depicted as leading complex lives. His opening chapter describes successful Traveller traders who conduct their businesses across borders and continents. He describes class and family structures and how conflicts and feuds emerge. He describes a society that Robert Putnam would depict as strong on binding social capital but exceedingly low in trust in and exceedingly disconnected from the wider society:

> One of the problems of living outside mainstream society is that there are limited means to pursue a legitimate grievance over a bad business deal or matters of a domestic nature. Travelling people generally prefer to sort out their affairs amongst themselves. The police, solicitors and the court system of 'country people' are regarded with suspicion. Instead, recognised family leaders will be prevailed upon to suggest a solution.

But sometimes the two sides can fail to reach a compromise or those who the most aggrieved feel unable to accept the proposed arbitration. A row can quickly spiral out of control before more level-headed figures can exert any influence over events. Sometimes there may be no obvious solution or common ground between the two sides of the dispute and a feud develops.[79]

Dillon's narrative includes successful but shady Traveller businessmen – some in suits with mobile phones – criminal gangs, cigarette smugglers, vicious feuds and conflicts and assaults associated with bare-knuckle boxing. Much of it ignores the social policy and racism issues emphasised by Traveller organisations. Traveller organisations for their part have been wary of discussing communal problems for fear that these be seized upon as justifications for anti-Traveller prejudice. Similarly, it has taken considerable time for equivalent racialised groups in other countries to feel able to publicly air their internal issues to the wider world. These might include gender equality issues, homophobia, domestic violence or crime – problems that affect all communities. Racism has obfuscated problems within Traveller communities, encouraging Travellers to keep these hidden, fearful of the stereotypes that blight their lives.

For all his disinterest in such issues (Travellers in *The Outsiders* are travellers), Dillon vividly highlights similar consequences of racism and segregation to those encountered by African-Americans. Television dramas such as *The Wire* portray a black urban poor with bleak prospects, the educational system that fails them and the communal pressures that deprive black children of educational opportunities. The America that elected Barak Obama also incarcerates about three-quarters of a million black men. Both African-Americans and Irish Travellers are far more likely than the wider population to be in prison, to be poor, to be in poor health, to be victims of violence and to die young.

Notes

1 *Frontline* Blog, 28 June 2010 (at: www.rte.ie/frontline/entry/the_travelling_community_and lifestyle).
2 Email to author 4 July 2010.
3 More than 50 per cent of the workforce were in agriculture in 1926, still over one-third in 1961 but less than one-fifth by 1980 (see T. Garvin, *The Evolution of Irish Nationalist Politics* (Dublin: Gill & Macmillan, 1982), p. 22).
4 T. H. Marshall used the concept of social citizenship in the post-Second World War era to envisage universal rights to welfare as citizenship rights. Subsequently, the lesser enjoyment of such rights by some groups in society has been depicted as differential social citizenship.

5 See N. Crowley, 'Travellers and Social Policy', in S. Quin, P. Kennedy, A. O'Donnell and G. Keily (eds), *Contemporary Irish Social Policy* (Dublin: University Dublin College Press, 1999), p. 247.
6 *Ibid.*, p. 248.
7 *Report of the Task Force on the Travelling Community* (Dublin, Official Publications, 1995), p. 58.
8 *Ibid.*, p. 63.
9 *Ibid.*
10 *Ibid.*, p. 290.
11 *Ibid.*
12 *Report of the Commission on Itinerancy* (Dublin: Official Publications, 1963), p. 290.
13 J. O'Connell, 'Ethnicity and Irish Travellers', in M. McCann, S. O'Siochain and S. Ruane (eds), *Irish Travellers: Culture and Ethnicity* (Belfast: Institute for Irish Studies, 1994), p. 111.
14 *Irish Times* (21 May 2001).
15 D. Goldhagen, *Hitler's Willing Executioners: Ordinary Germans and the Holocaust* (London: Abacus, 1996), p. 41.
16 *Task Force*, p. 76.
17 K. Boyle and B. Watt, *International and United Kingdom Law Relevant to the Protection of the Rights and Cultural Identity of the Travelling Community in Ireland; Paper commissioned by the Task Force on the Travelling Community* (Colchester: Human Rights Centre University of Essex, 1995).
18 *Task Force*, p. 83.
19 Ruling of Lord Frazer in *Mandla* v. *Dowell Lee* (1983), cited in Boyle and Watt, *International and United Kingdom Law*.
20 Department of Justice, Equality and Law Reform, *The First Progress Report of the Committee to Monitor and Co-ordinate the Implementation of the Recommendations of the Task Force on the Travelling Community* (Dublin: Official Publications, 2000), p. 8.
21 *Ibid.*
22 J. Barry, B. Herity and S. Solan, *The Travellers' Health Status Study* (Dublin: Health Research Board, 1989).
23 Pavee Point (1999), based on *The Travellers Health Status Study* (1989) and *Economic and Social Research Institute Report No. 131* (1986).
24 Pavee Point Women (2000) 'Primary Health Care for Travellers Project', in E. Sheehan (ed.), *Travellers: Citizens of Ireland* (Dublin: Parish of the Travelling People), p. 128.
25 Crowley, 'Travellers and Social Policy', p. 245.
26 *Ibid.*, p. 129.
27 *Report of the Task Force*, p. 142.
28 *Ibid.*
29 DJELR, *First Report*, p. 48.
30 *Ibid.*
31 *Irish Times* (7 June 2001).
32 Pavee Point Women, 'Primary Health Care', in Sheehan, *Travellers*, p. 129.
33 Keleher *et al.*, *Our Geels All Ireland Traveller Health Study* (Dublin University College Dublin/Department of Health and Children, 2010).

34 *Ibid.*, p. 165.
35 *Commission on Itinerancy*, p. 64.
36 The Review Body noted that as a result of reforms by the Department of Education in 1970 Travellers had the same right of admission to all schools as other children (Travelling People Review Body, *Report of the Travelling People Review Body* (Dublin: Official Publications, 1983)).
37 *Task Force*, p. 173.
38 *Ibid.*, p. 184.
39 *Irish Times* (1 May 2001).
40 *Irish Times* (11 September 2001).
41 The president's residence in Dublin.
42 However, the previous president, Mary Robinson, did, on a number of occasions, promote the inclusion of Travellers through such symbolic measures.
43 *Report of the Travelling People*, p. 60.
44 This comment was made in a discussion with the author in 2000. The official explained that some figures on primary education were available because of records associated with a grant scheme based on the numbers of Traveller children enrolled.
45 The Department of Education Working Group on Post Primary Education of Traveller Children estimated that 80 per cent of Traveller children did not attend any secondary school during the 1989–90 school year.
46 An ad hoc group of Vocational Education Chief Executive Officers reported in 1993 that only 100 Traveller children aged 12 to 15 years of age were attending mainstream second-level schools out of the estimated 2,000 eligible to do so (about 5 per cent). Of these between 12 and 15 years of age 1,400–1,600 out of a total group estimated at between 200 and 2,400 do not continue their education.
47 *Task Force*, p. 184.
48 Department of Education and Science, *Guidelines on Traveller Education in Primary Schools* (Dublin: Official publications, 2002), p. 5.
49 N. Hourigan and M. Campbell, *The Teach Report: Traveller Education and Adults: Crisis, Challenge and Change* (National Association of Travellers' Centres, 2010), p. 23.
50 *Ibid.*, p. 70.
51 *Ibid.*, p. 117.
52 Interview with former TD 2000.
53 *Irish Times* (7 November 2001).
54 *Irish Times* (22 June 2000).
55 DJELR, *First Report*, pp. 1, 13.
56 *Ibid.*
57 Citizen Traveller fact sheet (2000).
58 An advertisement by Citizen Traveller described the 2002 Act as racist. The minister of justice, equality and law reform announced an immediate review of the funding of the group which was subsequently disbanded.
59 G. O'Toole, *Feasibility Study for the Establishment of a Traveller Led Voluntary Accommodation Association* (Dublin: Irish Traveller Movement, 2009), p. 15.
60 'Anger in Ballina over purchase of house for Travellers', *Nenagh Guardian* (19 September 2008).

61 'Both sides waiting on judgement over ballina house' *Limerick* leader (14 May 2009).

62 'Inquiry begins as house bought for Travellers destroyed by fire', *Irish Times* (6 July 2009).

63 *Task Force*, p. 82.

64 W. McPherson, *The Stephen Lawrence Inquiry: Report of an Inquiry by Sir William McPherson of Cluny* (London, Stationery Office, 1999).

65 DJELR, *First Report*, p. 94.

66 The Irish National Co-ordinating Committee for the European Year Against Racism (1997) framework programme, cited in Crowley, 'Travellers and Social Policy'.

67 Government of Ireland, *First Report by Ireland as Required under Article 40 of the Covenant on the Measures Adopted to Give Effect to the Provisions of the Covenant – International Covenant on Civil and Political Rights* (Dublin: Stationery Office, 1992).

68 Human Rights Commission, *Travellers as an Ethnic Minority under the Convention on the Elimination of Racial* Discrimination (Dublin: Human Rights Commission, 2004), p. 12.

69 *Ibid.*, p. 14.

70 *Ibid.*, p. 2.

71 Sections 6(2) (h) and (i) of the 1998 Employment Equality Act.

72 Race Relations (Northern Ireland) Order, 1997.

73 Human Rights Committee, *Travellers as an Ethnic Minority*, p. 11.

74 Equality Authority, *Traveller Ethnicity* (Dublin: Equality Authority, 2006).

75 Human Rights Committee, *Travellers as an Ethnic Minority*, pp. 12–14.

76 Cited in Pavee Point, *Irish Travellers and Roma: Shadow report: A response to Ireland's Third and Fourth Report on the International Convention on the Elimination of All Forms of Racial Discrimination (CERD)* (Dublin: Pavee Point, 2011), p. 14.

77 Hourigan and Campbell, *Teach Report*, p. 92.

78 *Ibid.*, p. 86.

79 E. Dillon, *The Outsiders: Exposing the Secretive World of Ireland's Travellers* (Dublin: Merlin, 2006), p. 118.

8

Racial nation, ethnic state

This focus of this chapter is upon the academic literature on racism in Ireland that has (mostly) emerged during the last decade. In effect, this literature has sought to understand how and to what extent racism has informed and defined Irish responses to immigrants and ethnic minorities. Analyses of the Referendum and other Irish responses to immigration have variously emphasised state racism drawing on David Goldberg's conception of the racial state or, alternatively, the role of ethnic nepotism, the primacy of solidarity with co-ethnics.[1] The emphasis here is upon the macro-levels of the Irish state, the Irish nation and Ireland's dominant ethnos as distinct from on-the-ground experiences of racism and institutional barriers to the recognition and redress of these examined in the next chapter.

Earlier chapters of this book have highlighted how notions of Western racial superiority coexisted with interchangeable meanings of the terms of race and nationality. Over time, it became less usual to describe nations as different races. Essentialist nationalisms that fostered such thinking became less prevalent and, in effect, ethnicity might be understood as a politically correct replacement for ideas of race-as-nation put forward by nationalists in Ireland and elsewhere. The term ethnicity came to be used to denote cultural differences between and sometimes within nation states. In the case of the Republic of Ireland, the dominant ethnic identity came to be institutionalised as the dominant national identity. In this sense, the Irish state remains into the twenty-first century very much an ethnic state.

Castles and Davidson distinguish between three kinds of nation state. First, they identify a sovereignty perspective whereby an ethnic group that controls a bounded territory becomes a nation. Second, they distinguish the *kulturnation*, a nation defined by its culture (in the sense that *kutlur* was depicted in Chapter 2) and by the state. As they explain it: 'Romanticism portrayed individuals as part of an organic whole; freedom meant not individual rights but acceptance of one's role in a greater organism. The state was the embodiment of this superior meaning, which only could be interpreted by great leaders'. Both kinds are explicitly grounded in the dominance of some majority ethnic group but differ in how this dominance came to be manifested in the state. The third *staatnation*, or civic nation defines community in terms of obedience to the same laws and institutions within a given territory.[2] However, in practice (Castles and Davidson give France as an example), civic nations are likely to be grounded in underlying presumptions about cultural homogeneity.[3] Some accounts of civic nations envisage these as emerging from ethnic nations.[4] But an ethnic nation can only be considered as a civic nation if it sets aside ethnic rules of belonging.

Early twentieth-century Irish antipathy to the *kulturnation* ideal (see Chapter 2) had much to do with Catholic rejection of state worship and the republican character of Irish nationalism. In this context, the new Irish state did not engage in any explicit efforts to define an Irish 'race' although it continued to engage in an explicit Irish-Ireland cultural nation-building project. This was supplanted from the 1950s by an economic development nation-building project that seemed to de-emphasise ethnic 'rules of belonging'.[5] Dominant ideological conceptions of Irishness changed over time so as to apparently discard essentialist nationalism in favour of a more lightly worn sense of national identity. Yet, somehow a nineteenth-century definition of Irishness was found to have considerable political salience in the early twenty-first century. As a result of the 2004 Referendum on Citizenship the immediate right of children born in the Republic of Ireland to become part of the Irish republican *demos* effectively depended upon being born into the national *ethnos*.[6]

Much of the recent writings on racism in the Irish case are the work of sociologists. These are unsurprisingly focused on structural explanations of racism. A number of these have drawn on David Theo Goldberg's *The Racial State* (2002) to argue that the Irish state, like other modern states, is inherently racist in its preoccupations and that whenever it comes to organise and regulate its population underlying racisms, embedded in its laws and practices, come to the fore. Various Irish-based academics, most notably Ronit Lentin, have depicted Ireland as a racial state and a racist state as Goldberg defines these terms. At the same time such accounts emphasise how manifestations of racism have shifted over time in Western societies. Goldberg and Lentin marry accounts of how racism has become historically embedded in the institutions of Western states with Michel Foucault telling of intersections between the caring and coercive functions of modern states.

This book includes several case studies where the Irish state can be seen to play a role in the mobilisation of racism while never presuming that racism can be simply attributed to or blamed upon the state. How this role might be understood has emerged as a key issue within the academic literature on the Irish case. Much of this draws on theories of the racial state, whereas the emphasis in this book has been instead upon the wider social and cultural contexts within which racism finds expression and comes to be exploited. Here the focus includes how Irish nation-building has come to narrowly define ethnic solidarities and addresses some forms of exclusion as expressions of ethnic nepotism – in essence solidarities with co-ethnics – that have insidious racist consequences even if explicit racist intent is denied.

Racism and the state

Lentin has argued that that the state is the leading actor in creating anti-immigrant sentiment in Ireland. This argument draws upon critical race theory where the emphasis is upon how the state might be understood as an institution that racialises its populations.[7] As depicted by Lentin and her sometimes co-author Robbie McVeigh racism 'is essentially dialectical – it names a coherent set of relationships which situate different people in terms of notions of race and which result in very different life experiences for those people'.[8] Her sociological focus is on how the structure of social relations in Ireland has become racialised through the institutions and practices of the state. The key event in her account (and indeed in many other analyses of racism in Ireland) has been the 2004 Referendum on Citizenship. In her analysis the emphasis is upon how the state choreographed the referendum outcome rather than the wider Irish society which voted by a huge majority to remove the birthright to Irish citizenship from the Irish-born children of immigrants. As argued by Lentin: 'State racism culminated in the 2004 Citizenship Referendum, in which, at a majority of four to one, the Irish electorate voted for the removal of birthright citizenship to children of migrants'.[9]

Her argument draws upon two theoretical sources: the racial state theories of David Theo Goldberg and the bio-politics theories of Michel Foucault also cited by Goldberg.[10] Both these theoretical approaches emphasise how states come to impose (as distinct from influence) exclusionary societal rules of belonging. The combination of both these theoretical approaches as deployed by Lentin has been draw upon in a number of other academic accounts of racism in Irish society.[11]

Goldberg posits modern nation states as 'racial states', that construct national homogeneity through constitutions, border controls, the law, policy making, bureaucracy and governmental technologies (a term borrowed from Michel Foucault) such as census categorisations, curriculum and invented histories and the use of cultural ceremonies. Much of what he means might be exemplified by the focus of Chapter 3 on exclusionary nation-building although the conceptual approach underpinning that account (see below) is somewhat different. Goldberg argues that modern states, each in their own way, are defined by their power to exclude (and include) in racially ordered terms.

He posits two traditions of thinking about what he calls 'racial states'. The first, naturalism encompasses the presumed scientific and religious 'proofs' of biological inferiority described in Chapter 2. It also encompasses essentialist nationalist (the nation depicted as a race) claims of superiority over out-groups within and without the nation. The second tradition emphasised by Goldberg, historicism, elevates Europeans over primitive or underdeveloped others as a victory of progress.[12] An Irish example of such thinking detailed in Chapter 1 is the belief that Irish missionaries to Africa were bringing civilisation. Goldberg argues that historicism – belief in the superiority of so-called advanced cultures over so-called outmoded or primitive ways of life – has become more prevalent than naturalism – the belief in biologically rooted superiority – within modern states. Other frameworks noted in Chapter 2 also understand cultural racism to have superseded beliefs in claims about biological superiority and inferiority as the prevalent (and more acceptable) face of racism. In Lentin's summary, the modern state's historicist progressivism aims, through amalgamation and assimilation, to assist its non-white racial others to 'undo their uncivilized conditions'. As Goldberg puts it, beneath its liberalism, historicism camouflages racism, and is ultimately about the ordering zeal of modernity.[13]

Lentin's application of Goldberg's model of naturalist and historicist racism mirrors the accounts contained in Chapter 3 of how notions of the Irish 'race' emerged in opposition to colonialist depictions of the Irish race as inferior and accounts of how anti-Semitic and anti-Traveller prejudice found expression within Irish nation-building:

> While naturalism Irish-style is exemplified in English colonialism, from the seventeenth century onwards, racializing the Irish, casting them as bestial, and incapable of progress, Irish historicism creates its own 'racial inferiors' through, firstly, the ongoing racialization of Irish Travellers, conceived as 'Irish national' though not always as 'white'.[14]

Lentin uses Goldberg's archetype to insist that Ireland is a racial state that has become a racist state. The way that both define this term has not travelled beyond some sociologists into wider academic or popular discourse. An early use of the term is in Michael Burleigh and Wolfgang Wipperman's 1991 book *The Racial State*, which refers to the German state under Nazi rule.[15] In Goldberg's writings Nazi Germany is also described as a racist state. But so too, Lentin insists, is Ireland.[16]

Goldberg and Lentin argue that the workings of racism within the processes of the state and the manipulation of racism by the state have become increasingly and 'infuriatingly' complex. Both argue that the insidious persistence of racism long after the overt versions practised by Nazi Germany or apartheid-era South Africa were discredited warrant use of the terms 'racial state' and 'racist state' to describe modern Western states. The distinction Goldberg makes between racial states and racist states might be summarised between latent tendencies towards the racial sorting of populations – a product of naturalist and historicist legacies embedded in its laws and institutions – and acting upon such tendencies (through 'specifically racist policies and practices') as a racist state.[17]

In Chapter 2 Adam Lively's metaphor of pouring old wine into new bottles was employed to describe how justifications for racism became reinvented. When defences of racism as the will of God (to justify colonialism and slavery) lost ground, new proofs about the scientific validity of racism (to justify eugenics) found favour only to be replaced by presumptions of cultural superiority and inferiority. Shifting justifications for racism were mirrored by changing ways in how race thinking influenced the sifting of populations. As put by Goldberg, naturalism's 'violence of an imposed physical repression' gave way to historicism's 'infuriating subtleties of a legally fashioned racial order' where the law is committed to the 'formal equality of treating like alike (and by extension the unlike differently).'[18] What changed then was how racism became justified, how racism became manifested and also how racism in its different stages might come to be mobilised by the state.

Lentin argues that the Irish state has demonised asylum seekers and promoted a sense of crisis – what Etienne Balibar refers to as crisis racism[19] – to legitimise new coercive state practices such as direct provision and deportations. But this is just one element, she argues, of a wider coercive repertoire of techniques or 'technologies' available to the state and their use warrants defining Ireland as a racial state. In Lentin's summary:

> Ireland has evolved from being, like other nation-states, a 'racial state' – in which 'race' and 'nation' are defined in terms of each other – evident, for instance, in the ethnically narrow framing of the Constitution of Ireland – to a racist state, where governmental 'biopolitics' and technologies of racialising indigenous groups and regulating immigration and asylum

dictate the discursive and practical construction of Irishness's otherness. This argument is explicated through an examination of the controversy surrounding Irish citizen children whose parents are migrants, and the 2004 Citizenship Referendum, which, this article argues, is a turning point in the recent history of racism in Ireland.[20]

The language here – 'biopolitics' and 'technologies of racialising' – is drawn from the 'governmentality' theory of Michel Foucault who argued the role of the state in modern societies has expanded to have jurisdiction over the biological life of the nation. In Breda Gray's summary, governmentality is defined as 'the many heterogeneous and pervasive ways in which the conduct of individuals and populations is shaped and directed. It incorporates both the notion of governing and those modes of thought (*mentalité*) that enable governance.[21] The state, from this perspective is not viewed as a centralised or cohesive entity but a diffuse locus of power. In Lentin's grafting of Foucault's governmentality perspective onto racial state theory:

> Race no longer serves one group against another, but becomes a 'tool' of social conservatism and of state racism: a racism that society practices against itself, an internal racism, that of constant purification and social normalisation. In constructing homogeneities, the state therefore is not only denying its internal heterogeneities, it is also a normalising, regulating biopower state. As opposed to scapegoat theories of racism, which argue that under economic and social duress, sub-populations are cordoned off as intruders, blamed and used to deflect anxieties, Foucault's theory of racism is an expression of an ongoing social war nurtured by biopolitical technologies of purification. Thus racism is internal to the bio-political state. Foucault concludes on an ominous note. While the deadly play between a power based on the sovereign right to kill and biopolitical management of life was exemplified at its worst in the Nazi state, it is not housed there alone but appears in all modern states, and racism is intrinsic to the nature of all modern, normalising states and their biological technologies, occurring *in varying intensities* (italics added), ranging from social exclusion to mass murder.[22]

Foucault took race to mean race-as-nation in the sense defined by Ernest Renan in *Qu'est-ce qu'une nation?* (see Chapter 2). His *Society Must Be Defended* focused upon the emergence of ideas of race within the West aimed at distinguishing countries from one another and governing their populations. In such settings 'race' was not pinned to any stable biological meaning (by contrast, say, with the scientific racisms that created categories based upon phenotype).[23] The late nineteenth century, he argued, saw the emergence of state racism aimed at policing the biological life of the nation. At the more extreme end of this race-as-nation continuum was the practice of eugenics. In effect, the nation was being defended from internal biological threats from elements of the poor, the mad, the diseased and the deviant.[24] Colonialism as practiced by the West institutionalised other forms of race thinking and these, according to Foucault, also boomeranged back upon the West. Chapter 1 gave the example of Victorian race thinking about the urban poor, the 'people of the abyss' depicted as a race apart. The result, Foucault argued, was that the West began to practise something akin to colonisation, or internal colonisation, upon itself.[25] Unsurprisingly, such biopolitics also came to be directed at the foreign bodies of immigrants.

In lectures delivered the year after those collected in *Society Must Be Defended* were given – published as *Security, Territory and Population* – Foucault placed considerable emphasis on the practice of government prior to the development of the modern state. For all that controlling human populations within specific territories became integral to the functions of the state, Foucault was adamant that government cannot simply be reduced to what states do.[26]

Ethnic nepotism and the state

State racism and the kinds of coercive biopolitics depicted by Foucault can be identified in how Travellers, asylum seekers and some other groups have been treated by the Irish state. However, the Irish state has also actively promoted large-scale labour migration from countries that joined the EU in 2004. These quickly came to outnumber other immigrants living in the Republic of Ireland. The Irish state could have continued to control these by means of work permits for a number of years (as did most existing EU states) but instead allowed immediate unrestricted access to migrants from new member states.

It quickly became apparent that nobody, certainly not the government, knew quite how many migrants from Poland, Lithuania and other Eastern European countries had come to Ireland. It was also the case that nobody knew for sure how many Chinese migrants lived in Ireland. Most of these had arrived on student visas and various estimates put their numbers as between 11,601 – those identified by the 2006 census – and 80,000, the best guess of the Chinese embassy.[27] If state racism concerns the biopolitics of security, territory and population, it seems that the majority of immigrants living in Ireland were in many respects ungoverned bodies. It appears that state scrutiny was specifically directed at some racialised populations (non-European labour migrants and asylum seekers) while others (migrant workers from EU countries) received relatively little care or coercion. This is not to say that such migrants were exempt from racism. Kevin Howard identifies racism in manifestations of banal nationalism – distinctions between 'natives' and 'invaders' drawn at a communal level that play out within local conversations and the local media – that point to grass-roots equivalents to the kinds of cognitive distinctions between 'us' and 'them' institutionalised in distinctions between nationals and non-nationals.[28]

What came to be most intensively policed were not borders but access to Irish citizenship. A number of analyses (including by this author) emphasise efforts to mobilise racism in support of the government's case for 'commonsense citizenship'.[29] These highlighted various statements by Michael McDowell, the then Minister of Justice, which insinuated that African asylum seekers were exploiting Irish maternity hospital services and a 'loophole in the constitution' in seeking to have Irish-born children entitled to Irish citizenship. The main political party in government ran a campaign in 2004 using the slogan 'commonsense citizenship'. However, the crucial cognitive distinction in the debate leading up to the referendum, made repeatedly by government officials, politicians and the media was a distinction between 'nationals' and 'non-nationals'. Immigrants were generally referred to as 'non-nationals'.

The term 'non-national' derived from the Irish Nationality and Citizenship Act (2001) that superseded the Aliens Act (1935). It systematically replaced the term 'alien' in Irish legislation and was used by the Department of Justice Equality and Law Reform (DJELR) in security debates – in reports about crime, human trafficking and illegal immigration – and by the Department of Enterprise and Employment to describe immigrant workers. By 2004 the 'national–non-national' dualism had become the prevalent common-sense conceptual framework for political and media debates about immigration. Racial state theories as these have come to be applied in the Irish case do not address tendencies towards solidarity with co-ethnics and fellow citizens that I refer to as expressions of ethnic nepotism.[30] Steve Garner, in his analysis of the Citizenship Referendum quotes a statement by Senator John Minihan (a member like McDowell of the Progressive Democrats) as exemplifying the government's case for the Referendum:

> People with no social, historic or cultural links to Ireland should not be able to freely confer Irish citizenship on their children. These children currently born in Ireland will in turn, be able to confer Irish citizenship on their own children and grandchildren even if they never reside in Ireland.[31]

It was from such Irish-born foreign bodies that the Irish nation, to paraphrase Foucault, had to be defended.

The 2004 Referendum outcome, whereby 80 per cent of the Irish nationals who participated voted to remove the birthright to citizenship from the Irish-born children of immigrants, has been *the* crucial event in the governance of immigrants within Irish society. The referendum outcome did not affect those immigrants who could trace Irish ancestry. Millions descended from the Irish Diaspora not born in Ireland remained entitled to become Irish citizens but Irish-born children of immigrants who did not have Irish blood had no right to become naturalised. The latter fall outside the Irish nation, which seems intent on remaining an ethnic nation. Naturalisation rates for applicants for Irish citizenship are exceedingly low by international standards. For example, in 2009 the UK and Australia refused to grant citizenship to 6 per cent or less of long-term resident candidates who applied.[32] In 2009 Ireland refused applications for naturalisation from 47 per cent of applicants. In this context the exclusion of migrants from the Irish nation can be seen to have been fostered by the state. The rationale for promoting such ethnic nepotism has been outlined by David Goodhart in the following terms:

> The justification for giving priority to the interests of fellow citizens boils down to the pragmatic claim about the value of the nation-state. Without fellow-citizen favouritism, the nation-state ceases to have much meaning. And most of the things liberals desire – democracy, redistribution, welfare states, human rights – only work when one can assume the shared norms and solidarities of national communities.[33]

Goodhart argues that citizens share mutual obligations with one another and that there are inevitable limits to the solidarity human beings are willing to express towards others. Solidarities with fellow citizens, he argues, come easier than with non-citizens.[34] Solidarities with co-ethnics come easier than with those from other ethnic groups just as solidarity with family members come easier than solidarity between those without kinship bonds. 'To put it bluntly', Goodhart argues 'most of us prefer our own kind'.[35]

Kenan Malik has highlighted close similarities between Goodhart's presumptions and the 'unsavoury claims' of what Frank Salter terms ethnic nepotism theory.[36] Ethnic nepotism theory ultimately makes similar assertions to nineteenth-century essentialist understandings of national identity. In Salter's account of 'genetic interests' the blood and soil territorial imperative of romantic nationalism is repackaged as a selfish-gene territorial imperative. Salter like Goodhart argues that diversity undermines the moral consensus on which social solidarity rests.[37] For all that the socio-biology theory behind such claims is dubious it is difficult to dispute the assertion that many Irish nationals care more about what happens to other Irish nationals than to what are termed 'non-nationals'. As Chapter 4 noted, an important impetus for the 2004 Citizenship Referendum were public concerns about the fate of Irish citizen children who were deported. Once such children were no longer Irish citizens – those born after 2004 – public outcry at such deportations became more muted. In this sense the biopolitics of the Referendum enacted the kind of socio-biological prescriptions advocated by Salter and Goodhart.

Within the Irish ethnic state, where most citizens are part of the dominant ethnic group, feelings of solidarity that exclude non-citizens proved easy to rouse in 2004. Lentin and writers such as Paul Gilroy would argue that the 'technical, anthropological language of "ethnicity" and "culture" is just another way of speaking about "race"'.[38] In so far as the Referendum was about bolstering *jus sanguine* definitions of Irishness this seems to be case. However, the entity that defended the Irish nation from 'non-nationals' was a self-professed ethnic state.

Security, territory, population and racism

Governmentality meant for Foucault the circumstances, institutions, forms of knowledge and practices that allowed for the exercise of power. In his lectures published as *Security, Territory, Population* where, he developed his concept of governmentality, he depicted efforts to control populations ('power that has the population as its target') as dependent upon a complex ensemble of institutions, procedures, analyses, reflections and tactics as these have played out over the past few centuries. In Foucault's account the modern state was the result of such efforts. In this sense, the development of government preceded the modern state and governmentality remained something wider than the state. He was trenchantly critical of accounts that depicted the state as a monolithic unified entity:

> the state, doubtless no more today than in the past, does not have this unity, individuality, and rigorous functionality, nor, I would go so far as to say, this importance. After all, maybe the state is only a composite reality and a mythicized abstraction whose importance.[39]

The core feature of modernity was not, he continued, the state's takeover of society but rather the 'governmentalization' of the state. While government came to be increasingly presented as synonymous with the state it was more the case that the state came to be entangled within a wider web of practices, knowledges *and* institutions that were manifested both internal and external to the state. According to Foucault, security, territory and population were the objects of government *before* preoccupations with 'race' emerged in the West.[40] In this context racial knowledges (beliefs that there were such things as races, ideas of race-as-nation) – became an aspect of how societies defined and policed themselves. Societal responses to immigrants (the foreign bodies) were, for Foucault, a subset of the internally focused preoccupations with bio-politics. And again this bio-politics could not be reduced to that which was defined by the state. In this context racisms constituted one element – as forms of knowledge and practices – in the care and coercion of populations within a given territory. In different times and places race and racism (however defined) have played greater or lesser roles in the practices of states and wider governmentality. What then of the Irish case?

Racism, modernisation and social hygiene

Race thinking became part of Irish nation-build prior to the formation of the Irish state. Whether through nationalist histories, the Gaelic linguistic revival or academic debates on what constituted a nation (considered in Chapters 2 and 3) specific societal rules of belonging were proposed that came to be institutionalised within the new state. Beliefs in Irish cultural and race-as-nation ethnic distinctiveness preceded an Irish state. These came to be institutionalised in a post-independence ethnic state. The role of the Irish state in governing what it was to be Irish – through for example school curricula and the promotion of the Irish language – institutionalised elements of a wider cultural politics. Elements outside the jurisdiction of the state included leisure and religion. Crucially the Church and the GAA – the main sporting organisation – were both organised at parish level. So too were the schools which were owned and controlled by the Church. Such institutions were integral to pre-independence nation-building and to intergenerational reproduction of identities (senses of local and national belonging) after independence. In this context nation-building can hardly be defined in terms of acts by the state or government understood solely in terms of what the state does. Certainly the state has institutionalised definitions of belonging. The constitution, legislation and state practices define and police definitions of Irishness through the mechanisms of citizenship but such definitions can hardly be understood to have originated within or to have been confined to those elements of government invested in the state.

The rules of belonging that apply within Irish society are sociologically wider than might be encompassed by definitions of citizenship, ethnos or race. Furthermore these can be seen to change over time. State efforts to regulate, care for and coerce populations strive for different outcomes at different times. The lives of the poor came under scrutiny during the nineteenth century. The Irish poor experienced equivalents of the social hygiene introduced to civilise their equivalents elsewhere. For example, in an essay entitled 'Race and Class in the Language of Charity in Nineteenth-Century Dublin' Margaret Preston describes a context where, one's class was as final as 'caste', where discourses of the poor as a 'race apart' applied in Dublin as in London and became internalised in Catholic as well as Protestant philanthropy.[41] Philanthropic efforts to govern the lives of the poor coexisted with the expansion of education and other forms of social policy aimed at governing populations.

It was only from the early 1960s Travellers became the focus of social policies explicitly aimed at assimilating them in such terms. Economic development rather than the intergenerational reproduction of culture (the Irish language) and religion became the pre-eminent nation-building project of the last half-century. The 1963 Report of the Commission on Itinerancy is no less a key text of developmental nation-building than the 1958 *Economic Development* report that is usually emphasised in accounts of post-1950s modernisation.[42] In this context Travellers became racialised as enemies of progress. Travellers were displaced from the rural economy that sustained them by economic modernisation and the mechanisation of agriculture. They became increasingly urbanised and found themselves increasingly in conflict with the inhabitants of new suburbs and bunga-lows on the outskirts of towns such as Ennis.

In *Becoming Conspicuous: Irish Travellers, Society and the State 1922–70* Aoife Bhreatnach argues that the state played a role in deepening the social distance between Travellers and the rest of the Irish population. This occurred to a considerable extent as the role of the state in education and social housing expanded. The increasingly regulated lives of the settled poor came to differ increasingly from those of Travellers. Increasing state regulation of work and trading along with the expansion of education and slum clearance rendered Travellers increasingly conspicuous. As argued by Bhreatnach:

> Niches occupied by travellers were eroded not only by increased intol-erance, or a wave of vast impersonal 'modernisation', but by persistent government regulation of various aspects of Irish social organisation. Such regulation also served to make Travellers increasingly distinctive and, often, unacceptably different.[43]

Lentin and McVeigh assert in their 2006 book *After Optimism? Ireland, Racism and Globalisation* that Anti-Traveller prejudice in Ireland 'has constantly carried with it a genocidal logic'.[44] Yet, for all that Travellers in Ireland have been racialised and excluded from the ongoing processes of nation-building, there are crucial differences between an impetus towards assimilation and one towards genocide. The sole evidence of genocidal logic marshalled by Lentin and McVeigh, a passing reference to a call by a deputy Lord Mayor during the 1980s for the incineration of Travellers, is hardly compelling, and less so again when one considers that Belfast is not part of the Republic of Ireland.[45] Chapters 6 examined the communal undercurrents of anti-Traveller violence in County Clare. Clearly violence forms part of the repertoire of anti-Traveller racism as it does in the case of other manifestations of racism examined in the previous chapter. Such violence is at times ignored by the state but it is hardly orchestrated by the state.

Lentin also argues that state policies towards Travellers which denied their ethnicity (and therefore the legitimacy of their claims to have experienced racialised discrimination) exemplified the intersections between coercion and care that Foucault had in mind:

> While the racial state deprives Travellers of their chosen 'ethnic' status which would allow them to name their discrimination 'racism', it does so in the pretence of caring, based on a Foucauldian 'biopolitics', according to which the role of the state is to 'manage', and in this case, assimilate and settle the Traveller population, but ultimately aiming to segregate them.[46]

The politics of Traveller exclusion described in Chapter 6 were communal rather than state led and found expression within local politics rather through central government. Yet, state policies and guidelines – outlined in the report of the Commission on Itinerancy and its successors to some extent defined the contours of communal exclusions. The somewhat fanciful proposals considered by Clare County Council, to intern and re-educate all Traveller in the mid-west region in a camp at Knockalisheen are closer to what Lentin and McVeigh refer to as genocidal logic than anything that subsequently transpired. The notion of a regional internment centre recalled efforts by the Australian state to forcibly assimilate Aboriginal people of the kind depicted in the 1930s-set movie *Rabbit Proof Fence* where children were forcibly removed from their families. What transpired was no less destructive in intent to Traveller ways of life, a cocktail of care and coercion, neglect and discrimination. Segregation in schools coexisted with poor-quality education. Coercive efforts to settle Travellers coexisted with discriminations designed by local politicians that prevented Travellers from accessing housing. If the state fostered assimilation, assimilation failed because of local communal and local political 'go move shift' vetoes on proposals to settle Travellers. As spatial conflicts between settled suburbanites and Travellers deepened so too did anti-Traveller racism.

The 1995 Report of the Task Force on the Travelling People seemed to usher in a new era of anti-discriminatory policies. However, the apparent gains – evident in equality legislation and statutory obligations to provide accommodation for Travellers were undermined by an anti-Traveller realpolitik within local government. With the passing of further legislation in 2002 central government undermined obligations placed upon local authorities to address the accommodation needs of Travellers. As the Irish state developed an anti-racism institutional infrastructure during the first decade of the twenty-first century it also responded to anti-Traveller political populism, be it by shutting down the Citizen Traveller campaign when it described the Housing Miscellaneous Provisions Act (2002) as racist, undermining the ability of Travellers to make complaints under equality legislation without having to take cases to court, imposing draconian cuts upon the Equality Authority in 2007 because it supported Travellers in legal actions against the state or by threatening to remove funding from a Traveller organisation because it expressed solidarity with Roma (see Chapter 10).

Clearly the Irish state is implicated in anti-Traveller racism. From the establishment of the Commission on Itinerancy in 1960 onwards a veneer of care and considerable coercion of Travellers by local authorities and from 2002 by central government can be identified. Chapter 7 illustrates how denial of Traveller ethnicity was very much bound up with the political influence of anti-Traveller racism. For example, the Report of the Task Force on the Travelling People (1995) accepted Traveller cultural distinctiveness but fudged recognising Traveller ethnic distinctiveness. The report apparently rejected the assimilationism of the Commission on Itinerancy but it was clear from the 'Minority Report' of local government representatives appended to the Report of the Task Force that beliefs in Traveller cultural inferiority – historicist racism a Goldberg describes it – influentially persisted among at least some members of the Task Force.

While the Task Force identified 400 recommendations aimed at addressing discrimination and barriers faced by Travellers in Ireland it did not identify racism as a contributing factor in any of these. In the absence of ethnic recognition none of these barriers or discriminations were identified as racist.

Racism, migration and foreign bodies

Decisions by the Irish state to restrict the entry of Jewish refugees before, during and after the Holocaust suggest the salience of racial state theories. Chapter 3 describes an exclusionary process of nation-building within which Jews came to be ideologically depicted as enemies of the Irish nation, prior to the formation of the Irish state. It identified anti-Semitism within the Catholic press, trade unions and also considered manifestation of communal anti-Semitism in Limerick in 1904 that was stoked by Fr Cregh's assertion that Jews were enemies of the Church and exploiters of Irish people worse than Cromwell. He advocated the use of boycotts, a strategy linked to agrarian emancipatory politics (against colonial oppressors) as one to free the people of Limerick from supposed exploitation of Jews. With the formation of the state, anti-Semitism found overt expression in the words and deeds of some senior officials, whose anti-Semitism was tolerated by others. In the case of the extreme anti-Semitism of Charles Bewley, the only criticism was the extent of his obsession with Jews, not his anti-Semitism per se.

The analysis in Chapter 4 of Ireland's response to the Holocaust is that even though deValera was far from anti-Semitic his sometimes advocacy of Jewish refugees had to be by political stealth, given the extent of anti-Semitism at the time. So while Oliver J. Flannagan was atypical among post-independence politicians in making anti-Semitic statements his perspective was not contested by others. The persistence of influential anti-Semitism within the Department of Justice, personified by Peter Berry, suggests a pronounced institutional racism, unlikely to have been contested within the organisation. The trail of evidence for institutional (i.e. state-fostered) anti-Semitism dries up after the late 1950s when Ireland's ratification of the UN Convention on the Status of Refugees challenges the autonomy of the Department of Justice to set policies of keeping Jews out of Ireland. Most likely the post-Holocaust normative challenges to anti-Semitism – still prevalent in many Western countries – began also to have an influence on what officials felt they could say or commit to writing without being challenged. It seems that institutional anti-Semitism was the work of a small number of influential committed Jew haters. Yet the institutional climate was such that until the late 1950s it was unlikely that overt expressions of anti-Semitism by officials would have been challenged.

If Jews ceased to be a racialised group, responses to asylum seekers came to mirror in many respects how Jews were treated as enemies of the nation. In the absence of available archives it is difficult to identify to what extent the organisational culture of the twenty-first century DJELR resembles that of the Department of Justice that presided over the exclusion of Jews before, during or after the Holocaust. To considerable extent its security governance brief has remained unaltered.[47] The DJELR presided over the development of a patently coercive asylum system whereby punitive measures were promoted as a means of discouraging refugees from exercising their rights under UN conventions ratified by the Irish state. The DJELR was a key actor in orchestrating the 2004 Referendum on Citizenship.

The decision to hold the referendum can be located within a distinct sequence of security governance measures orchestrated by the DJELR. The first phase consisted of efforts to defend Irish sovereignty against asylum seekers through the ramping up of border controls by means of carrier liability legislation and the introduction of direct provision to deter applications for asylum (represented by the then minister of justice as welfare tourism). Direct provision fostered internal barriers in two ways. First, punitively low levels of benefit (held to the same low level year after year from 2000 to 2012) served to materially isolate asylum seekers from wider Irish society. Second, the creation of a parallel 'direct provision' welfare system for asylum seekers (operated by the DJELR, an entity with hitherto no track record in the provision of welfare goods and services and one charged with advocating the deliberate exclusion of asylum seekers from Irish society) administratively isolated them from the wider social policy system.

The second phase (the regulation of citizenship and residency) culminated in the 2004 Referendum on Citizenship. It began with a legal challenge to a 1987 High Court interpretation of the Constitution. The 1987 ruling (*Fajouou* v. *Minister of Justice*) blocked the deportation of non-citizens who had an Irish citizen child. The child's meaningful right to enjoy Irish citizenship required that its family be also allowed to reside in the state. This ruling had subsequently allowed for the regularisation of a significant number of asylum seekers and other immigrants with Irish-born children. A DJELR 'policy decision' was made to begin to refuse leave to remain to asylum seeker families in the knowledge that this would trigger a further test case in the Supreme Court.[48] In April 2002 the 1987 ruling was overturned in the High Court (*Lobe* v. *Minister of Justice*). On 23 January 2003 the Supreme Court upheld this ruling, in essence holding that the Irish citizen child of non-citizens could be deported with its parents unless the non-citizen parent agreed to be deported without their child. This ruling was effectively superseded by the June 2004 Referendum on Citizenship that removed the existing birthright to citizenship from the Irish-born children of non-citizens.

Theories of racism in context

One problem with the kinds of theoretical approaches considered in this chapter according to Steve Loyal and Kieran Allen is for all that 'questions of racialisation are insightfully discussed', 'endemic tendencies of modernity to exclude others' revealed and 'restrictive forms of ethnic nationalism' exposed, the accompanying analyses 'are pitched at a very high level of generality'. There also exists, they suggest, within some of the literature on racism in the Irish case something of a tendency to transmute 'the complex and contradictory attitudes of the indigenous population into a flattened metaphysical formula about a fear or dislike of the other'.[49] Racism and exploitation, they argue, finds expression in specific material contexts. Here the state comes to orchestrate categories for migrants that racialise some (the asylum seekers unwanted by the state), exploit others (immigrant workers on permit systems that foster their economic exploitation as bonded labour) yet privilege some (high-skilled and professionals from some countries of origin).

Some accounts of racism Ireland that draw upon Goldberg's racial state archetype argue the need for greater nuance. Rebecca King-O'Riain, drawing on Irish case studies of census, citizenship and language policy (all potentially instruments of a racial state) argues that these illustrate that there is no consistent 'logic' to state racialisation. Such policy areas, she argues, display contradictory goals, some exclusionary, others inclusive.[50] Her argument is that race and racialisation are strongly determined by the state but bleed into other realms of social life not controlled or shaped directly by the state. Goldberg himself argues that race, however states might seek to define and codify it, it is 'ultimately uncontainable'. In an important sense glossed over in accounts that portray the racial state as some kind of monolithic entity, states reflect societal racisms. As put by Goldberg with a degree of nuance absent from much of the Irish literature that draws on his work:

> In shaping the state's personality, racial configurations likewise mould the sorts of personhood rendered possible or permissible within the global frames and flows between modern states, though not in any narrowly deterministic sense.[51]

In a 2010 article Alistair Christie concluded that while it was hard to argue against the increasing significance of the politics of 'race' in Ireland it was important to recognise how government policies and practices were often inconsistent and contradictory:

> there is no consistent logic to the racialisation by the state in Ireland, rather racially repressive legislation co-exists with laws that encourage

greater social justice and equality. In addition to this inconsistency in state policy making, there are also unintended consequences and gaps in legislation which the State fails to predict and/or control.[52]

Theories of racism or ethnic nepotism offer, at best, only partial explanations of responses to immigration. Such theories are, however, necessary because the kinds of grass-roots experiences of racism detailed in the next chapter require contextual explanations that focus upon wider society and, of course, the actions and inactions of the state.

Notes

1 On racial state perspectives, see R. Lentin and R. McVeigh, *After Optimism: Ireland, Racism and Globalisation* (Dublin: Metro Eireann, 2006) and A. Christie, 'From Racial to Racist State: Questions for Social Work Professionals Working with Asylum Seekers', *Journal of Applied Social Studies*, 7(2) (2006), pp. 35–49; on ethnic-nepotism, see B. Fanning, *New Guests of the Irish Nation* (Dublin: Irish Academic Press, 2009) and B. Fanning, 'Integration Policy Convergence and Welfare Ethnic Nepotism in the Republic of Ireland', in Andrzej *Suszycki* (ed.), *Welfare Citizenship and Welfare Nationalism in the New Europe* (Helsinki: NordWel, 2011).

2 A. D. Smith, *National Identity* (Harmondsworth: Penguin, 1991), p. 8.

3 Stephen Castles and Alastair Davidson, *Citizenship and Migration: Globalisation and the Politics of Belonging* (London: Macmillan, 2000), pp. 13–15.

4 A. Poole, 'In Search of Ethnicity in Ireland', in B. Graham (ed.), *In Search of Ireland* (London: Routledge, 1997), p. 132.

5 B. Fanning, 'From Developmental Ireland to Migration Nation: Immigration and Shifting Rules of Belonging in the Republic of Ireland', *Economic and Social Review*, 41(3) (2011), pp. 395–412, p. 400.

6 S. Garner, 'Babies, Bodies and Entitlement: Gendered Aspects of Citizenship in the Republic of Ireland', *Parliamentary Affairs*, 60(3) (2007), pp. 437–51, p. 443.

7 Garner, 'Babies, Bodies and Entitlement', p. 447.

8 R. Lentin and R. McVeigh, 'Irishness and Racism – Towards an E-Reader, *Translocations*, 1(1) (2006), pp. 22–40, p. 24.

9 R. Lentin, 'Ireland: Racial State and Crisis Racism', *Ethnic and Racial Studies*, 30(4) (2007), pp. 610–27, p. 610.

10 Goldberg, *The Racial State* (Oxford: Blackwell, 2002), pp. 105–6.

11 For example, Christie, 'Racial to Racist State'.

12 Goldberg, *Racial State*, p. 43.

13 *Ibid.*, pp. 92–3; Lentin, 'Ireland: Racial State', p. 612.

14 Lentin, *ibid.*

15 M. Burleigh and W. Wipperman, *The Racial State* (Cambridge: Cambridge University Press, 1991).

16 Christie, 2010, p. 5.

17 A. Christie, 'Whiteness and the Politics of "Race" in Child Protection Guidelines in Ireland', *European Journal of Social Work*, 13(2) (2010), pp. 199–215, p. 201.

18 Goldberg, *Racial State*, pp. 200–38.

19 E. Balibar, 'Racism and Crisis', in Etienne Balibar and Immanuel Wallerstein (eds), *Race, Nation, Class: Ambiguous Identities* (London: Verso, 1991) pp. 217–27.

20 Lentin, 'Ireland: Racial State', p. 611.

21 B. Gray, 'Governing Integration', in B. Fanning and R. Munck (eds), *Globalisation, Migration and Social Transformation: Ireland in Europe and the World* (London: Ashgate, 2011), p. 94.

22 Lentin, 'Ireland: Racial State', p. 614.

23 M. Foucault, *Society Must be Defended* (London: Penguin, 2003), p. 77.

24 *Ibid.*, pp. 82–3.

25 *Ibid.*, p. 103.

26 M. Foucault, *Security, Territory, Population: Lectures at the Collège de France 1977–1978*, ed. M. Senellart (London: Palgrave, 2007), p. 108.

27 B. Fanning, *Immigration and Social Change in the Republic of Ireland* (Manchester: Manchester University Press, 2011), p. 61.

28 K. Howard, 'National Identity and Moral Panic and East European Folk Devils', in Fanning and Munck, *Globalization*, p. 168.

29 B. Fanning and F. Mutwarasibo, 'Nationals/Non-Nationals: Immigration, Citizenship and Politics in the Republic of Ireland', *Ethnic and Racial Studies*, 39(3) (2007), pp. 439–60; Garner, 'Babies, Bodies and Entitlement', p. 438.

30 B. Fanning, *New Guests of the Irish Nation* (Dublin: Irish Academic Press, 2009), pp. 181–7.

31 Cited in Garner, 'Babies, Bodies and Entitlement', p. 441.

32 As highlighted by the Immigrant Council of Ireland (www.immigrantcouncil. ie). The comparisons here are like for like: applicants who met long-term residency requirements and thus eligible to apply (see Fanning, *Immigration*, p. 168).

33 D. Goodhart, 'The baby boomers see sense' (*Observer*, 24 February 2008).

34 D. Goodhart, 'Discomfort of Strangers' *Prospect*, June 2004.

35 *Ibid.*

36 K. Malik, *Strange Fruit: Why Both Sides Are Wrong in the Race Debate* (Oxford: One World, 2007), pp. 263–4.

37 F. K. Salter, 'Introduction', in F. K. Salter (ed.), *Welfare, Ethnicity and Altruism: New Findings and Evolutionary Theory* (London: Frank Cass, 2004) p. 5.

38 See P. Gilroy, Between Camps: Nations, Cultures and the Allure of Race (London: Allen Lane, 2000).

39 Foucault, Security, p. 108.

40 In *Security, Territory and Population* Foucault does not mention race or racism even once, whereas in *Society Must Be Defended* the role of race thinking in ordering internal populations is strongly emphasised. The reason is that the former is in fact concerned with the emergence of governmentality in the post-medieval period whereas the latter is focused on an era when race-as-nation discourses had become prevalent.

41 M. Preston, 'Discourse and Hegemony: Race and Class in the Language of Charity in Nineteenth-Century Dublin', in T. Foley and S. Ryder (eds), *Ideology and Ireland in the Nineteenth Century* (Dublin: Four Courts Press, 1998).

42 Government of Ireland, *Economic Development* (Dublin: Stationery Office, 1958).

43 A. Bhreatnach, *Becoming Conspicuous: Irish Travellers, Society and the State 1922–70* (Dublin: University College Dublin Press, 2006), p. 5.

44 R. Lentin and R. McVeigh, *After Optimism? Ireland, Racism and Globalisation* (Dublin: Metro Éireann Publications, 2006), p. 131.

45 This criticism of hyperbolic assertions about genocidal logic is shared by a published review of *After Optimism*: 'What begins as an effective illustration – backed up with many examples – of the prevalence of anti-Travellerism … Ends in the assertion (with only one example to back it up involving a Lord Mayor of Belfast who in the 1980s called for the "incineration" of travellers) that widespread incitement of hatred towards Travellers belies a supposed all-consuming state inspired genocidal logic' (A. Ní Mhurchú, *Translocations*, 3(1) (2008), 176–9, p. 177).

46 Lentin, 'Ireland: Racial State', p. 615.

47 On security governance perspectives within the DJELR, see Fanning, *Immigration*, pp. 43–7.

48 D. O'Connell and C. Smith, 'Citizenship and the Irish Constitution', in U. Fraser and C. Harvey (eds), *Sanctuary in Ireland: Perspectives on Asylum Law and Policy* (Dublin: Institute of Public Administration, 2003) p. 265.

49 S. Loyal and K. Allen, 'Rethinking Immigration and the State in Ireland' in. pp. 213–14.

50 R. King-O'Riain, 'Re-Racialisling, the Irish State through the Census, Citizenship and Language', in A. Lentin and R. Lentin (eds), *Race and State* (Cambridge: Cambridge Scholars Press, 2006), p. 275.

51 Goldberg, *Racial State*, p. 274.

52 Christie, 'Whiteness', p. 201.

9

Experiences of racism

This chapter examines cases studies of how racism is understood and experienced by victims of racist violence, harassment and various forms of discrimination. As distinct from the kinds of academic understandings and debates set out in the previous chapter, it draws upon 2011 research by the Immigrant Council of Ireland (ICI) and other studies of racism.[1] The aim in setting out case studies in some detail is to capture a sense of the dynamics of incidents of racist harassment, violence and anti-social behaviour; the challenges encountered by victims in accessing meaningful support; and, no less crucially, the consequences of such incidents on the lives of victims and their families. Other sources drawn upon include print and social media. The aim of this chapter is to offer concrete examples and to explore some of the difficulties and challenges in getting racism taken seriously.

Experiences of racism are inevitably subjective. Often the person who perceives herself as a victim cannot be sure about the motivations of those who she perceives as perpetrators. A person may be quite unaware that they are being discriminated against or that the motivation for such discrimination is racist or – as the academic theories discussed in the previous chapter would have it – she is the victim of some kind of state or institutional racism where, even if there are no identifiable perpetrators, the outcomes she experiences differ from what might otherwise be expected. Sometimes racism works like a toxic substance. The damage it does is cumulative. Experiences of ongoing racist abuse or discriminations can affect how victims perceive new situations. African participants in the ICI research described unrelenting experiences of racism. Filipino respondents described feelings of anxiety and insecurity that were the product of experiences of racist verbal abuse on the streets, harassment and violence, bullying at work that they saw made possible by their insecure immigration status and by racism in Irish society. Various experiences with immigration officials, at work, on the streets and in the neighbourhoods where they lived produced a sense of insecurity and anxiety. Collectively such experiences produced a climate of insecurity and anxiety.

Interpretations of events and experiences by victims or their advocates are inevitably influenced by prevalent understandings of racism. As noted in Chapter 1 such understandings evolve over time, so that what one generation regards as a manifestation of racism or, indeed of some other form of discrimination (for example, homophobia) might not be acknowledged in the same way by an earlier generation. Such societal understandings of racism are normative.

In this context, anti-racism activists and researchers and artists have often sought to deepen understandings of the experiences and consequences of racism. Their aim, like equivalent opponents of discrimination encountered by women, people with disabilities, lesbians and gay men, has been to shift societal perceptions of what constitutes acceptable social behaviour, as a means of combating various forms of discrimination. For example, in the UK and the US normative and institutional understandings of racism have clearly deepened since the 1960s. Until then racist segregation of the kind referred to as apartheid in South Africa pertained in schools, in restaurants and on public transport in most parts of the US. Shifting American understandings of racism influenced other Western countries. In the UK activism against forms of discrimination deemed to be racist and a growing awareness of how damaging racism could be to social cohesion led to anti-racist legislation such as the Race Relations Act. Even before Ireland came to host its own black immigrant population, some decades later, the resultant normative shifts in Britain and America had some degree of influence on Irish understandings of racism.

My own formative experiences included watching Alex Haley's *Roots* and repeat showings of Sidney Poitier's *In the Heat of the Night* on Irish television, reading *To Kill a Mockingbird* by Harper Lee and learning as a teenager to recite the lyrics of Grandmaster Flash and the Furious Five's seminal *The Message*. Irish society experienced the shifting portrayals in Western popular culture of black people in recent decades whether the elevation of black characters in American crime dramas from caricature pimp (*Starsky and Hutch*) to politically correct dignified police captains (*NYPD Blue*) to flawed complex African-Americans (*The Wire*). British television, readily available in Ireland, also documented shifting portrayals of race and racism. Black and ethnic minority families have been consciously portrayed in programmes such as *EastEnders*. Irish schoolchildren learn about Martin Luther King and Nelson Mandela's respective struggles against segregation and apartheid but they may also listen to 50 Cent and Jay Z. Many who have never heard of the literature cited in the previous chapter have absorbed understandings of racism.

Yet being aware that racism exists hardly confers knowledge of the experience of racism no more than being aware of poverty is the same as being poor. An apparent consensus among Irish elites and opinion formers that racism was reprehensible preceded large-scale immigration. Yet, this came to be accompanied by narrow institutional understandings of racism and denials of experiences of racism. As earlier chapters in this book illustrate, Irish society has proved to be by no means exempt from Western racisms. Earlier chapters on the experiences of Travellers and Jews describe how Irish society had its own unresolved histories of racism. Many Irish people have come to imbibe racist beliefs. Many new immigrants in Ireland have come to experience racism manifested in very similar ways to that experienced by immigrant black and ethnic minorities in other countries.

Immigrant perspectives on racism

In August 2010 Lebeta Debela a 22-year-old asylum seeker was attacked by two men while out running in the outskirts of Limerick city. The assault received considerable local media coverage; Lebeta from Ethiopia had recently finished first in a half-marathon in Limerick city and had won a number of other races as a Limerick Athletics Club member. The attack occurred near the Knockalisheen asylum centre where he lived. He received head injuries. The assault left him unconscious. The story was reported in the local print media and radio and was picked up by the Ireland's main newspapers. Little of this coverage speculated whether the assault was racially motivated or not.[2] A number of articles quoted Lebeta's Irish coach who described how other members of the club were upset by the attack: 'In a couple of weeks we hope he will be back to himself again. He is such a quiet young boy, everybody is mad about him. All his training companions are always very keen to run with him and I'd say everybody is upset at what happened.'[3]

Unlike such Irish media coverage, an article on the same story, drawing on the same interview sources by an African-based journalist considered whether the assault was motivated by racism. It quoted a Garda superintendent who in his statement addressed the issue of racism:

> We would be very concerned about a serious assault. If there was a racist undertone to it, that would be a particularly distressing and worrying development, if this victim was targeted because of his race. We are very anxious to try and identify the culprits.

It also quoted the Limerick Athletics Club press officer as stating that he was not aware of any racial motive for the attack while also saying that the athlete had nothing other than his running gear on him at the time, the inference being that the motive was unlikely to have been robbery.[4] Online debate in Limerick among bloggers focused on the prevalence of violent crime in Limerick and law-and-order issues, but again did not consider racism as a motive.[5]

Yet, a 2009 study undertaken on behalf of the Fundamental Rights Agency (FRA) placed Ireland among the worst five of the EU's twenty-seven member states where people of African origin had experienced racist crime or victimisation such as theft, assault or harassment. Sub-Saharan Africans in Ireland, a category that would include Lebeta Debela, ranked second highest across the EU in the percentage (39 per cent) of respondents who avoided certain places for fear of being assaulted, threatened or being harassed. Across the EU only the Roma in Poland were more likely to avoid certain places out of fear than black Africans in Ireland.

African and Filipino participants in the 2011 ICI study articulated such fears. A number of Filipino focus group participants recalled that they had experienced considerable hostility when they first came to Ireland around the turn of the millennium but that overt expressions of racist verbal abuse had risen again since the start of the economic crisis. Some participants in the Filipino focus group believed that Filipinos and other immigrants were particularly at risk from robbery and assault, that they were more likely than non-immigrants to be targeted by criminals and that Filipinos who experienced assaults and robberies were being attacked because they were immigrants:

It's like when we came (first), now we are going through it all over again for the past two years, since the start of the recession. [Annabelle]

Two Filipino nurses were walking outside the Mater private hospital. They tried to get the bag of one and had a blade. The Gardaí caught the men and she testified in court. She was supposed to go back to work for a month before moving to the USA but she feared going back so she resigned early. [Concepta]

Our friends have been burgled. Most have been burgled at this stage. Most have the feeling it's serious now, it's escalating. They complained to the Gardaí but the Gardaí think nothing can be addressed. The Filipino and Indians are targeted because we've jobs. It's not really nice to say that. [Daphne]

After Sunday mass, our friend was with her 3-year-old girl. They held a knife to the neck of the child and took everything. They always target immigrants. [Mary]

There is a feeling that they are targeting us now. [Concepta]

In 2009, our friend Jamie was going to work. He was near Griffith College and he was physically mugged. He lost consciousness and was rushed to A & E. He was very bruised and bloody. He also had a haemorrhage. He was so frightened he moved to the USA. He had been in Ireland since 2000/2001. This could be a racist attack. I think he felt it was a racist attack. It happened at the start of the recession. [Annabelle]

If Filipinos perceived that racism towards them was on the rise, African participants in the same study spoke of racism as an unrelenting constant in their lives. For example, one African participant who was the citizen of another EU country considered that racist verbal abuse was far more prevalent in Ireland than there:

I get abused in Ireland almost every day – that doesn't happen in Germany. For example, if I'm driving the car in Lucan or Blanchards-town, and if I stop at the lights, someone walking by will shout 'black bastard'. This happens every second day, on the bus or when I'm off duty. Not a month has gone by since I've come to Ireland when I haven't heard abuse. [Adam]

A number of other African participants who were also bus drivers described experiences of racist harassment, including experiences of racism from customers that they found to be extremely distressing. A number of examples are set out below. In the first example Adam describes an incident in July 2010 where he received racist abuse and was spat upon and where the Gardaí managed to arrest his assailants. As a result of the incident he became ill and could not work for several weeks. The incident occurred at night en route from Dublin 15 to the city centre:

There were 3 guys about 22 years old, an elderly woman and a girl at the bus stop. The guys had cans of beer. As they got on the bus, I told them they couldn't drink on the bus. They said they wouldn't. They got on without paying and went upstairs. I asked them to come down to pay on the PA system. They shouted 'What do you want you black bastard?' One of them came downstairs to pay for two of them and said the third person wouldn't come down to pay. I said I wasn't going to drive until I was paid. Another came down and started shouting 'What does this nigger want?' The third arrived down and said 'Let's go, we've no money'. They then wanted their money back. I said I could issue a refund but not give the money back. All three became abusive and started banging at the door and shouting 'Bring the nigger out, we'll kill him'. I rang the depot but no one answered. I pressed the Panic button. One of them put his hand in the small hole to open the door. All the passengers were quiet. I held onto his hand and then released it. He then spat in my face and left the bus. That was the last trip of the evening.

Simon described a similar incident from August 2010 where he received racist verbal abuse, was urinated upon from upstairs in the bus above his cabin and was upset by what he felt was a lack of subsequent support from management. Simon argued that unless a zero-tolerance approach was taken to such incidents these would only increase:

> Towards the end of my shift (11.15 p.m.), 10 youths aged 18–20 years of age were going into town. They were a bit drunk and didn't want to pay. I didn't move. I stayed for 10 minutes without moving. Two girls from the group came downstairs to pay. Two guys then came downstairs shouting 'fucking nigger, what are you doing here?'. I rang control. I was told to stay in the cabin and make sure they pay. They went upstairs and I started driving. When I was half way to town I saw some liquid coming down through the cabin ceiling. They were peeing from above.

Caleb described three incidents which occurred in early 2011 in which he experienced racist abuse. During the previous year, 2010, he reckoned he encountered such abuse about twice a week or about a hundred times that year. In the first two of the following examples he described difficulties in having this recognised as such from his supervisor who inferred that racist abuse was no different from any other kind of verbal abuse:

> (1)
> Early on a Saturday morning, I was coming up to the square. Three men got on the bus, they were Eastern European I think. They had two buggies. I asked them to fold the buggies and to keep the kids on their lap. They said yes OK, we will just get on first. They sat down and I reminded them to fold the buggies. They replied 'Fuck off, just do your job you fucking black bastard'. I called the garage who called the Gardaí. I sat there until they arrived and kicked the guys off the bus. The inspector then asked, 'Is the problem solved?'. After duty I told him, that the problem was solved as they were off the bus but they didn't abuse the bus but me; they abused me racially. The inspector replied 'We all get that – it could have been me'.
> (2)
> A young woman was getting on a non-wheelchair accessible bus. I told her she had to fold the buggy. She replied 'Why don't you go back to where you came from you black bastard'. I pulled over the bus and called the Gardaí. This is very hard to prove as I have no evidence. She'll lie and say she didn't say that... Dublin Bus told me it could have happened to anyone.
> (3)
> At the bus stop was a disabled woman in her early thirties. She never signalled that she wanted the bus. I pulled in. As I closed the door she jumped on and shouted 'Black bastard, you nearly killed me! Go back to where you came from black monkey'.

Some of these incidents were triggered when black drivers insisted that passengers pay their fares or otherwise obey the rules. Other members of the group stated that they had experienced similarly frequent levels of racist abuse. Sidney stated that when he worked on Nightlink buses or drove at weekends that he encountered two or three incidents of racist abuse per night. Roger felt that management did not understand the stress induced by experiences of racism:

> Some management look at it as nothing. It has a huge effect on our health. I used to have a problem every day. Every time I'd challenge someone to pay I'd get racial abuse. Even if I look at other drivers in cars, I get abuse. I had pain in my head, neck and shoulders. I even had chest pains. In 2010 I went to the GP and told him every time I get angry I get pain. He told me if I keep taking on everything, I'm going to die. Now I don't challenge. People in charge don't care either.

There have been some high-profile cases where racism has been acknowledged as a motivating factor in fatal assaults. A 29-year-old Chinese student of English, Zhao Liu Tao was assaulted in Dublin on 27 January 2002. It was reported that a five-member gang which included a 14-year-old boy, two 16-year-olds and an 18-year-old had been drinking on waste ground in the Beaumont area of north Dublin. The five were reported as making racist taunts and a fracas followed. One of the youths struck Mr Zhao with a metal bar. He died three days later in Beaumont Hospital. The case came to trial in March 2003 and one youth was convicted of manslaughter.[6] In 2008 two Polish men, Mariusz Szwajkos and Pavel Kalite were stabbed to death in Drimnagh.[7] The case came to trial in May 2010 and one man was convicted of murder. In both cases a gang of young people were linked to the incident.

When Amataya, a participant in the ICI study, described being racially assaulted at a bus stop in Dublin he felt that the dynamics of the incident recalled reports of the killings of Mariusz Szwajkos and Pavel Kalite. In that case both Polish men were killed following an assault by a group of teenagers that included girls who, as he understood it, played a role in triggering the attack. In his case the young teenage girl shouted at Amataya, 'You broke the glass of my car' (there was no car) which instigated the physical assault by male members of the group. One of them punched Amataya on the forehead. He fell down and replied that he did not know what she was talking about. He tried to run away but the male who had punched him gave chase. When he lost his footing and fell in the middle of the road his assailant kicked his back near his kidney. Somehow he managed to stand up and cross the road to the petrol station. He dialled 999 and reported the incident. After forty-five minutes the Gardaí arrived at the petrol station. He explained what had occurred and asked them were these kinds of incidents common? They replied that such incidents were uncommon.

While waiting for the Gardaí to arrive at the petrol station he asked the East Europeans working there were such incidents common. They replied yes and described a couple of similar attacks that had previously occurred nearby. In his subsequent letter to the Gardaí he described how other immigrants he knew considered such experiences to be common. He had heard accounts of such incidents from many immigrants including, Indians and other Asians, Africans, South Americans and Europeans. In each case their assailants were Irish.

In March 2011 Toyósi Shittabey, a 15-year-old black youth, was stabbed to death in an incident in Tyrelstown in Dublin 15 that many commentators have described as racist.[8] Two white Irishmen were arrested following the fatal assault. In the immediate aftermath the killing received considerable media coverage. Some of this speculated that killing had a racist motive but, because the case had yet to come to court and also arguably because of reluctance to acknowledge and discuss racism, much of this was circumspect. By contrast, internet discussion Toyosi's killing by other young people, immigrants and white Irish people was less guarded.

For example, an article entitled 'Racist killing of Toyosi Shittabey in Tyrelstown' on the Gombeen Nation blog attracted 149 postings in the period after his death.[9] These included posts from residents of the area, some from young people who knew the victim, posts that described other incidents of racist violence, expressions of sympathy to Toyosi's family and many expressions of anger that the apparently racist nature of the killing was not taken seriously enough and that the perpetrators had been released on bail. A number of postings noted that one of the perpetrators had been previously charged with incitement to hatred – using the word 'nigger' during an assault on two immigrants in 2000 during which one was stabbed a number of times – a decade earlier, posting links to media accounts of that incident. The flow of debate shifted from expressions of shock and grief (with a few posting from friends or acquaintances of the victim) to posts about the nature and extent of racism in Irish society, expressions of concern that the perpetrators would not be charged with murder and sufficiently punished. Then the debate shifted towards broader questions of evidence – including the need to distinguish between allegations about the behaviour and motivation of the perpetrators and what could be proved in court. Among these were the following postings (edited to include clarifications in brackets and some spelling corrections to phone-text postings) from black teenagers and mothers of black children about their experiences of racism.

The fears of black and other immigrant parents that their children will encounter racism are well founded. A study published by the Teachers' Union of Ireland (TUI) around the time of Toyosi's death involving 332 second-level and third-level (Institutes of Technology and Further Education Colleges) teachers found that 28 per cent were aware of racist incidents that had occurred in their school or college during the last month. African children were identified as particularly vulnerable to such incidents.[10] Online responses to Toyosi's killing posted on Gombeen Nation addressed the experiences of racism by children and young people:

> I looked at your face Toi and tears rolled from my face. I am a foreign mom with a 9 year old son. He loves Ireland, his Irish friends, my home is a home to all. I have a fear that like you he too will face the cruelty for the 'excuse' some have, that God created black people for white men to eradicate. Where is the justice in all this when laws overlook the pain you suffered, when the likes of Paul (one of the perpetrators) can live on Irish streets as men. You came to Ireland with hopes I am sure, to be a free man, a man that can enjoy a (foot)ball without looking over your shoulder and fulfil all your dreams. I pray for you and your family and all the young people out there – let the light of your life shine through, keep an eye on my son and all the foreign young people who love and feel they belong in Ireland. [Anonymous]

> Man, this is still pissing me off
> 'cause if y'all came to our country yeah
> We would'nt be acting like this at all
> This fucking racism that people be going on about is everywhere end before the irish government could see this, they had to kill our mate Toy
> Toy's death is significant in all the black people in Ireland's lives.
> Not only Irish people are racist. When I walk down the road Polish people will give me looks and shout words of abuse.
> And when I was on the bus with my mates a bunch of Irish kids turned around and said yo 'Africa's that way', that made me so MAD.
> We knew they hated us but don't mean you go killing us now.
> When y'all went to America and shit we ain't complaining and when white people made us slaves, we forgave them, but still you go and kill Marin Luther King, but we still forgiving as it is.
> THIS COUNTRY IS FUCKED UP MEHANN (KMT)

> You're a bit ignorant if you don't see what we're all talking about here, we're talking about how racism is becoming worse EVERYWHERE in Ireland, not just Tyrelstown. We didn't call ALL IRISH racist, a majority aren't but there shouldn't be any at all. How would you know what anyone is thinking?
> Some Irish if they see a (non)Irish person they'd be mad inside but they

wouldn't carry out any abuse because they know better. It's still racist. Every single person in your family could be racist and it wouldn't show. Racism could also be *visa versa* – not all foreign people are happy with whites and for all racist people out there is related to a black person because African people were the first on the surface of the earth, which just makes Adam and Eve black. This theory spouts a lot of queries? We might never know. [written by 13-year-old, Toy's mate]

This story is so sad.
I was guilty of skipping over the story when it first came up on the news, but when I sat down to read it properly it really struck a chord.
Like some of the other posters I'm baffled as to why he is facing man-slaughter charges and not murder. IT WAS MURDER. The scumbag should not have been on the streets in the first place.
My husband is black and my child is mixed race. This stuff scares me. It's hard to believe that while think I have the most beautiful family in the world, someone else out there would kill them based on the colour of their skin.
My heart goes out to that boy's mother. She will never be the same again. I truly hope the Irish stand up behind this case and make sure that knacker gets his just desserts. Make an example of him. Racism is not acceptable.
When I first started seeing my husband, we went on one date in town. In Temple Bar three absolute junkie knackers came up to us. One of them roared at the top of his voice: 'One in four of those c**ts has AIDS'. I almost fell out of my standing. I was seriously gobsmacked that people sill behaved in such a vile racist manner. I wouldn't mind if he was an upstanding, well dressed fully educated member of society with a valid point but he was an absolute moron. He was so enraged seeing a white girl with a black man. It was that whole mentality, they are taking our jobs they're taking our women. Grow up! I was angry at first. Then I just felt sorry for them. Losers, obviously dragged up!
God bless Toyosi's family Kelly

Many experiences of racism occur in the neighbourhoods where victims live. A 2007 estate management study by Fingal County Council (covering the Dublin 15 area where Toyosi was killed) identified a problem of racist intimidation, whereby some immigrants allocated local authority housing were 'being targeted for ongoing harassment'. Such harassment included 'the sending of projectiles into their street space, name calling, damage to possessions and racist bullying to their children at school'. The Fingal study located such harassment within a wider context of anti-social behaviour and intimidation that meant that residents were afraid to name anti-social households as they feared they would become subjected to abuse. Racist harassment of some tenants occurred alongside other incidents of anti-social behaviour, and as such could be to some extent viewed as part of a wider issue.[11] The Fingal study identified some 'racial tensions' in Blanchardstown:

> The problems centred on one area of new housing, part of a new infill to an established estate, were a group of non-indigenous families were allocated housing. According to community representatives from the area, local people in adjoining areas of the existing estate were assured that they would be given special consideration to the new housing. In the event the houses were allocated in accordance with the Council's scheme of letting priorities and a number were allocated to people from Ethnic minorities. Soon after taking up residence, these families were targeted for racial harassment, damage to property and verbal abuse.[12]

It must be noted that claims that 'indigenous' residents had been turned down for housing were unfounded. On examination it was found that none had applied. In effect the claim that immigrants were taking houses from local people was a species of urban myth, invoked to promote and justify hostility towards immigrants.

A 2008 study, *Building Integrated Neighbourhoods* published by the NCCRI identified racially motivated anti-social behaviour as a problem in all areas covered by the research. They were the Dublin City Council, Dublin South Council, Dundalk Town Council and Ennis Town Council areas. Racially motivated anti-social behaviour was identified as a problem in both local authority social housing and private housing developments, particularly in low-income areas.[13] Various UK studies suggest that incidents of racist harassment of people where they live can only be addressed through a focus on perpetrators as well as victims. Such studies find that perpetrators, most of whom are groups of minors or families, tend to perceive their harassment of black and ethnic minority neighbours as endorsed by the community within which they live. Research undertaken by the ICI in 2011 highlighted experiences of racist violence, harassment and anti-social behaviour. With the exception of 'Dexter' who is Filipino, the other victims of the incidents described below were black Africans. In all these cases the perpetrators were minors and sometimes were young children.

Arthur described receiving ongoing racist abuse from the children of their next-door neighbours. His family have been living in Clonskilla in Dublin since 2005. In 2008 their next-door neighbours' young children began calling him and other members of his family names. Even though these children were very young they engaged in constant harassment of Arthur's family by means of racist verbal abuse and by coming onto their property. One of the children aged about 6 years of age took to urinating at their window in front of his daughter in addition to using racist terms of abuse. They also experienced some harassment from those children's parents. As a result of various incidents, the family went on holiday for two weeks and left loud music playing while they were away. This meant that Arthur and his family had difficulty getting to sleep.

Arthur called the Gardaí three times to deal with their neighbours. In the absence of proof no charges were made against the neighbours. The abusive behaviour of their neighbour's children continued. Arthur and his wife began to take photographs every time the children crossed over the boundary onto their property. They then provided the photographs to the Gardaí. One local Garda who was supportive asked Arthur did he want to press charges. Arthur just asked him to talk to the neighbours and tell them he had documented proof of their harassment. The Garda did so and the children admitted what they had done and the harassment came to an end.

Adam described events that occurred when the car of a black woman he knew was being robbed in Blanchardstown. She called the Gardaí while the attempted robbery was taking place. However, the Gardaí stated they were unable to immediately respond to the incident. So she took a stick and ran after the kids. An Irish person saw this and rang the Gardaí. The Gardaí arrived immediately. Adam believed that the Gardaí took crime against black people less seriously than other crimes: 'You call the Gardaí to protect you but they don't. No matter what colour, what citizenship, they're supposed to protect the public.'

From early 2000 Andrew's council house in Tallaght and car were vandalised on a number of occasions. Car windows were broken on a number of occasions and their car was damaged repeatedly while parked outside their home. The damage was so severe and incidents were so frequent that their car had to be replaced on six occasions. Every week it seemed there was another incident. Andrew believed that a group of teenagers from the area aged about 14 or 15 years of age were responsible for the damage. But there were also some younger children in the group which harassed his family. This group engaged in ongoing verbal abuse, calling him,' 'black monkey' and 'nigger' telling him 'we do not want you here.' Andrew tried to talk to the parents of these children. The parents were aware of this behaviour but did nothing about it. Often the group of teenagers would sit on his car. Andrew recalled: 'They would crowd around the car, I would say nothing. I was fed up.'

The harassment appears to have escalated over time. Their house was robbed a number of times. On one occasion where Andrew, his wife, his children and his brother-in-law and sister-in-law were in the house a teenager broke a car window. Previous damage had occurred while he and his wife were out at work.

In May 2002, while the family were away overnight their house was robbed and all their possessions – beds, furniture and personal possessions – were stolen. The family left their house never to return. One of the Gardaí who responded to this incident advised the family to leave as this was 'a bad area'. Andrew remembers this Garda as being unusually supportive. He had come to the house before in response to various earlier incidents. He gave the family his business card and said he would provide information to the Council if needs be. Most of the time Andrew found the Gardaí to be unsupportive. Each time something happened, Andrew reported it to the Gardaí. It often took up to three hours for them to come. They used to call the Gardaí almost every weekend. The Gardaí tried to talk to the teenagers who were harassing them 'two or three times' but this resulted in no reduction of the harassment. The family also reported incidents to the Council. After their home was robbed in May 2002 they moved from the area.

When asked whether he felt his experiences in Tallaght were unusual he replied that in Tallaght they were the only African family in an all-Irish neighbourhood. However, Andrew described how he knew of several other African families who had had similar experiences of racist harassment and damage to their property in other parts of Tallaght and Clondakin. One friend's family similarly experienced two years of harassment before moving out of their council house. This family moved to Navan.

More than eight years later, in July 2010, Andrew's family was finally allocated a council house in south Dublin. Since moving there they have experienced one racist incident. Their car was parked in front of their neighbour's house. The neighbour, a middle-aged woman, came and banged on their door. When Andrew opened the door she shouted: 'I am living in my country, I'm Irish, you are not from here'. This incident happened at night. The woman was drunk and Andrew has only seen her once since.

Dexter had been living in west Dublin for several years with his family. The first incident occurred in 2009 when he arrived home from church on Sunday with his family. He heard a bang on the car. It had been hit by a stone. He got out and saw a group of children and teenagers aged between 12 and 15 throwing stones at his 3-year-old child. The teenagers used abusive language, including terms such as 'chinky eyed' and shouting 'you don't belong here'. His children were not hit by any of the stones thrown at them. Dexter picked up a stone and threw it at one of the teenagers. It hit him. Dexter spoke to the boy's parents. He told them what the boy had done and told them they were responsible for the behaviour of their children. These parents took action and did not let their son play near Dexter's house any more.

However, the harassment of Dexter and his family by the group of children continued. In 2010 at Halloween, the gang threw stones and fire crackers at his house. Over time the gang got bigger and Dexter and his family were still being harassed by the gang when he was interviewed in February 2011. Since the harassment began, Dexter no longer allows his children to play outdoors.

Dexter first complained to the Gardaí about this harassment in April 2009 but received limited support from that time until February 2011 when he recounted his experiences. He made numerous complaints about incidents. Garda patrols apparently responded to some incidents but the Gardaí never visited Dexter or his family at home:

> I called the Garda station in April 2009. The Gardaí said they'd send around a squad car. Sometimes they do, sometimes they don't. They send around unmarked cars sometimes.
>
> I phone the Gardaí every night and they have done nothing so far. They have never come to the house. After two weeks I went to the Garda station. I went to the station twice. It always happens at night so they say they will deal with it in the morning. Sometimes they lodge a report, sometimes they don't. Now I don't phone the police. Since 2009 I have called more than fifty times. No Garda has ever come to the house. It used to affect me when I was at work. I feel useless, I'm the father of a family and I can't protect the family.

Dexter stated that several other Filipino families of his acquaintance had experienced similar racist harassment in west Dublin. The ICI has highlighted a number of cases where the Gardaí have apparently ignored or inadequately responded to experiences of racist harassment and anti-social behaviour. Gardaí statistics arguably identify only a small percentage of racially motivated crimes that occur in Ireland. Yet research has indicated that significant percentages of black and ethnic minority populations have experienced or witnessed racist incidents, which should – if incidents were comprehensively reported and recorded number in their thousands. For example, a government-funded survey in 2004 found that 18 per cent of respondents had personally witnessed racist behaviour in Ireland.[14] A 2005 study by the Economic and Social Research Institute (ESRI) that 35 per cent of black Sub-Saharan African respondents had experienced racist harassment on the street, on public transport or in public places. The same study also found that some 19.5 per cent of

Table 9.1 Numbers of yearly recorded racially motivated incidents by category

Incident type	2007	2008	2009	2010
Minor assault	50	45	30	36
Assault causing harm	17	12	13	7
Harassment	11	9		7
Criminal damages	42	29	22	22
Public order offences	57	42	34	26
Drunkenness offences	6			
Menacing phone calls		5		
Incidents covered by Prohibition of Incitement to Hatred Act (1989)	13	15	10	
Total number of offences identifiable by Category	196	157	109	98
Overall total of racially reported incidents per annum	214	173	128	122

Source: Garda data (PULSE) collated by the Central Statistics Office
Note: Table 9.1 does not identify incidents where the total within a category is fewer than five per annum

respondents described being treated badly by the Gardaí on at least one occasion.[15] The 2005 ESRI study also found that black Africans were more likely than other non-EU migrants to experience harassment by neighbours or on the street but least likely to report such an incident to the police.[16] The number of racially motivated incidents officially recorded by the Gardaí has fallen year on year, from 214 incidents in 2008 to just 122 in 2010 (see Table 9.1). Yet, immigrants interviewed in studies such as ICI believe that that racist violence, harassment and anti-social behaviour has in fact risen since the beginning of the economic crisis.

Racist harassment involving minors and children emerged as a serious problem for some participants in the ICI research. There has, to date, been no Irish research that focuses on perpetrators but it is clear that efforts to contest racist harassment and anti-social behaviour need to focus on perpetrators as well as victims. A Home Office study of the perpetrators of racial harassment in the UK includes profiles of different age groups of children found to participate in racist harassment. These are noted here because of the apparent prevalence of similar kinds of perpetrators in the Irish case, as identified by our research:

- 15–18-year-olds likely to have parents with racist views living in areas where such views are prevalent. They may have black friends in school but not outside of school. They join in anti-social behaviour and racist harassment carried out by older youths so as to become accepted by them.
- 11–14-year-olds, also likely to have grown up in an area where racist views are prevalent and regularly expressed. They are likely to be low-achievers who receive little educational input from their parents. They are likely to have low self-esteem and to bully children weaker than them in order to gain prestige from their peers who they are unable to impress in other ways. Together with their peers, and especially older youth, they may engage in continual harassment and violence towards neighbouring families and particular individuals at school. They are also abusive and threatening towards people they pass on the street. They may engage in physical violence.
- 4–10-year-olds. Racism is part of the language with which they have grown up. Family members are likely to hold, and regularly express, racist views and condone or, at least fail to condemn, racist harassment. Such children are likely to be low-achievers in school. They are most likely to engage in racist harassment in school when they feel they can get away with it and in the neighbourhood where they live.[17]

ICI case studies give examples of racist harassment of immigrant families by neighbouring families. Again research undertaken on behalf of the Home Office in the UK finds that particular kinds of family found to be perpetrators of racist harassment. These tend to be problem families who are constantly abusive and threatening towards neighbours in general who 'tend to act as unit, encouraging and reinforcing each other's behaviour'. Young children from such families who racially harass neighbours are likely to be doing so with the approval of their parents. Older perpetrators are likely to feel they have the approval of their communities.

Institutional contexts

Many of these accounts of racism quickly shade into accounts of responses to racism, to difficulties experienced by victims in having their experiences of racism taken seriously. In almost all of the aforementioned ICI case studies (the experiences of Adam, Andrew and Dax and, as recounted earlier in the chapter, those of Amataya) victims of racism experienced what they considered was inadequate support from the Gardaí. The Gardaí have put in place a number of policies to address racially motivated crime. These are detailed in the next chapter. However, some black victims of racist violence, harassment and anti-social behaviour have experienced forms of institutional racism. At a March 2011 consultative event organised by the Gardaí one community representative present stated that Toyosi Shittabey was Ireland's equivalent to Stephen Lawrence.[18] The inquiry into the response by the Metropolitan Police in London to Stephen's death identified how the police in effect took the murder of a black teenager less seriously than it might have taken the killing of a white person and how the police tended to treat black victims of crime as if they were perpetrators.

There is no evidence that the Gardaí have not taken Toyosi's killing seriously. Yet, there are indications that some racially motivated harassment against black people have not been taken seriously, that some black people do not believe they will be treated fairly. At the same Garda Siochana consultative event one black participant described what occurred when a black friend had reported a dispute with a white couple. When the Gardaí arrived the black complainant was asked to produce proof of identity and immigration status. The Gardaí did not ask him about his complaint but instead asked the white couple to explain what had happened.

Experiences of racism are often cumulative in the sense that a specific incident is interpreted in light of the victims' wider experiences. Some African participants in the ICI research describe unrelenting experiences of racism at work, on the streets and in the communities where they lived. In effect, they may anticipate racism; expectations that their experiences will not be taken seriously may result in an unwillingness to report incidents. Just as many black Africans were found by the FRA to avoid certain areas it may also be the case that people who anticipate experiencing racism may seek to avoid a range of social situations, so that racism impedes the choices they make in a range of ways. It is also likely that the life chances of black Africans are influenced by cumulative experiences of racism. The 2006 census undertaken at a time when overall rates of unemployment were about 4 per cent found unemployment among Nigerian men to be about 50 per cent. The census also found that some 41 per cent of Nigerians in Ireland were educated to degree level. A study by the ESRI found that black people in Ireland were nine times more likely to be unemployed than white people. It may be that many marginalised black people in Ireland are able to identify multiple occasions when they encountered barriers as a result of racism.

Most black Africans living in Ireland arrived as asylum seekers just before or after the turn of the millennium. Many experienced what is described in Chapter 5 as structural racism. They were deliberately accorded lesser rights by the state, including no right to work or access to employment training. They became a racialised population in the politics of the citizenship referendum. More recently a very high proportion of these have had their applications for citizenship turned town because of a decision of the minister of justice to refuse citizenship to persons who have claimed benefits or become known to the police. Ireland is unusual in that minor offences such as cycling through red traffic lights have resulted in applications for citizenship being turned down. Other jurisdictions such as the UK, Canada and Australia, set a much higher threshold that only take into account serious offences in turning down applications for citizenship. Victims of racism who have contacted the ICI have been unwilling to make formal complaints because they fear that by coming to the attention of the Gardaí (as victims rather than offenders) they may have their application for naturalisation turned down.

Had Toyosi Shittabey lived, he may well have fulfilled the promise that those who knew him identified. However, in some crucial respects his options would have been more limited than many other Irish children. Because he was not an Irish citizen – even though he had grown up in Ireland – he would not have been allowed to attend third-level education unless he was able to pay the same high fees charged to non-EU citizens. Many of generation 1.5, the rising generation of immigrant teenagers who are growing up Irish but are not Irish citizens, face similar barriers. Migrants from EU countries have similar entitlements to third level education as Irish citizens. Those most likely to be denied such entitlements are non-whites who have come to Ireland from outside the EU.[19]

Notes

1 Interviews in this chapter cited from author's fieldnotes. See also B. Fanning, B. Killoran and S. Ní Bhroin, *Taking Racism Seriously: Racist Harassment, Violence and Anti-social Behaviour in Twenty-first Century Ireland* (Dublin: Immigrant Council of Ireland, 2011).
2 'Club members condemn attack' *Irish Times* (10 August 2010); 'Ethiopian runner hospitalised after attack', *Irish Examiner* (10 August 2010).
3 Interview/podcast on Limerick Live95fm radio (9 August 2010).
4 Wilfred Mulliro, 'Ethiopian athlete attacked, hospitalized in Ireland' *Alshahid Network/Ethiopian Review* (11 August 2010).
5 Limerick's Independent News Blog, accessed 30 August 2010.
6 *Irish Times* (28 January 2001).
7 *Irish Times* (10 May 2010).
8 *Sunday Tribune* (11 April 2010).
9 'Racist killing of Toyosi Shittabey in Tyrelstown', Gombeen Nation (http://gombeennation.blogspot.com, accessed 3 September 2010).
10 Teachers' Union of Ireland, *Results of the Behaviour and Attitudes Survey on Racism, Interculturalism and Resources for Minority Ethnic Students Incorporating*

Recommendations of the TUI Equality Council (Dublin: TUI, 2010).

11 E. Bergin, *Managing To Do Better: A Review of Estate Management Practice in Fingal County* (Dublin: Fingal County Council), p. 37.

12 *Ibid.*, p. 59.

13 D. Silke, M. Norris, F. Kane and B. Portley (2008), *Building Integrated Neighbourhoods: Towards an Intercultural Approach to Housing Policy and Practice in Ireland* (Dublin: NCCRI), pp. 94–5.

14 Millward Brown IMS, 'Presentation of Research Findings on Racism and Attitudes to Minority Groups', 2004, Know Racism (at: www.knowracism.ie).

15 F. McGinnity, P. J. O'Connell, E. Quinn and J. Williams, *Migrants' Experience of Racism and Discrimination in Ireland: Results of a Survey Conducted by the Economic and Social Research Institute for the European Union Monitoring Centre on Racism and Xenophobia* (Dublin: ESRI, 2006).

16 *Ibid.*, p. 40.

17 R. Sibbett, *The Perpetrators of Racial Harassment and Racial Violence: Home Office Research Study 176* (London: Home Office, 1997), pp. 78–80.

18 The McPherson Report defined institutional racism in the following terms: 'The collective failure of an organisation to provide an appropriate and professional service to be people because of their colour, culture or ethnic origin. It can be seen in processes, attitudes and behaviour which amount to discrimination through unwitting prejudice, ignorance thoughtlessness and racist stereotyping which disadvantage ethnic minority people (*The Stephen Lawrence Inquiry: Report of an Inquiry by Sir William McPherson of Cluny* (London: Stationery Office, 1999)).

19 Barriers to citizenship are addressed in detail in B. Fanning, *Immigration and Social Cohesion in the Republic of Ireland* (Manchester: Manchester University Press, 2011) and in various reports produced by the ICI (at: www.iimmigrant-council.ie).

10

Responses to racism

This chapter examines the main political, legal and institutional responses to racism in Ireland. By the time the first edition of this book had appeared in 2002 those in various Western countries had begun to abruptly shift. Multiculturalism had become an internationally derided term, yet many responses to racism in Ireland and elsewhere continued to be influenced by multiculturalism. During the 1990s Irish policy debates about racism and diversity predominantly focused on Travellers. The Prohibition of Incitement to Hatred Act (1989) was an anomaly. It was introduced to prevent the publication of racist materials in Ireland on behalf of racist organisations elsewhere; this was before the internet. Equality legislation progressed during the 1990s. The Equal Status Act (2000) prohibited discrimination in the provision of goods and services on nine grounds including 'race'. To some extent multiculturalism became institutionalised within the Irish state with the formation of the National Consultative Committee on Racism and Interculturalism (NCCRI) in 1998. The NCCRI was formed to act as an expert body to develop 'an integrated and strategic approach to racism, to focus on its prevention and to foster interculturalism within Ireland', to inform policy development and 'seek to build a consensus through dialogue in relation to the issues of racism and interculturalism' and 'to promote the understanding and celebration of cultural diversity within Ireland'.[1] If racism was the problem, interculturalism was the solution that came to be advocated.

Interculturalism prevailed as the dominant concept within Irish policy debates on racism until 2008 when the NCCRI was closed down. In the early years of the twenty-first century there had been backlashes against multiculturalism in countries such as the UK and the Netherlands and the post 9/11 West more generally.[2] To some extent these were driven by a moral panic about Islam that was mostly absent in Ireland.[3] Yet there were ideological equivalencies between the liberal challenges to multiculturalism in such countries and hostility to goals of promoting cultural recognition as a means of contesting anti-racism in the Irish case. Travellers came to be treated as enemies of Irish modernity, despised by some liberals who otherwise disapproved of racism and discrimination. So too has Islamophobia become normatively acceptable among some Western liberals, who are otherwise opposed to racism and discrimination.[4] Both might be understood as expressions of the kind of historicist racism identified by David Theo Goldberg and (as I describe it) as manifestations of ethnocentric liberalism whereby liberalism as the dominant value culture behaves like an ethnos.[5]

From the election of Barack Obama to the rising profile of black and ethnic minorities in Western popular culture the notion that Western societies *are* multicultural seems to have become embedded. Alongside such recognition apparent normative rejections of racist speech and overt forms of racist discrimination can be identified. Yet, inequalities resulting from racism – examples include educational attainment, access to employment, health status and treatment by the criminal justice system – are often discounted. At the same time, new forms of anti-immigrant politics have emerged in various Western countries, often expressed by left or social democrat political parties whose members viewed themselves as natural opponents of racism. The problems experienced by asylum seekers and some other migrants were not ones of institutional racism – where racism was evident in unequal access to services – but of structural racism whereby overt discrimination against groups with lesser rights than citizens came to be promoted by the same governments charged with formulating anti-racism policies. Such inconsistencies between normative opposition to racism and state policies that promote structural racism have played out in Ireland as in other countries. How these might be understood conceptually was examined in Chapter 8. The focus here is upon specific policy responses to racism that have emerged in the Irish case.

Interculturalism

Some of the key ideas and approaches that influence Irish anti-racism can be traced to work undertaken by Traveller organisations during the 1990s to promote cultural recognition of Travellers by the state in general and within specific areas of policy, notably education. In response to such activism the *Report of the Task Force on the Travelling People* (1995) emphasised the need to break with past assimilationist public policies. Such a break occurred, if only in the realms of official discourse, when integration replaced assimilation as the stated intent of such policies. This new official discourse also emphasised the need for multicultural policies and practices to acknowledge the cultural distinctiveness of Travellers. However, the Travellers' organisations, which pressed for such acknowledgements, distinguished between the need for multiculturalism (a necessary focus on Traveller cultural identity) and interculturalism, a term employed to refer to a stronger multiculturalism which as an ideal type acknowledged, and contested, the inequalities of power and status that underpinned cultural assimilation and marginalisation.

Multiculturalism is a term that became employed in a number of ways to refer to a range of ideas and practices that relate to acknowledgements of and responses to social diversity. It was understood to stand in opposition to presumptions of societal monoculturalism. Multiculturalism, broadly conceived, was understood to be critical of and resistant to monocultural presumptions of social homogeneity.[6] Within the literature on multiculturalism that emerged during the 1990s – the kind that influenced Irish debates at the time – a range of multicultural possibilities ranging from weak or 'managed' multiculturalisms to radical or strong multiculturalisms were identified. Goldberg, a stern critic of the former, gave the example of a weak multiculturalism within which the imagery of diversity proliferated but where the aim was to manage diversity rather than contest inequalities. Culture could be commodified within the market (he gave the example of the United Colors of Benetton) or within in the education system (through the acknowledgement of diversity within the curriculum) without challenging inequalities experienced on the basis of race or ethnicity. He argued that an emphasis on equality grounded only in liberal individual rights to equal treatment provided an inadequate basis for a strong multiculturalism. Here, minority communities might expect protection from inequality only as individual citizens. Citizenship might become equated with tolerance of minority cultures but no more than that. Goldberg's critique, and that of many other commentators, was that weak multiculturalism would not address the underlying social inequalities caused by racism.

In the post 9/11 era multiculturalism came to be blamed for undermining social cohesion in a number of Western countries. It is important to note that this was primarily an ideological argument. Both the Netherlands and Great Britain – where the rejection of multiculturalism became explicitly politicised – at best practised a kind of weak multiculturalism. This was characterised by tolerance of minority cultures rather than intolerance of the inequalities many black and ethnic minorities encountered. The resultant weak multiculturalism – the kind that was blamed internationally in the post 9/11 era for ruptures to social cohesion

– offered symbolic inclusion to minorities but ignored inequalities. As put by Trevor Philips, chairman of the Commission for Racial Equality in the United Kingdom in 2004:

> Celebrating diversity, but ignoring inequality, inevitably leads to the nightmare of entrenched segregation. Half a century after legal segregation was outlawed in the US, nine out of 10 African-American children are in black-majority schools; nine out of 10 whites live in areas where the black population is negligible. Guess whose schools underachieve, and whose districts are poorer.

Symbolic measures, such as the promotion of positive images of minorities or the celebration of exoticism, were always unlikely to be sufficient to challenge racisms in society. Racialised perceptions of minorities were unlikely to be shifted by measures that did not acknowledge and contest the racism and discrimination experienced by such minorities. As put in 1986 by Godfrey Brandt – giving the example of multicultural education programmes that celebrated diversity but ignored inequality – within the following dialogue:

> Schools: We're all equal here.
> Black students: We know we are second class citizens, in housing, employment and education.
> Schools: Oh dear. Negative self image. We must order books with Blacks in them.
> Black students: Can't we talk about the immigration laws or the National Front?
> Schools: No that's politics. We'll arrange some cultural evenings.[7]

Here, according to Brandt weak multiculturalism effectively denied the existence of racism and potentially legitimised it. He contended that multicultural education needed to acknowledge the experiences of those communities which were the victims of racism. This could not be possible unless teachers were equipped with the skills to challenge racism and change the bias of traditional ethnocentric education; 'Positive change and development in this context is seen as coming through dual action. The "multiculturalising" of the curriculum content and the consciousness raising of teachers who would then be able to positively use the new material.'[8] Similar debates played out in the Irish case particularly with respect to the failure of education systems to meet the needs of Travellers.[9] An emphasis upon intercultural education by Traveller organisations emerged in part as a concern about the perceived inability of weak multiculturalism to address the racism and exclusion which they had experienced.[10] Various statements on intercultural education within Irish

policy debates acknowledged the shortcomings of weak multiculturalisms. A major report on intercultural education by the Irish National
Teachers' Organisation (INTO referred to the problem of racism in just
one paragraph.[11] The report discussed 'name-calling, bullying, taunting
and teasing from other children' but otherwise adhered to the kind of
weak multiculturalism challenged by Brandt.

However, the INTO report did emphasise equal rights and participation in education for all, the need for anti-discrimination measures and for
the expansion of the Department of Education's refugee support service
to address the needs of all non-EU ethnic minority children, including
asylum seekers. It emphasised a right for children from minority communities to learn his or her mother tongue and that ethnic minority parents
be actively involved in the development of intercultural education
in schools.[12] What came to be implemented fell short of such aspirations.[13] Various subsequent education initiatives that included a focus
on racism emphasised the promotion of cultural awareness as distinct
from changes in how education was delivered. Since 2007 a number of
reports have highlighted risks of educational disadvantage among black
children. These include a 2007 study of the Dublin 15 area where the
highest proportion of black Africans reside and a countrywide study
by the Economic and Social Research Institute (ESRI), which found that
immigrant children were disproportionately found in schools designated
as disadvantaged.[14]

Institutional politics

The very title of the government agency established in 1998 to address
racism in Irish society, the National Consultative Committee on Racism
and Interculturalism (NCCRI), suggested the emergence of a paradigm
within which interculturalism had been cast as the solution to racism in
Irish society. It was used by non-governmental organisations (NGOs) at
times to argue for policies that addressed the structural contexts of racism
and used at times by politicians and state bodies to mean pretty much the
weak multiculturalism derided by Goldberg, Brandt, Irish Traveller organisations and many campaigners against racism in Ireland. The NCCRI
saw its role as promoting the mainstreaming of anti-racism and intercultural approaches within government policy. From the government's
perspective it provided a mechanism for responding to the demands of
NGOs and immigrant organisations. In a retrospective assessment by the
Chairperson of the NCCRI, Anastasia Crickley:

The space occupied has been likened to a tightrope, not part of government, but needing to communicate and relate well with politicians and
officials, not competing for NGO space, but needing strong partnership
and engagement with the voices, groups and needs of that sector, NCCRI
could not be all things to all people and the tightrope was sometimes
slippery.[15]

The NCCRI, in its efforts to 'develop a common space between government and broader civil society where consensus and agreement could be
reached on combating racism', mirrored the wider consensual corporatist
governance approach of the Irish state.[16] Consensus proved elusive, in
so far as 'some in civil society', according the Philip Watt the Director
of NCCRI, 'wanted a more adversarial approach' to addressing racism.[17]
Some of the work of the NCCRI with other bodies took place behind the
scenes. The NCCRI encouraged the adoption of good practice by others
and tended to avoid conflict.

Perhaps the main visible exception to this was its consistent advocacy
of ethnic status for Travellers and its insistence that Travellers experienced racism. Travellers were referred to as an ethnic minority in NCCRI
statements and reports. The key individuals in the NCCRI, Crickley and
Watt had previous worked for Traveller organisations. NCCRI advocacy
of interculturalism had emanated from policy work done by Traveller
organisations during the 1990s.

The NCCRI successfully promoted voluntary commitments to challenge
racism in areas such as sport and politics. It worked to get bodies such
as the Gardaí to introduce commitments to address racially motivated
crime. For example, the Annual Plan of the Gardaí in 2000 referred to
'initiatives on policing in an inter-cultural society'.[18] The Gardaí set up a
Racial and Intercultural Office. It provided anti-racism and intercultural
awareness training. It supported community groups. The NCCRI funded
some research on racism and upon the needs of immigrant communities.
It monitored racist incidents and produced many policy reports. Little of
this work might be described as moving beyond the weak multiculturalism that interculturalism was claimed to differ from.

Key initiatives included the establishment of Know Racism in 2001
and the preparation of Planning for Diversity: The National Action Plan
against Racism 2005–2008 (NPAR).[19] Know Racism in essence was an
anti-racism awareness programme. It engaged in a series of advertising
campaigns, funded television programmes, distributed 1.3 million copies
of a direct-mail leaflet entitled 'What you can do against racism' and
funded a range of community group and NGO anti-racism initiatives. It
provided funding to events such as Holocaust Memorial Day (inaugurated

in Ireland in 2003). The leaflet encouraged people to challenge racism, stated that racism was against the law and proclaimed that, 'Ireland is increasingly a multicultural society. This is a strength.'[20]

The 'intercultural framework' underpinning NPAR incorporated five principles. These were 'effective protection and redress against racism', 'economic inclusion and equality of opportunity', 'accommodating diversity in service provision', 'recognition and awareness of diversity' and 'full participation in Irish society'.[21] For all that the NPAR was a government policy, much of its emphasis was upon getting other sectors such as the media, sport and the arts to 'promote interaction and cultural diversity'.[22] For all that NPAR emphasised benchmarks and targets, it identified little or nothing that could be measured. There was little overt focus on institutional barriers and structural barriers experienced by immigrants due to lesser rights. Rather, the emphasis was upon 'accommodating diversity in service provision'.[23] What this might mean in practice was generally intangible. Nevertheless there was a distinct focus on addressing racially motivated crime with a recommendation to consider the introduction of sentencing policy for racially aggravated offences and for consideration of the concept of 'hate crime'.[24]

In addition to such official anti-racism a number of NGOs and some state-funded bodies were more adversarial. In particular, the Irish Human Rights Commission (IHRC) and the Equality Authority, bodies with specific remits under Irish law, have made forceful criticisms of the failures of the Irish state to address racism and inequalities addressed by legislation. Because these had statutory responsibilities they were arguably in a stronger position to be critical insiders – both were funded by the minister of justice. The Equality Authority's remit was determined by the Employment Equality Act (1998) and the Equal Status Act (2000). Both of these prohibited discrimination on grounds including race, ethnicity and membership of the Travelling Community. The statutory mandate of the IHRC was derived from the 2000 and 2001 Human Rights Commission Acts. Under the 2000 Act it had a specific statutory remit to ensure that Irish law and policy met the standards of best international practice. In effect, the function of the IHRC was to recommend measures that it considered would strengthen, protect and uphold human rights in Ireland.[25]

A key NGO strategy has been to press the Irish state to comply with international treaty obligations, notably in relation to the UN Convention on the Elimination of All Forms of Racial Discrimination (CERD). Ireland had signed the Convention in 1968 but had failed to ratify it. Once CERD became ratified the Irish state was obliged to make periodic reports detailing actions it had taken to address racist discrimination. NGOs, including Traveller organisations, submitted shadow reports taking the Irish government to task on issues such its unwillingness to recognise Traveller ethnicity, the treatment of asylum seekers and the inadequacy of monitoring systems, be it of racist incidents or of how services measurably respond to ethnic minorities. For example, the IHRC in a 2005 submission to CERD pressed for the breakdown of census and other data that would allow inequalities experienced by Travellers and immigrant ethnic groups to be identified.[26] To some extent, CERD offered a forum to address the kinds of racism identified in Chapter 8 that were mostly ignored in policy debates about racism mediated by the NCCRI.

Pro-migrant NGOs developed what Pauline Cullen refers to 'a strategic repertoire aimed at influencing institutional and discursive opportunities'. They built alliances of various non-state actors 'eager to gain credibility with and expertise about' new immigrant communities. These have come to include anti-poverty, women's rights, NGOs and faith community organisations as constituent members of campaigns mobilised by a smaller number of groups with a distinct remit in advocacy on behalf of migrants.[27]Reports by umbrella single-issue groups made up of such members, notably CADIC (Coalition Against Deportation of Irish Children) formed in response to the 2004 referendum on citizenship or NGO submissions to the UN and other bodies such as CERD, are typically endorsed by many such groups.

To a considerable extent such NGO activists have driven governmental institutional responses to racism. They do so partly by mobilising international norms. The commitment to establish the NCCRI came about during the European Year Against Racism (1997). The Irish government's commitment to draw up the National Action Plan Against Racism was made at the World Conference on Racism in Durban in 2001. Behind the scenes NGOs pressed for such responses and through their international alliances with anti-racist and human rights groups in other countries these worked to put pressure on the Irish state to fulfil various commitments to address racism set out in conventions and agreements it had adopted. In their submissions to CERD, Traveller organisations, Irish NGOs and sympathetic statutory bodies such as the IHRC have presented a united front and have consistently made similar criticisms of the failures of the Irish state to address racism. These criticisms have included the denial of Traveller ethnicity, criticism of lack of action to address institutional barriers experienced by Travellers in the areas of health and education, the treatment of asylum seekers in 'direct provision' and the lack of provisions under criminal law that addressed racist offences.

Various conflicts played out in submissions to CERD. The Irish govern-ment denied that Travellers were an ethnic group (see Chapter 7) and were strongly criticised by NGOs. NGOs were also strongly critical of the treatment of asylum seekers by the Irish state and of the unwillingness of the state to put anti-racism on a statutory footing. Adversarial challenges to the Irish government at CERD contrasted with the consensual corpo-ratist style of Irish policy debates. In effect NGOs endeavoured to shame the Irish state before the international community while seeking to cajole government departments within national-level debates. Sometimes dealings between NGOs and Irish officials were fraught. Various members of pro-migrant NGOs have reflected upon high levels of antipathy they experience in the dealings with civil servants.[28] There were at times consid-erable gaps between the perspectives of Department of Justice, Equality and Law Reform (DJELR) officials who regarded migration as primarily a security issue and NGOs focused on the rights of migrants that campaigned against state-fostered barriers to their participation in Irish society.[29]

This was the tightrope that NCCRI leaders referred to. The NCCRI could advocate good practice but the interculturalism it practised could not challenge many institutional barriers that pro-migrant organisa-tions had identified. Yet, for all that it appeared to sit on the fence, the NCCRI advocated positions – particularly in support of Travellers – that ran counter to those of the government. The underlying reality was a wider political and institutional antipathy to such goals and the likeli-hood of muscular responses from the minister of justice to state-funded organisations that were perceived to challenge the state. When the Citizen Traveller campaign argued that the Housing Miscellaneous Provisions Act (2002) was racist it had its funding withdrawn by the minister of justice.[30] In July 2007 the Irish government deported a community of Roma living on a roundabout on the M50 motorway. The main expres-sion of solidarity towards them came from Pavee Point, a Traveller NGO affiliated with Roma communities in international networks. Pavee Point worked with Crossscare, a Catholic pro-migrant organisation, to provide material support for the Roma and to facilitate negotiation.[31] As a result, the minister of justice, threatened a review of state funding received by the Traveller organisation.[32]

In 2008 Niall Crowley the chief executive of the Equality Authority resigned when the budget of the Authority was cut by 43 per cent. Around the same time other state-funded bodies had received only minor cuts.[33] Crowley argued the budgetary reductions amounted to a deliberate effort to hobble a body that had become a thorn in the side of the government. As argued by Crowley:

The only credible explanation I can see for what has been done to the Equality Authority appears to be that the casework strategy implemented by it, particularly in relation to allegations of discrimination in the public sector, has been experienced as a threat by senior civil servants and/or Government. It would further appear that the independent voice of the Equality Authority has had to be silenced for becoming an awkward witness to the inequality and discrimination in our society.

Much of this casework related to discrimination against Travellers. Crowley, a former director of the Traveller organisation Pavee Point, argued that the Equality Authority was being victimised for doing well what it was established to do. In 2006 the Equality Authority actively supported a case taken by a Traveller family with the help of the Irish Traveller Movement against local authorities, the commissioner of An Garda Síochána, the Director of Public Prosecutions, a district justice *and* the Attorney General. The case backed by the Equality Authority challenged public order legislation that, it argued, had a disproportionate and discriminatory impact on Travellers. Again in 2006 it supported a case taken by two Travellers against South Dublin County Council, the Minister of the Environment, Heritage and Local Government and the Attorney General. All these unsuccessfully opposed the participation of the Equality Authority in the case. According to Crowley: 'It was made clear to us that this was at the instigation of the Department of Justice, Equality and Law Reform'.[34] Under Crowley, the Equality Authority pushed the envelope of its statutory brief in challenging discriminations perpetrated by the Irish state. As put by Crowley:

> Although government and public sector officials remained at ease with according people rights not to be discriminated against, they became increasingly adverse to those rights actually being exercised – in particular by individuals against the public sector.[35]

In 2007, 67 per cent of Equality Authority cases filed under the Equal Status Acts related to allegations of discrimination of people availing of public services. Crowley argued that these allegations were experienced as a threat by government and senior civil servants and that this was the major reason why funding of the Equality Authority was so drastically cut. His vision of an Equality Authority that would, if necessary, challenge state authoritarianism was not one shared by the DJELR and its ministers.

In 2008 the Irish state effectively dismantled its institutional mechanisms for addressing racism. Alongside efforts to neuter (as Crowley put it) the Equality Authority the IHRC experienced serious funding cuts which it argued impeded its ability to fulfil its statutory remit. The

NCCRI was closed down in 2008 as was Know Racism. Also in 2008 the National Action Plan Against Racism was discontinued.[36] The cuts in 2008 amounted to what the NGO Alliance Against Racism – a platform that combined some thirty NGO, faith community, Traveller and immigrant-led bodies – called 'an attack on the human rights infrastructure of the State'.[37] A 2011 report to CERD by the Shadow Alliance argued that since the demise of National Action Plan Against Racism and the NCCRI in 2008 the Irish state lacked the means for strategic responses to racism, a focal point for anti-discrimination and anti-racism measures as well as a forum for national debate on these matters. In effect, the NGO Alliance Against Racism argued that the Irish state had deliberately undermined efforts to address racism and to meet its obligations under the UN Convention on the Elimination of All Forms of Racial Discrimination.[38]

From 2007 the state intercultural infrastructure of the Irish state became effectively superseded by the establishment of the Office of the Minister of State for Integration. Travellers were explicitly excluded from the remit of integration policies and, in effect the anti-multiculturalism evident in refusals to acknowledge Traveller ethnicity became further entrenched. The Office of the Minister of State for Integration in effect replaced the NCCRI and Know Racism. However, the commitment of the Irish state to integration policy was short-lived. Once it had produced an integration strategy document (one similar to the National Action Plan Against Racism in its lack of specific targets or in placing obligations upon the state) – and it had disbursed a small amount of grant aid to various projects the Integration Office began to wind down.[39]

Institutional responses to racism

When it comes to addressing racist discrimination some areas – notably those covered by the Employment Equality Act (1998) and the Equal Status Act (2000) – appear straightforward. Racist discrimination in the provision of goods and services (including public services) can be legally challenged. So too can experiences of racism in employment. However, it remains less clear how other manifestations of racism are being success-fully challenged. One key anomaly is that the Gardaí Síochána are not covered by the Equal Status Act (2000). It is also the case that the work of the Equality Authority has been severely cut back in recent years. It no longer tends to offer an advocacy service on individual cases but pursues test cases aimed at influencing how the courts and others respond to particular issues.

A cursory review of media reports of court hearings would indicate that the majority of racist crime is primarily dealt with under a range of other legislation, in particular the Criminal Justice (Public Order) Act 1994, Non-Fatal Offences Against the Person Act 1997 and Criminal Damage Act 1991.[40] Anti-social behaviour is defined under Irish law as any behaviour that causes or is likely to cause danger, injury, loss or fear including violence, threats, intimidation, coercion and harassment. It is defined as such under the Housing Act 1966 (as amended), the Housing (Miscellaneous Provisions Act) 1997 and the Residential Tenancies Act (2004).

The Prohibition of Incitement to Hatred Act 1989 was never intended to cover a wide range of criminal offences where incitement is not a factor, including the majority of cases involving assaults, harassment including verbal abuse and criminal damage. Such criminal acts are for the most part dealt with under existing public order, criminal damage and offences against the person legislation. The weakness in this approach is that such general legislation in Ireland does not recognise racism as an aggravating circumstance when it comes to sentencing. A decade after it was first introduced, just one case involving an alleged breach of the Act had been referred to the Director of Public Prosecutions (DPP). In March 1999 a Mayo county councillor was acquitted of inciting hatred towards Travellers at Galway District Court. In September 2000 the first conviction under the Act was secured against a Dublin bus driver. Earlier that month the minister of justice, equality and law reform acknowledged that the Act was ineffective and stated that new legislation was necessary.[41] The Act was ineffective, in part, because the extensive burden of causal proof required to demonstrate that racist acts had been incited. Since then there has been a rise in cases prosecuted under the Act. However, these amount to a small number of identified racially motivated offences.

The UK's Crown Prosecution Service (CPS) – the equivalent of the Director of Public Prosecutions in the Republic of Ireland – has published a prosecution policy for racist crime. It did so for the following stated reasons:

> We want people to know what they can expect from us when we prosecute racist or religious crime and hope this will help them have greater confidence in the criminal justice system.[42]

In the UK, as in Ireland there is no single criminal offence of racist crime. There are a number of different offences where it may be necessary to prove that there was a racist element. Racism as defined by the CPS can be experienced by any group or people who are defined by reference to their race, colour, nationality (including citizenship), ethnic origin (including

Travellers) or less visible minorities (groups such as Jews or Sikhs). The key issue is the identification of racially aggravated offences. Here the onus is to prove first that the offender has committed an offence and second that the onus is to prove that the offence was racially aggravated.

Basic offences might include assault, harassment or public order offences, such as causing people to fear violence or harassment. More severe sentences can be imposed when such offences are charged as being racially motivated. In essence there is a requirement to prove that the accused person:

- Either demonstrated hostility to the victim because the victim belonged to or was thought to belong to a particular racial or religious group – for example, using racist language when assaulting someone.
- Was motivated by hostility towards the victim for the same reasons – for example, the accused admitting to the police that he threw a brick through an Asian shopkeeper's window because he disliked Asians.

According to the CPS, motive is always difficult to prove and most prosecutions for alleged racist offences end up being prosecuted as basic offences. The key difference with Irish law is that when racism can be proved this will result in more severe sentencing.

'Racially aggravated offences' is a concept which does not exist under Irish law. In the absence of legal definitions of racially aggravated offences much depends on how institutions define and understand racism and interpret their role to address it. For example, some Gardaí reports offer definitions of 'racially motivated crime' that define this as 'any incident, which is perceived to be racially motivated' by either the victim, a member of An Garda Síochána, a person who was present and who witnessed the incident or person acting on behalf of the victim'.[43]

Research undertaken by the Home Office in the UK addressed a similar context (more than a decade ago) where institutional understandings of racism were somewhat vague. Police officers tended to subjectively interpret complaints about racism within the wider context of their own experience. For example, complaints about racist harassment by neighbours were often treated as neighbourhood disputes, where both parties were seen as perpetrators. Often responses to assaults focused on the basic offence and no consideration was given to the alleged racist motivations of these. Many racial incidents recorded by the police involved reports of verbal racial abuse in the street. Even where such abuse was accompanied by threatening behaviour the police were inclined to see this as a fairly normal aspect of life in areas 'where people were not nice to each other'. In short, 'the police were not quite sure why the victims bothered to report such things'.[44] Such verbal abuse was seen to go with the territory.

The Gardaí have put in place procedures, overseen by the Garda Racial and Intercultural and Diversity Office, whereby all racially motivated incidents that come to their attention are meant to be recorded on the PULSE system. These are then required to be individually followed up by the Racial and Intercultural Office. In addition each area has designated Garda ethnic liaison officers who are responsible for liaising with ethnic minority communities an 'hard to reach' groups, informing ethnic minorities of Gardaí services and monitoring racist incidents and the delivery of appropriate policing services to ethnic minority communities.[45] Furthermore the Gardaí have put in place procedures for victim support and family liaison to keep victims informed of progress in investigations and 'to ensure that they are afforded appropriate and relevant emotional, psychological, information and support'.[46] In some divisional areas the Gardaí hold regular clinics to reach out to immigrant communities. One example of such good practice is a regular clinic held at the mosque at Clonskeagh in Dublin after prayers on Fridays. However, various case studies outlined in this chapter find that some victims perceive the Gardaí as unresponsive or uninterested in their experiences of racism. There is clearly a disjuncture between the experiences of victims of racism and institutional acknowledgement of the nature of and extent of racism. A 2004 report by the NCCRI (following consultation with the Gardaí Síochána) considered that the reasons for the under-reporting included negative perceptions of police by recent migrants to Ireland, a reluctance to report crime out of fear that it might jeopardise residency in Ireland and, crucially, inconsistencies in the way the Gardaí respond to racist crime.[47]

Challenges

Since the demise of the NCCRI and Know Racism there has been a policy leadership vacuum in driving institutional responsiveness to racism. Much of this work was about winning hearts and minds. This sought to persuade Irish people and Irish institutions that racism was wrong. The experience of other countries is that such efforts only go so far. As put by Trevor Phillips, director of the Commission for Racial Equality about the British experience:

> The prevailing orthodoxy for 40 years was that we could not change the behaviour of the majority community until we changed its attitudes. Some of us now think differently. What matters is what people do rather than what they say they think. That is why the CRE is now focusing on delivery of race equality outcomes – measured in numbers of people

employed and resources distributed – rather than on declarations of goodwill. [48]

In the Irish case there is little institutional focus on the measurement of outcomes needed to identify and address institutional barriers. The National Action Plan Against Racism 2005–2008 got as far as urging accommodation of diversity in service provision. In the Irish case there has been no shortage of declarations of goodwill. In the absence of specific efforts to meaningfully accommodate diversity efforts to challenge the responsiveness of public services towards black and ethnic minorities have been perceived by public service providers as threats. This has been the experience of the Equality Authority in its efforts to support cases under equality acts by Travellers. Other examples can be identified through case work undertaken by NGOs such as the Migrants Rights Centre Ireland (MRCI) and the Immigrant Council of Ireland (ICI).

Since the closure of the NCCRI the MRCI and the ICI have emerged as the most significant pro-migrant organisations. Much of their work holds public service providers to account. The MRCI has produced a number of qualitative studies that examine in detail how immigrant workers have been exploited in the labour market and how various institutional barriers render migrants vulnerable to exploitation. Much of this research is drawn directly from MRCI case work that documents barriers and exploitation encountered by clients and the outcomes of such advocacy work. MRCI research and campaigns have also explicitly focused on experiences of racism. For example, in 2011 it published a study of racial profiling and its impact on migrant workers and their families.[49]

The ICI has predominantly focused upon supporting applications by migrants for residency status and citizenship. Again it has used its case work as the basis of research and in doing so has highlighted institutional barriers experienced by non-EU migrants – many of these black Africans – in their efforts to obtain Irish citizenship. For example, ICI research has revealed that some 47 per cent of applications for Irish citizenship were refused by the DJELR when comparable 2009 refusal rates for citizenship by naturalisation in other countries were less than 9 per cent in the UK, less than 3 per cent in Canada, 9 per cent in Australia.[50] According to the DJELR in 2009 applications from Nigerians outnumbered those from any other country of origin. Nigerian applicants for Irish citizenship also experienced the highest refusal rates.[51] This refusal rate was presumably greater than the overall 47 per cent of applications for naturalisation that were turned down.

In 2011 the ICI undertook the study of experiences of racism upon which much of Chapter 9 is drawn. The aim was to enable the ICI to take on the role of the NCCRI of promoting anti-racist practice in policing and other public services. Research published by both the MRCI and the ICI provides the best available evidence for considering questions of state racism of the kind highlighted in Chapter 8. But the work of both also attests to the importance of presenting real world reformist challenges to state practices.

The dilemmas faced by the ICI and MRCI are similar to those of the Equality Authority and the NCCRI. Neither are statutory bodies. Nor do they depend upon the state as their main source of funding. Yet both have to strike a balance between criticism of the state and establishing positive working relationships that enable them to advocate successfully on behalf of their clients with the DJELR and other government departments.

Neither are immigrant-led organisations. A key issue in the Irish politics of anti-racism has been the marginality of immigrant-led organisations with the pro-migrant sector. A recurring theme in conversations I have had with leaders of immigrant-led organisations over the last decade has been the difficulties they have faced in obtaining recourse. In essence, such groups compete with others in the Irish voluntary sector for state grants and philanthropic funding. Even before the economic crisis such immigrant-led groups faced steep competition in winning funding criteria and over the years a number of immigrant-led groups have collapsed.

A number of African-led organisations have emerged to promote the inclusion of immigrants. These include the New Communities Partnership, AkiDwa and the Africa Centre. The New Communities Partnership by 2011 consisted of a network of '117 minority-led groups'. Much of its work has focused upon communication, leadership and business training. Most of its funding, for example for voter awareness work in advance of the 2009 local government election comes directly or indirectly from the state (for example from local government).[52] The Africa Centre's core mission has been to advance 'attitudes, policies and actions that promote justice, social inclusion and meaningful participation for African communities in Ireland'. It has published research on immigrant political participation and African civic participation.[53] Most of its funding comes from Irish NGOs working in Africa but it has also attracted funding from the UK (Joseph Rowntree) and the EU.[54] AkiDwa is an African immigrant women's network that includes Muslim and Christian members. It has run campaigns and undertaken research on the needs of victims of genital mutilation, domestic violence and so-called honour killings. A number of African women candidates who stood in the 2009 local government elections were members of AkiDwa.[55]

Often these do not foreground racism in their efforts to promote the economic, social and, crucially, political inclusion of black people in Ireland. In 2003 and 2004 the Africa Centre undertook action research aimed at encouraging political parties to respond to immigrants as potential voters in local government elections (where non-Irish citizens can vote) and to recruit immigrant party members and candidates. This work built on one of the major achievements of the NCCRI, securing the adoption of an anti-racism protocol by all political parties in the run-up to the 2002 general election. The idea for this work came from Fidèle Mutwarasibo, a founding member of the Africa Centre who later became policy officer for the ICI.

Mutwarasibo's Ph.D. thesis on new migrant political entrepreneurs (a category to which he belongs) examines the challenges and complexities of immigrant political mobilisation. His interviews with leading black African activists in politics and immigrant-led organisations foreground wider preoccupations with creative resistance and with finding opportunities to express agency as distinct from the importance in defining barriers as racist and defining activism as anti-racist.[56] The exemplar of the kind of positive creative resistance identified by Mutwarasibo is perhaps Rotimi Adebari, a former asylum seeker who was elected as councillor in the 2004 local government elections, became Ireland's first black mayor (of Portlaoise) in 2007, was re-elected in 2009 and how stood as an independent candidate in the 2011 general election.

Adebari's 2011 campaign like his earlier ones was designed to win support to the wider local community, as distinct to appealing primarily to immigrant voters.[57]Other African candidates in the 2009 local government elections were typically members of immigrant-led networks such as AkiDwa but the more successful of these were also members of Irish-led organisations and community groups. In interviews prior to the 2009 election African (and other immigrant candidates) stressed that they could only get elected if they appealed to the wider community (rather than just to fellow immigrants) and in their campaigns they emphasised the importance of local issues (for example, employment, difficulties faced by local businesses, childcare, street lighting, the threatened closure of a local hospital, public transport, drug problems and anti-social behaviour).

One of Fine Gael's African candidates consequently objected to the term 'immigrant candidate' as an exclusionary label, which she felt implied that she was not really a local person.[58] Just five out of ten black African candidate interviewees who stood in the 2009 local elections identified concerns about racism as a motivation for becoming involved in politics.[59] Yet, one of the ten (at a post-election meeting of candidates who stood in 2009) recalled that whenever she was interviewed by the local media about racism in the community where she lived she deflected the question in saying that she was proud to be a number of the community.[60] Racism, she reflected, was all too real in her experience but emphasising this would undermine her chances for election. This is not to suggest that those five who did not emphasise racism as a motivation for entering politics when interviewed exhibited some kind of false consciousness. Rather it endorses Mutwarasibo's findings that some putative black leaders focused pragmatically and idealistically on opportunities for agency and inclusion, seeing racism as part of the problem and seeing anti-racism measures as just part of the solution to the marginalisation that their communities experience. In effect, their understanding of racism – and of the stakes involved in becoming preoccupied with racism – differed considerably from that of many of the academics who have written about racism in the Irish case (see Chapter 8).

Anti-racism in Ireland as elsewhere cannot be viably defined as the opposite to any one thing. Various ideals might be understood to oppose racism but there is no single political project, however abstract or utopian, that can be understood as holistically anti-racist, given the range of insidious consequences racisms can exert, in combination with other forces, upon the lives of people. The coalitions against racism that have emerged in Ireland during the last decade have involved groups that would disagree ideologically on many issues: groups motivated by human rights ideals, socialists, faith communities, and liberals, mobilised by various ideals of human solidarity and universalism. Academics who write about racism in theory have contributed to understandings of how insidious racism can be, how intrinsic it may be to the structure of social relations and how embedded it can be in institutional practices of the state. Yet, much of this literature on the Irish case is poor at suggesting remedies and often appears to deride those who walk the tightrope, including participants of the institutional politics of anti-racism and immigrant activists whose style of politics differs by necessity from the archetypes of anti-racist politics in some other countries.

Various NGO campaigns have sought to promote responsiveness among Irish political parties towards immigrants in advance of the last two local government elections in which non-citizens can vote. Yet, nowhere are immigrants sufficiently numerous to create the kinds of black and ethnic minority driven local politics that has proved influential in parts of urban Britain. The most likely future site of such politics may be Dublin 15, particularly in the Tyrelstown area where Toyosi Shittabey was killed in 2010. A year earlier three African candidates competed with one another in Tyrelstown for election to Fingal Council. Had just one of these stood, an African might conceivably have been elected by an electorate that included a significant proportion of Africans. The spatial distribution of immigrants in Ireland is such that elsewhere candidates are unlikely to be elected in local government elections by appealing primarily to fellow immigrants for support. Immigrant candidates have tended to empha-sise community and local issues rather than focus directly on racism, in the way that immigrant politicians relying on immigrant votes in other countries can do so. Yet, as Chapter 9 illustrated, local communities are the sites of much of the racism experienced by some immigrants. In his focus on community and in his ability to appeal to Irish voters as a 'local', Rotimi Adebari has been both role model and outlier.

Although Ireland has a large immigrant population the proportion of immigrants who are Irish citizens is small. As a result mainstream politics can effectively ignore Ireland's black and ethnic minority communities. During the run-up to the 2011 election Fidèle Mutwarasibo noticed that canvassers for the various political parties going door to door in his neighbourhood were not calling at his house. He surmised that this was happening because it did not occur to the canvassers that he was an Irish citizen because he was black. In the week before the 2011 election the ICI held a media event outside Leinster House (the seat of the Dáil) where immigrants who were Irish citizens gave interviews to the press and recorded YouTube videos. In 2011 an estimated 35,000 immigrants were Irish citizens, fewer than one in ten of Ireland's migrant population and well under 1 per cent of the Irish population. In this context, efforts by the ICI to promote fair and transparent access to citizenship for long-term denizens is crucially important. Most applicants for Irish citizenship come from outside the EU and the majority of applicants being turned down at the time of writing are black Africans. The fact that large numbers of these are being denied Irish citizenship works to undermine the responsiveness of mainstream politics to the concerns of the so-called 'new Irish'.[61]

The problems of racism in the Irish case cannot be reduced to one of phenotype racism (for all that Chapter 9 gives vivid examples of the experi-ences of some black people) and cultural racism as experienced by white groups such as Travellers and Roma. The 2004 referendum on citizenship revealed the salience of nineteenth-century race-as-nation thinking upon twenty-first century conceptions of Irishness in two ways. First, most Irish citizens, some 80 per cent of those who voted, effectively did so to protect the ethnic nation from immigrants. These tolerated large-scale immigra-tion but did not consider the Irish-born children of immigrants as Irish. Second, to some extent, the politics of the referendum became explicitly focused on defending Irish citizenship from black mothers and their babies. Much has been written about this. Analyses of the 2004 referendum have become a staple of most writings on immigration and racism in Ireland. Yet, it is unclear to what extent phenotype racism affected the result of the referendum. As put by Steve Garner, from the available knowledge 'there can only be speculation into the intentions of the referendum voters'.[62] Yet, the referendum outcome gave the DJELR an apparent mandate to turn down a large proportion of applications for citizenship because it so strongly endorsed a mono-ethnic definition of the Irish nation. In this context, the problem of racism cannot be separated from the politics of Irish ethno-national identity and the ethnic nepotism it appears to license.

This still-dominant sense of an Irish 'us', its inscription on the Irish ethnic politics of security, territory and population, sets the context for and imposes limits upon how racism might be contested in the Irish case. Insisting that black people and other immigrants can be no less Irish than members of the Irish ethnos is a necessary precondition for dealing with racism in Ireland.

Notes

1 Goals of the NCCRI are set out in its various reports published in the ten years of its existence (1998–2008) (and at: www.nccri.ie). Cited from Education Disadvantage Committee, *The Traveller Education Strategy – As Part of an Intercultural Education Strategy in Ireland* (Dublin: NCCRI, 2004), p. 2.

2 C. Joppke, 'The Retreat of Multiculturalism in the Liberal State: Theory and Policy', *British Journal of Sociology*, 55(2) (2004), pp. 237–57, p. 249.

3 See B. Fanning, *Immigration and Social Cohesion in the Republic of Ireland* (Manchester: Manchester University Press, 2011), pp. 33–7.

4 C. Joppke, 'Limits of Integration Policy: Britain and Her Muslims', *Journal of Ethnic and Migration Studies*, 35(3) (2009), pp. 4353–72, p. 467.

5 B. Fanning, 'Integration Convergence and the Irish Case', in B. Fanning and R. Munck (eds), *Globalization, Migration and Social Transformation: Ireland in Europe and the World* (Farnham: Ashgate, 2011), p.115.

6 D. T. Goldberg, *Multiculturalism: A Critical Reader* (Oxford: Blackwell, 1994), p. 7.

7 G. Brandt, *The Realization of Anti-Racist Teaching* (London: Farmer, 1986), p. 115.

8 *Ibid.*, p. 118.

9 M. Kenny (2000) 'Travellers, Minorities and Schools', in E. Sheehan (ed.), *Travellers Citizens of Ireland* (Dublin: Citizen Traveller, 2002), pp. 140–3, p. 142.

10 J. O' Connell, *Reach Out: Report by the Dublin Traveller Education Development Group on the 'Poverty 3' Programme* (Dublin: Pavee Point, 1994), p. 31.

11 Irish National Teachers' Organisation, *The Challenge of Diversity* (Dublin: Irish National Teachers' Organisation, 1998), p. 59.

12 *Ibid.*, p. 51.
13 For criticisms of the poor focusing on racism and interculturalism in teacher training and on the school curriculum, see IHRC, *CERD Submission* (Dublin: IHRC, 2005), pp. 25–6 (and at: www.ihrc.ie).
14 E. McGorman and C. Sugrue, *Intercultural Education: Primary Challenges in Dublin 15* (Dublin: Department of Education and Science, 2007); E. Smith, M. Darmody, F. McGinnity and F. Byrne, *Adapting to Diversity: Irish Schools and Newcomer Students* (Dublin; ESRI, 2009). For an overview on findings of education and segregation facing black children, see B. Fanning, *Immigration and Social Cohesion in the Republic of Ireland* (Manchester: Manchester University Press, 2011), pp. 106–23. For an overview of issues affecting immigrant children in Irish schools (including those relating to racism), see M. Darmody, N. Tyrrell and S. Song (eds), *The Changing Faces of Children in Ireland: Exploring the Lives of Immigrant and Ethnic Minority Children* (Rotterdam: Sense, 2011).
15 A. Crickley, 'Reflection on NCCRI's Role and Work 1998–2008', in NCCRI, *Reflection*, p. 5.
16 Philip Watt, 'Foreword', *ibid.*, p. 3.
17 *Ibid.*
18 Garda Siochana, *Annual Plan for 2000* (Dublin: Official Publications, 2000).
19 Department of Justice, Equality and Law reform, *Planning For Diversity: The National Action Plan Against Racism 2005–2008* (Dublin: Stationery Office, 2005).
20 Know Racism, *Final Report on Activities 2001–2003* (Dublin: Know Racism, 2003).
21 *Ibid.*, p. 27.
22 *Ibid.*, p. 34.
23 *Ibid.*, p. 45.
24 *Ibid.*, 75.
25 Irish Human Rights Commission, *CERD Submission* (Dublin: IRHC, 2011), p. 3 (at: www.ihrc.ie).
26 Irish Human Rights Commission, *CERD Submission* (Dublin: IHRC, 2005), p. 21 (at: www.ihrc.ie).
27 P. Cullen, 'Irish Pro-Migrant Nongovernmental Organizations and the Politics of Immigration' *Voluntas*, 20 (2009), pp. 99–128, p. 105.
28 This is based on various conversations with pro-migrant activists over the years and from witnessing expressions of antipathy towards them from some senior civil servants on a few occasions.
29 For an account of the security governance perspectives of the DJELR, see B. Fanning, *Immigration and Social Cohesion in the Republic of Ireland* (Manchester: Manchester University Press, 2011), pp. 43–7.
30 The Housing Miscellaneous Provisions Act 2002. See Una Crowley, 'Boundaries of Citizenship: The Continued Exclusion of Travellers', in Katy Hayward and Muris MacCarthaigh (eds), *Recycling the State: The Politics of Adaptation in Ireland* (Dublin: Irish Academic Press, 2007), p. 89.
31 See www.paveepoint.ie.
32 *Irish Times* (27 July 2007).
33 Crowley argued that the budget cutback of the Equality Authority stood in stark contrast to that of equivalent organisations such as the National Disability Authority (a 2 per cent cutback), the Legal Aid Board (a 1 per cent cutback),

or the Data Protection Commissioner (a 9 per cent cutback) (N. Crowley, open letter of resignation, 11 December 2008).

34 N. Crowley *Empty Promises: Bringing the Equality Authority to Heel* (Dublon: Farmer, 2010), pp. 90–2.

35 *Ibid.*

36 See JJELR, *Planning for Diversity: The National Action Plan Against Racism 2005–2008* (Dublin: Stationery Office, 2005), pp. 5–12.

37 NGO Alliance Against Racism, *Shadow Report in response to the Third and Fourth Periodic Reports of Ireland under the UN International Convention on the Elimination of All Forms of Racial Discrimination* (Dublin: NGO Alliance Against Racism, 2011), p. 1.

38 *Ibid.*

39 Office of the Minister of Integration, *Migration Nation: Statement in Integration Strategy and Diversity Management* (Dublin: Stationery Office, 2008).

40 NCCRI and the Equality Commission for Northern Ireland (2005). *Seeking Advice and Redress against Racism in Ireland* (at: www.nccri.ie).

41 Minister of Justice, Equality and Law Reform, preparatory conference.

42 CPS, Racist and Religious Crime: CPS Prosecution Policy (at: www.cps.gov.uk).

43 An Garda Síochána, Racial and Intercultural Newsletter, No. 3.

44 R. Sibbett, *The Perpetrators of Racial Harassment and Racial Violence: Home Office Research Study 176* (London: Home Office, 1997), p. 26.

45 Garda Ethnic Liaison Officer (ELO) information sheet (at: www.garda.ie).

46 Information on victim support, Crime Victims and Family Liaison Office (at: www.garda.ie).

47 An Garda Siochana, August 2004 in NCCRI/Equality Authority National Annual Report to the EUMC, October 2004.

48 T. Phillips, *Guardian* (28 May 2004).

49 Migrant Rights Centre Ireland, *Singled Out: Exploratory Study on Ethnic Profiling in Ireland and Its Impact on Migrant Workers and Their Families* (Dublin: MRCI, 2011) (at: www.mrci.ie).

50 Immigrant Council of Ireland, 'Citizen processes in need of overhaul', press release, 7 May 2009.

51 'Nigerians top of the list seeking Irish citizenship' *Metro Éireann* (5 November 2009).

52 www.newcommunities.ie, website accessed 4 April 2011.

53 B. Fanning, F. Mutwarasibo and N. Chadmayo, *Positive Politics: Participation of Immigrants and Ethnic Minorities in the Electoral Process* (Dublin: Africa Solidarity Centre, 2003); Theo Ejorh, *Inclusive Citizenship in 21st Century Ireland: What Prospects for the African Community?* (Dublin: Africa Centre, 2006).

54 www.africacentre.ie, website accessed 4 April 2011.

55 B. Fanning and N. O'Boyle, 'Immigrants in Irish Politics: African and East European Candidates in the 2009 Local Government Elections', *Irish Political Studies*, 25(3) (2010), pp. 417–35.

56 F. Mutwarasibo, '(New) migrant political entrepreneurs: overcoming isolation and exclusion through creative resistance in Ireland', unpublished (Dublin: University College Dublin, 2011).

57 www.rotimi.com, website accessed 4 April 2011.

58 B. Fanning, K. Howard and N. O'Boyle, 'Immigrant Candidates and Politics in the Republic of Ireland: Racialization, Ethnic Nepotism or Localism?, *Nationalism and Ethnic Politics*, 16 (2011), pp. 420–2.

59 *Ibid.*

60 At this event I presented findings of the above-cited research on immigrants in Irish politics to a group of more than twenty candidates who then shared their experiences in contesting the local government 2009 election.

61 For an analysis of such intersections between barriers to citizenship and Irish politics, see Fanning, *Immigration*, pp. 152–73.

62 S. Garner, 'Babies, Bodies and Entitlement: Gendered Aspects of Citizenship in the Republic of Ireland', *Parliamentary Affairs*, 60(3) (2007), pp. 437–51, p. 442.

Select bibliography

Ahmad, W. (ed.), *'Race' and Health in Contemporary Britain* (Buckingham: Open University, 1996).

Akenson, D. H., *Small Differences: Irish Catholics and Protestants 1815–1922* (Dublin: Gill & Macmillan, 1991).

Akenson, D. H., *The Irish Diaspora: A Primer* (London: Harman, 1993).

Back, L. and Solomos, J. (eds), *Theories of Race and Racism* (London: Routledge, 2000).

Balibar, E. and Wallerstein, I., *Race, Nation, Class: Ambiguous Identities* (London: Verso, 1991).

Barrington, R., *Health, Medicine and Politics in Ireland 1900–1970* (Dublin: Institute of Public Administration, 1987).

Barry, J., Herity, B. and Solan, S., *The Travellers' Health Status Study* (Dublin: Health Research Board, 1989).

Bauman, Z., *Modernity and the Holocaust* (London: Sage, 1996).

Bhreatnach, A., *Becoming Conspicuous: Irish Travellers, Society and the State 1922–70* (Dublin: University College Dublin Press, 2006).

Bielenberg, A. (ed.), *The Irish Diaspora* (London: Longman, 2000).

Binchy, D., 'Adolph Hitler', in B. Fanning (ed.), *An Irish Century: Studies 1912–2012* (Dublin: University College Dublin Press, 2012).

Boylan, C., *Black Baby* (New York: Doubleday, 1989).

Boucher, G., *The Irish are friendly but … A Report on Racism and International Students and Racism in Ireland* (Dublin: Irish Council for International Students, 1998).

Bowen, K., *Protestants in a Catholic State: Ireland's Privileged Minority* (Belfast: Queens University Press, 1983).

Boyle, K. and Watt, B., *International and United Kingdom Law Relevant to the Protection of the Rights and Cultural Identity of the Travelling Community in Ireland; Paper commissioned by the Task Force on the Travelling Community* (Colchester: Human Rights Centre, University of Essex, 1995).

Bradley, S., *From Bosnia to Ireland's Private Sector* (Dublin: Clann Housing Association, 1999).

Brandt, G., *The Realisation of Anti-Racist Teaching* (London: Falmer, 1986).

Brown, A., '"The Other Day I Met a Constituent of Mine": A Theory of Anecdotal Racism', *Ethnic and Racial Studies*, 22(1) (1999), pp. 23–55.

Burleigh, M. and Wipperman, W., *The Racial State* (Cambridge: Cambridge University Press, 1991).

Cashmore, E. (ed.). *Dictionary of Race and Ethnic Relations* (London: Routledge, 1995).

Castles, S. and Davidson, A., *Citizenship and Migration: Globalisation and the politics of belonging* (London: Macmillan, 2000).

Christie, A., 'From Racial to Racist State: Questions for Social Work Professionals Working with Asylum Seekers', *Journal of Applied Social Studies*, 7(2) (2006), pp. 35–49.

Christie, A., 'Whiteness and the Politics of "Race" in Child Protection Guidelines in Ireland', *European Journal of Social Work*, 13(2) (2010), pp. 199–215.

Cohn-Sherbok, D., *The Crucified Jew: Twenty Centuries of Christian Anti-Semitism* (London: Harper Collins, 1992).

Commission on Itinerancy, *Report of the Commission on Itinerancy* (Dublin: Stationery Office, 1963).

Cornwell, J., *Hitler's Pope: the Secret History of Pius XII* (London: Penguin, 2000).

Cronin, M., *The Blueshirts and Irish Politics* (Dublin: Four Courts Press, 1997).

Crotty, W. and Schmitt, D. E. (eds), *Ireland and the Politics of Change* (London: Longman, 1998).

Crowley, E. and McLaughlin, J. (eds), *Under the Belly of the Celtic Tiger: Class, Race, Identity and Culture in the 'Global Ireland'* (Dublin, Irish Reporter Publications, 1997).

Crowley, N., *Empty Promises: Bringing the Equality Authority to Heel* (Dublin: Farmer, 2010).

Cullen, P., 'Irish Pro-Migrant Nongovernmental Organizations and the Politics of Immigration', *Voluntas*, 20(2) (2009), pp. 99–128.

Curtis, L. P., *Apes and Angels: The Irishman in Victorian Caricature* (New York: New York University Press, 1971).

Darmody, M., Tyrrell, N. and Song, S. (eds), *The Changing Faces of Children in Ireland: Exploring the Lives of Immigrant and Ethnic Minority Children* (Rotterdam: Sense, 2011).

Department of Justice, Equality and Law Reform, *The First Progress Report of the Committee to Monitor and Co-ordinate the Implementation of the Recommendations of the Task Force on the Travelling Community* (Dublin: Stationery Office, 2000).

Department of Justice Equality and Law Reform, *Integration: A Two Way Process* (Dublin: Stationery Office, 2000).

Department of Justice, Equality and Law Reform, *Planning For Diversity: The National Action Plan Against Racism 2005–2008* (Dublin: Stationery Office, 2005).

Dillon, E., *The Outsiders: Exposing the Secretive World of Ireland's Travellers* (Dublin: Merlin, 2006).

Dillon, T. W. T., 'The Refugee Problem', *Studies*, 28(111) (1939), pp. 402–14.

Dominelli, L., *Anti-Racist Social Work* (London: Macmillan, 1998).

Dooley, B., *Black and Green: The Fight for Civil Rights in Northern Ireland and Black America* (London: Pluto Press, 1998).

Dunne, T., *Rebellions: Memoir, Memory and 1798* (Dublin: Lilliput Press, 2010).

Dunleavy, J. E. and Dunleavy, W., *Douglas Hyde: A Maker of Modern Ireland* (Oxford: University of California Press. 1991).

English, R. (ed.), *Unionism in Modern Ireland* (Dublin: Gill & Macmillan, 1996).

Ejorh, T., *Inclusive Citizenship in 21st Century Ireland: What Prospects for the African Community?* (Dublin: Africa Centre, 2006).

Fanning, B., *New Guests of the Irish Nation* (Dublin: Irish Academic Press, 2009).

Fanning, B., 'From Developmental Ireland to Migration Nation: Immigration and Shifting Rules of Belonging in the Republic of Ireland', *Economic and Social Review*, 41(3) (2011), pp. 395–412.

Fanning, B., *Immigration and Social Cohesion in the Republic of Ireland* (Manchester: Manchester University Press, 2011).

Fanning, B., 'Integration Convergence and the Irish Case', in B. Fanning and R. Munck (eds), *Globalization, Migration and Social Transformation: Ireland in Europe and the World* (Farnham: Ashgate, 2011).

Fanning, B., Howard, K. and O'Boyle, K., 'Immigrant Candidates and Politics in the Republic of Ireland: Racialization, Ethnic Nepotism or Localism?', *Nationalism and Ethnic Politics* 16(3/4) (2011), pp. 420–2.

Fanning, B., Killoran, B. and Ní Bhroin, S., *Taking Racism Seriously; Racist Harassment, Violence and Anti-Social Behaviour in Twenty-First Century Ireland* (Dublin: Immigrant Council of Ireland, 2011).

Fanning, B., Loyal S. and Staunton, C., *Asylum Seekers and the Right to Work in Ireland* (Dublin: Irish Refugee Council, 2000).

Fanning, B. and Mac Einri P., *Regional Resettlement of Asylum Seekers: A Strategic Approach* (Cork: Irish Centre for Migration Studies, 1999).

Fanning, B. and Mutwarasibo, F., 'Nationals/Non-Nationals: Immigration, Citizenship and Politics in the Republic of Ireland', *Ethnic and Racial Studies*, 30(3) (2007), pp. 439–60.

Fanning, B. Mutwarasibo, F. and Chadmayo, N., *Positive Politics: Participation of Immigrants and Ethnic Minorities in the Electoral Process* (Dublin: Africa Solidarity Centre, 2003).

Fanning, B. and O'Boyle, N., 'Immigrants in Irish Politics: African and East European Candidates in the 2009 Local Government Elections', *Irish Political Studies*, 25(3) (2010), pp. 417–35.

Fanning, B., Veale, A. and O'Connor, D., *Beyond the Pale: Asylum Seeking Children and Social Exclusion in Ireland* (Dublin: Irish Refugee Council, 2001).

Faughnan, P., *Refugees and Asylum Seekers in Ireland* (Dublin: Social Science Research Centre University College Dublin, 1999).

Faughnan, P. and Woods, M., *Lives on Hold: Seeking Asylum in Ireland* (Dublin; Applied Social Science Research Programme, 2000).

Feely, P. (ed.), *The Rise and Fall of Irish Anti-Semitism* (Dublin: Labour History Workshop, 1984).

Fisk, R., *In Time of War* (London: Paladin, 1985).

Foley, T. and Ryder, S. (eds), *Ideology and Ireland in the Nineteenth Century* (Dublin: Four Courts Press, 1998).

Foucault, M., *Society Must be Defended* (London: Penguin, 2003).

Foucault, M., *Security, Territory, Population: Lectures at the Collège de France 1977–1978*, ed. M. Senellart (London: Palgrave, 2007).

Fraser, U. and Harvey, C. *Sanctuary in Ireland: Perspectives on Asylum Law and Policy* (Dublin: Institute of Public Administration, 2003).

Garner, G., 'Babies, Bodies and Entitlement: Gendered Aspects of Citizenship in the Republic of Ireland', *Parliamentary Affairs*, 60(3) (2007), pp. 437–51.

Garvin, T., *The Evolution of Irish Nationalist Politics* (Dublin: Gill & Macmillan, 1982).

Goldberg, D. T., *Multiculturalism: A Critical Reader* (Oxford: Blackwell, 1994).

Goldhagen, D., *Hitler's Willing Executioners: Ordinary Germans and the Holocaust* (London: Abacus, 1996).

Gmelch, S. B., and Gmelch, G., 'The Itinerant Settlement Movement: Its Policies and Effects on Irish Travellers' *Studies*, 63(249) (1974), pp. 1–17.

George Boyce, D. and Day, A. (eds), *The Making of Modern Irish History: Revisionism and the Revisionist Controversy* (London: Routledge, 1996).

Gilroy, P., 'Race Ends Here', *Ethnic and Racial Studies*, 21(5) (1998), pp. 832–47.

Graham B. (ed.), *In Search of Ireland: A Cultural Geography* (London: Routledge, 1997).

Gray, B., 'Governing Integration', in in B. Fanning and R. Munck (eds), *Globalization, Migration and Social Transformation: Ireland in Europe and the World* (Farnham: Ashgate, 2011).

Healy, S. and Reynolds, B. (eds), *Irish Social Policy in Ireland* (Dublin: Oak Tree Press, 1998).

Hernstein, R. and Murray, C., *The Bell Curve: Intelligence and Class Structure in American Life* (New York: Free Press, 1994).

Helleiner, J., 'Gypsies, Celts and Tinkers: Colonial Antecedents of Anti-Traveller Racism in Ireland', *Ethnic and Racial Studies*, 18(3) (1995), pp. 532–54.

Hogan, E., *The Irish Missionary Movement: A Historical Survey, 1830–1980* (Dublin: Gill & Macmillan, 1992).

Hoppen, K. T., *Ireland since 1800: Conflict and Conformity* (London: Longman, 1990).

Hourigan, N. and Campbell, N., *The Teach Report: Traveller Education and Adults: Crisis, Challenge and change* (Dublin: National Association of Travellers' Centres, 2010).

Howard, K., 'National Identity and Moral Panic and East European Folk Devils', in B. Fanning and R. Munck (eds), *Globalization, Migration and Social Transformation: Ireland in Europe and the World* (London: Ashgate, 2011).

Husband, C., *Race in Britain: Continuity and Change* (London: Hutchinson, 1987).

Ignatiev, N., *How the Irish Became White* (London: Routledge, 1995).

Inglis, T., *Moral Monopoly* (Dublin: University College Dublin Press, 1998).

Irish Commission for Justice and Peace, *Refugees and Asylum Seekers: A Challenge to Solidarity* (Dublin: Irish Commission for Justice and Peace, 1997).

Jenkins, B. and Sofos, S. A. (eds), *Nation and Identity in Contemporary Europe* (London: Routledge, 1996).

Joppke, C., 'How immigration is changing citizenship: a comparative view', *Ethnic and Racial Studies*, 22(4) (1999), pp. 629–52.

Joppke C., 'The Legal–Domestic Sources of Immigrant Rights: The United States, Germany and the European Union', *Comparative Political Studies*, 34(4) (2001), pp. 339–66.

Lively, P., *Masks: Blackness, Race and the Imagination* (London: Chatto & Windus, 1998).

Loyal, S. and Allen, K., 'Rethinking Immigration and the State in Ireland', in A. Lentin and R. Lentin (eds), *Race and State* (Cambridge: Cambridge Scholars Press, 2006).

Kelleher, C. *et al.*, *Our Geels All Ireland Traveller Health Study* (Dublin University College Dublin/Department of Health and Children, 2010).

Kennedy, M., 'Our Men in Berlin: Some Thoughts on Irish Diplomats in Germany 1929–39', *Irish Journal of International Affairs*, 10 (1999), pp. 53–70.

Kennedy, M. and Skelly, J. M. (eds), *Irish Foreign Policy 1919–1966: From Independence to Internationalism* (Dublin: Four Courts Press, 2000).

Keogh, D., *Twentieth-Century Ireland: Nation and State* (Dublin: Gill & Macmillan, 1994).

Keogh, D., *Jews in Twentieth-Century Ireland* (Cork: Cork University Press, 1998).

King-O'Riain, R., 'Re-Racialising, the Irish State through the Census, Citizenship and Language', in A. Lentin and R. Lentin (eds), *Race and State* (Cambridge: Cambridge Scholars Press, 2006).

Kukathas, C. (ed.), *Multicultural Citizens: The Philosophy and Politics of Identity* (St Leonards: Centre for Independent Studies, 1993).

Lee, J. J., *Ireland 1912–1985 Politics and Society* (Cambridge: Cambridge University Press, 1989).

Lentin, R., 'Ireland: Racial State and Crisis Racism', *Ethnic and Racial Studies*, 30(4) (2007), pp. 610–27.

Lentin, R. and McVeigh, R., *After Optimism? Ireland, Racism and Globalisation* (Dublin: Metro Éireann Publications, 2006).

Lentin, R. and McVeigh, R., 'Irishness and Racism – Towards an E-Reader', *Translocations*, 1(1) (2006), pp. 22–40.

Longley, E. (ed.), *Culture in Ireland: Division or Diversity* (Belfast: Institute of Irish Studies, 1991).

Mac an Ghaill, M., *Contemporary Racisms and Ethnicities* (Buckingham: Open University Press, 1999).

McCann, M., O'Siochain, S. and Ruane. S. (eds), *Irish Travellers: Culture and Identity* (Belfast: Institute of Irish Studies, 1996).

McGinnity, F., O'Connell, P. J., Quinn, E., Williams, J., *Migrants' Experience of Racism and Discrimination in Ireland: Results of a Survey Conducted by the Economic and Social Research Institute for the European Union Monitoring Centre on Racism and Xenophobia* (Dublin: ESRI, 2006).

McGorman, E. and Sugrue, C., *Intercultural Education: Primary Challenges in Dublin 15* (Dublin: Department of Education and Science, 2007).

McLaughlin, J., *Travellers and Ireland: Whose Country, Whose History?* (Cork: Cork University Press, 1995).

McLaughlin, J., 'Nation-Building, Social Closure and Anti-Traveller Racism in Ireland', *Sociology*, 33(1) (1999), pp. 128–39.

McLoone, J. (ed.), *Being Protestant in Ireland* (Galway: Social Studies Conference, 1984).

McPherson, W., *The Stephen Lawrence Inquiry: Report of an Inquiry by Sir William McPherson of Cluny* (London, Stationery Office, 1999).

McVeigh, R., *The Racialisation of Irishness: Racism and Anti-Racism in Ireland* (Belfast: Centre for Research and Documentation, 1997).

Malik, K., *Strange Fruit: Why Both Sides are Wrong in the Race Debate* (Oxford: One World, 2007).

Manandhar, S., Friel, S., Share, M., Hardy, F. and Walsh, O., *Food, Nutrition and Poverty amongst Asylum Seekers in North West Ireland* (Dublin: Combat Poverty Agency, 2004).

Manning, M., *The Blueshirts* (Dublin: Gill & Macmillan, 1987).

Migrant Rights Centre Ireland, *Singled Out: Exploratory Study on Ethnic Profiling in Ireland and Its Impact on Migrant Workers and Their Families* (Dublin: MRCI, 2011).

Mooney, G., 'Remoralizing the Poor? Gender, Class and Philanthropy in Victorian Britain', in G. Lewis (ed.), *Forming Nation, Framing Welfare* (London: Routledge, 1999).

Moore, G., 'Socio-Economic Aspects of Anti-Semitism in Ireland: 1880–1905', *Economic and Social Review*, 12(3) (1981), pp. 187–201.

Moore, R., Turner, J., Nic Chártaigh, R., Quirke, B., Aman Hamid, N., Drummond, A., Kilroe J. and Frazer, K., *All Ireland Traveller Health Study; Qualitative Studies: Technical Report 3* (Dublin: University College Dublin/Department of Health and Children).

Mullally, M., 'Children, Citizenship and Constitutional Change', in Fanning (ed.), *Immigration and Social Change in the Republic of Ireland* (Manchester: Manchester University Press, 2007).

Murphy, T. and Twomey, P. (eds), *Ireland's Evolving Constitution* (Oxford: Hart).

Mutwarasibo, F. '(New) migrant political entrepreneurs: overcoming isolation and exclusion through creative resistance in Ireland', Ph.D. thesis (Dublin: University College Dublin, 2011).

Ni Shé, E., Lodge, T. and Adshead, M., *Getting to Know You: A Local Study of the Needs of Migrants, Refugees and Asylum Seekers in County Clare* (Limerick: University of Limerick, 2007).

Nolan, G., 'The education of refugee children: a review of Irish educational provision for refugee children in the light of international experience', M.Ed. thesis (Dublin: University College Dublin, 1997).

O'Connell, J., *Reach Out: Report by the Dublin Traveller Education Development Group on the 'Poverty 3' Programme* (Dublin: Pavee Point, 1994).

O'Connell, J., 'Myths of Innocence', in B. Baumgartl and A. Favell (eds), *A New Xenophobia in Europe* (London: Kluwer Law International, 1995).

O'Donnell, I., 'Imprisonment and Penal Policy in Ireland', *Howard Journal*, 43(1) (2004), pp. 253–66, pp. 262–3.

O'Farrell, P., *Ireland's English Question: Anglo-Irish Relations 1534–1970* (London: Batsford, 1971).

Ó'Gráda, C., *Jewish Ireland in the Age of Joyce: A Socioeconomic History* (New Jersey: Princeton University Press, 2006).

O'Mahony, P. and Delanty, G., *Rethinking Irish History: Nationalism, Identity and Ideology* (London: Routledge, 1998).

O'Regan, P., *Report of a Survey of the Vietnamese and Bosnian Refugee Communities in Ireland* (Dublin: Refugee Agency, 1998).

Parekh, P., *The Future of Multi-Ethnic Britain* (London: Runnymede Trust, 2000).

Quin, S., Kennedy, P., O'Donnell, A. and Keily, G. (eds), *Contemporary Irish Social Policy* (Dublin: University College Dublin Press, 1999).

Rattansi, A. and Westwood, S. (eds), *Racism, Modernity and Identity* (London: Polity, 1994).

Roth, A., *Mr Bewley in Berlin: Aspects of the Career of an Irish Diplomat* (Dublin: Four Courts Press, 2000

Ryan, D., 'The Jews of Limerick: Part One', *Old Limerick Journal* 17 (1984), pp. 27–30.

Ryan, D., 'The Jews of Limerick: Part Two', *Old Limerick Journal*, 18 (1985), pp. 36–40.

Sheehan, E., *Travellers: Citizens of Ireland* (Dublin: Parish of the Travelling People, 2000).

Sibbett, R., *The Perpetrators of Racial Harassment and Racial Violence: Home Office Research Study 176* (London: Home Office, 1997).

Silke, D., Norris M., Kane, F. and Portley, B., *Building Integrated Neighbourhoods: Towards an Intercultural Approach to Housing Policy and Practice in Ireland* (Dublin: NCCRI, 2008).

Sillitoe, K. and White, P. H., 'Ethnic Groups and the British Census: The Search for a Question', *Journal of the Royal Statistical Society*, 155(1) (1992), pp. 141–63.

Silverman, M. (ed.), 'Citizenship and the Nation-State in France', *Ethnic and Racial Studies*, 14(3) (1991), pp. 333–49.

Solomos, J., 'Race, Multiculturalism and Difference', in N. Stevenson (ed.), *Culture and Citizenship* (London: Sage, 2001).

Solomos, J. and Back, L. *Racism and Society* (London: Macmillan, 1996).

Sugden, J. and Bairner, A., *Sport, Sectarianism and Society in a Divided Ireland* (Leicester: Leicester University Press, 1993).

Task Force on the Travelling People, *Report of the Task Force on the Travelling Community* (Dublin, Official Publications, 1995).

Travelling People Review Body, *Report of the Travelling People Review Body* (Dublin: Official Publications, 1983).

Ward, E. '"A Big Show-off to Show What We Could Do" Ireland and the Hungarian Refugee Crisis of 1956', *Irish Studies in International Affairs*, 8 (1996), pp. 131–41.

Ward, T., 'Journeys in asylum space: a comparison of the socio-spatial production of asylum space in Norway and Ireland', M.Phil. thesis (Cork: Department of Geography and European Studies, 1999).

White, J., *Minority Report: The Protestant Community in the Irish Republic* (Dublin, Gill & Macmillan, 1975).

Williams, F., *Social Policy: A Critical Introduction: Issues of Race, Gender and Class* (Cambridge Polity, 1989).

Withol de Wenden, C., 'Immigration Policy and the Issue of Nationality', *Ethnic and Racial Studies*, 14(3) (1991), pp. 319–32.

Woods, M. and Humphries, N., *Seeking Asylum in Ireland: Comparative Figures for Asylum Seekers in Ireland and Europe in 2000 and 2001* (Dublin: Social Science Research Centre University College Dublin, 2001).

Index